FORD CAPRI 1300, 1600, 2000, OHC 1972-73 AUTOBOOK

Workshop Manual for
Ford Capri 1300 OHC 1972-73
Ford Capri 1600 OHC 1972-73
Ford Capri 2000 OHC 1972-73

by

Kenneth Ball
Graduate, Institution of Mechanical Engineers
Associate Member, Guild of Motoring Writers

and the

Autopress team of Technical Writers

AUTOPRESS LTD GOLDEN LANE BRIGHTON BN1 2QJ ENGLAND

The AUTOBOOK series of Workshop Manuals is the largest in the world and covers the majority of British and Continental motor cars, as well as all major Japanese and Australian models. For a full list see the back of this manual.

CONTENTS

ISBN 0 85147 413 6

First Edition 1973

Printed and bound in Brighton England for Autopress Ltd by G Beard & Son Ltd

ACKNOWLEDGEMENT

My thanks are due to The Ford Motor Company for their unstinted co-operation and also for supplying data and illustrations.

I am also grateful to a considerable number of owners who have discussed their cars at length and many of whose suggestions have been included in this manual.

Kenneth Ball
Graduate, Institution of Mechanical Engineers
Associate Member, Guild of Motoring Writers
Ditchling Sussex England.

INTRODUCTION

This do-it-yourself Workshop Manual has been specially written for the owner who wishes to maintain his car in first class condition and to carry out his own servicing and repairs. Considerable savings on garage charges can be made, and one can drive in safety and confidence knowing the work has been done properly.

Comprehensive step-by-step instructions and illustrations are given on all dismantling, overhauling and assembling operations. Certain assemblies require the use of expensive special tools, the purchase of which would be unjustified. In these cases information is included but the reader is recommended to hand the unit to the agent for attention.

Throughout the Manual hints and tips are included which will be found invaluable, and there is an easy to follow fault diagnosis at the end of each chapter.

Whilst every care has been taken to ensure correctness of information it is obviously not possible to guarantee complete freedom from errors or to accept liability arising from such errors or omissions.

Instructions may refer to the righthand or lefthand sides of the vehicle or the components. These are the same as the righthand or lefthand of an observer standing behind the car and looking forward.

CHAPTER 1

THE ENGINE

1 :1 Description

The Ford Type B overhead camshaft engine is a four cylinder water cooled unit, with cross-flow induction and exhaust. The cast iron cylinder block is integral with the upper half of the crankcase the lower half of which is formed by the pressed steel oil pan.

The valves are installed at a slight angle across the cylinder head and operated by an overhead camshaft driven by a toothed reinforced rubber belt from the crankshaft, the belt tension being maintained by a spring loaded idler pulley. The crankshaft runs in five steel backed liners in the main journal bearings of the crankcase.

Aluminium alloy flat top pistons are supported on H section forged connecting rods by piston pins which are a press fit into the little ends of the connecting rods and a floating fit in the bearing bores of the piston. The pistons have two compression and one oil scraper ring.

Also driven by the toothed rubber belt is a balance or auxiliary drive shaft which incorporates the skew gear for driving the distributor and oil pump shaft and a cam for operating the mechanical fuel pump.

A comprehensive system is fitted to ensure that these cars conform in all respects to current legislation with regard to fume emission and no trouble will be experienced in this respect provided that the makers settings are not disturbed.

Engine cooling is by a conventional arrangement of centrifugal pump and fan, with a thermostat ensuring a rapid warm up from cold and a pressurized radiator which also provides the hot water for the car interior heating system.

The lubrication system is from an oil pump located below the crankshaft, which draws oil from the pan through a filtering screen and forces it through a full flow filter to the main oil gallery and thence to the many areas of the engine in carefully regulated quantities. A general view of the oil distribution is given in **FIG 1 :1**.

The power units are supplied as required, in one of three categories, a 1.3, 1.6 or 2.0 litre. These engines are also available with high or low compression engines and there is a GT version of the 1.6 litre.

Many of the servicing operations which the owner may wish to do for himself can be carried out without removing the engine from the car, but as these jobs may be part of a full overhaul it may be convenient to describe first the removal of the engine and then the individual operations in the order most likely to be followed.

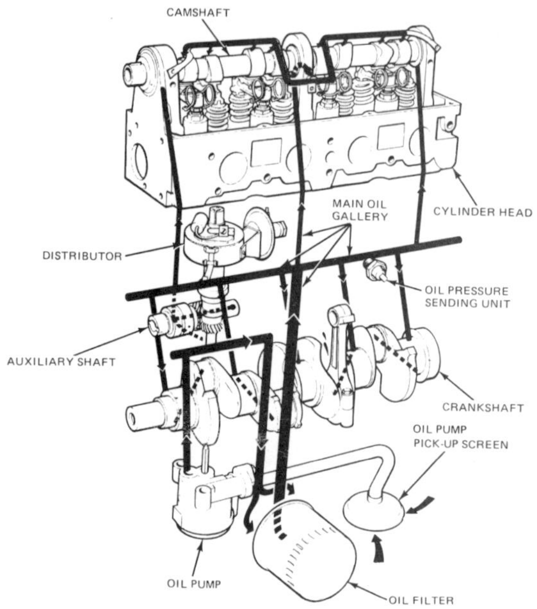

FIG 1:1 Diagram showing engine oil circulation

For the home operator who is not highly skilled there is much useful information for his guidance in 'Hints on Maintenance and Overhaul' at the back of this manual and reference to this section may assist in obtaining the best results from his efforts.

In the Appendix is a list of special tools that may be required to carry out certain operations successfully. They are listed under the country of origin with a part number common to two or all three countries or as an individual item. In nearly all the illustrations the USA tool is illustrated, however a simple check in the Appendix will give the equivalent for either the British or German models. If the tools are not listed enquiries should be made through the Ford agencies.

1:2 Removing the engine

Before commencing to describe this operation a warning must be given that any supports or lifting tackle used on the engine or chassis must be in sound condition and firmly based so as to ensure the safety of any one working underneath. Do not forget to lay a protective cover over the wings and other parts of the car likely to get scratched in the course of the work.

Remove the lower splash shield from the radiator and drain the cooling system. Remove the drain plug and drain the oil pan into a suitable container.

Mark the location of the hinges and remove the hood.

Disconnect the battery. Remove the air cleaner assembly from the carburetter.

Remove the radiator upper shield and disconnect the upper and lower radiator hoses and the hoses from the water pump and carburetter. Remove the radiator (see **Chapter 4**).

Disconnect the multiple wiring plug from the alternator, the accelerator cable and the fuel supply pipe (not forgetting to plug the end to prevent loss). Remove the two securing screws and lift off the bellcrank assembly from the inlet manifold.

Disconnect the coil primary wire and the HT cable. Disconnect the cables from the water temperature and oil pressure transmitters.

Raise the car and support it firmly or run it onto a ramp or over a pit.

Remove the starter and disconnect the exhaust pipe at the manifold.

On manual transmission models remove the flywheel and the flywheel housing lower attachment bolts.

On automatic transmission cars remove the lower front cover of the converter housing and disconnect the converter from the flexplate. Remove the screws securing the housing to the lower part of the cylinder block.

Disconnect the left and right engine mounting brackets.

Lower the car and support the gearbox or transmission with a suitable stand or jack before attaching lifting tackle and carefully raising the engine out of the car.

Transfer the engine to a work bench or, if possible, an engine stand.

Reinstallation:

This will be largely a reversal of the above procedure, but a few points must be remembered.

Fit a new seal over the exhaust pipe before lowering the engine into position.

Line up the dowels on the rear face of the cylinder block with their holes in the flywheel or converter housing. Line up also the exhaust manifold studs with the muffler inlet and the engine mounting studs in their brackets.

Very carefully insert the input shaft into the clutch, noting that it may be necessary to turn the crankshaft slightly to get the splines to mesh (Manual transmission only). Fit the upper screws securing the flywheel, or converter housing.

Remove the lifting slings and jacks under the transmission and raise the car. Fit the lower screws securing the flywheel, or converter, housing.

On automatic models fit the flexplate securing screws and tighten to 40-45 lb ft. Fit the housing front cover.

Fit the nuts to the engine mounting studs and tighten to 12-24 lb ft.

Fit the starter and connect the cables. Fit the nuts securing the exhaust pipe. Lower the car.

Reconnect: the fuel supply pipe, oil pressure and temperature transmitter cables, coil primary and HT cables.

Fit the bellcrank assembly to the inlet manifold, connect the throttle cable and adjust.

Reconnect the heater hoses to the choke and water pump, connect the radiator hoses.

Connect the multiple connector to the alternator.

Reinstall the radiator and fit the hoses. Reconnect the battery. Fill the crankcase with the correct grade of engine oil. Fill the cooling system.

Run the engine at a fast idle and check for leaks. Check the ignition timing and the carburetter idle adjustment.

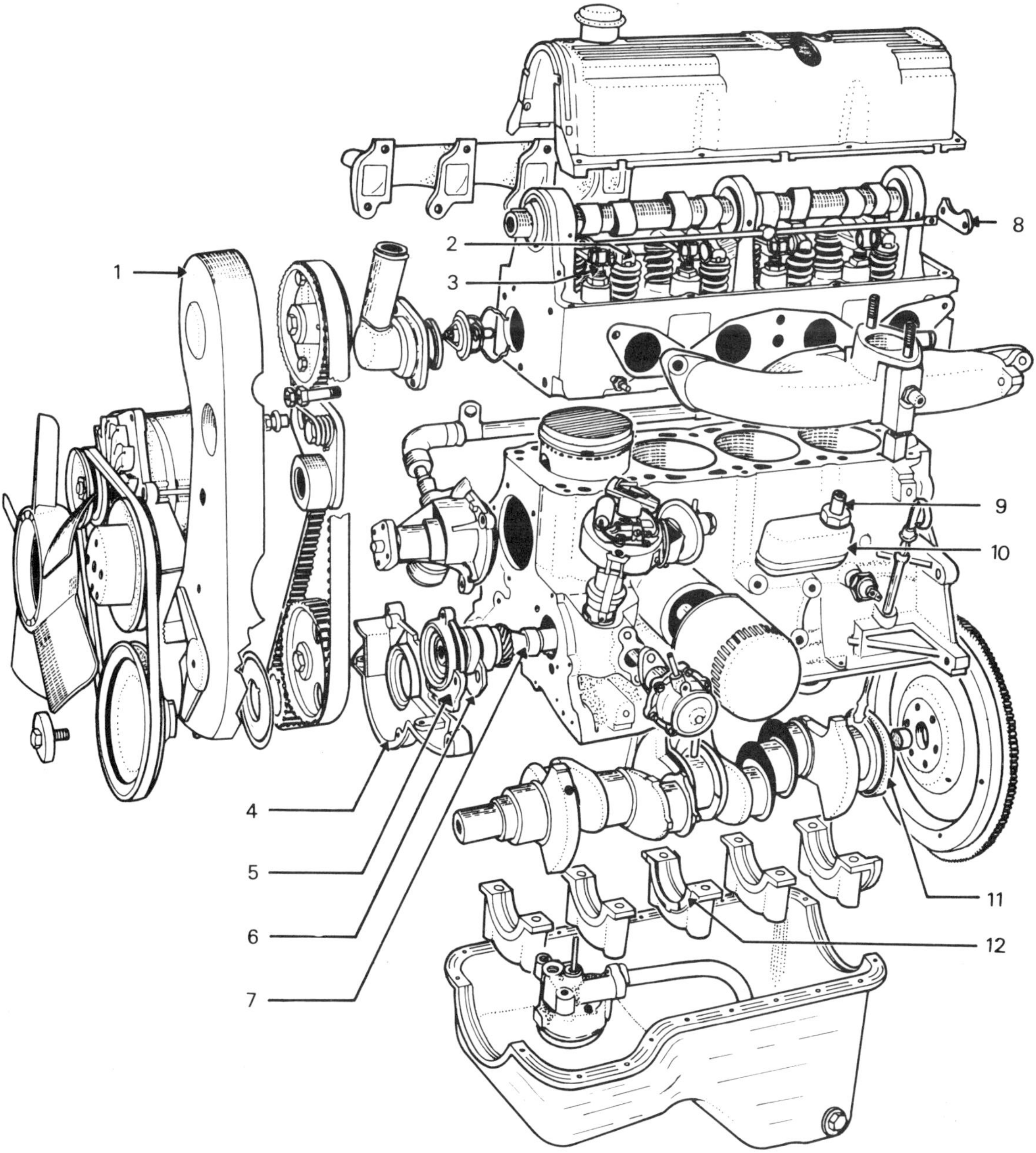

FIG 1:2 Exploded view showing main components of engine

Key to Fig 1:2 1 Timing belt guard 2 Cam followers 3 Fulcrum posts 4 Crankshaft timing cover 5 Balance shaft timing cover 6 Balance shaft thrust plate 7 Balance shaft 8 Camshaft thrust plate 9 Vent valve 10 Oil separator 11 Rear seal 12 Thrust washers (each side)

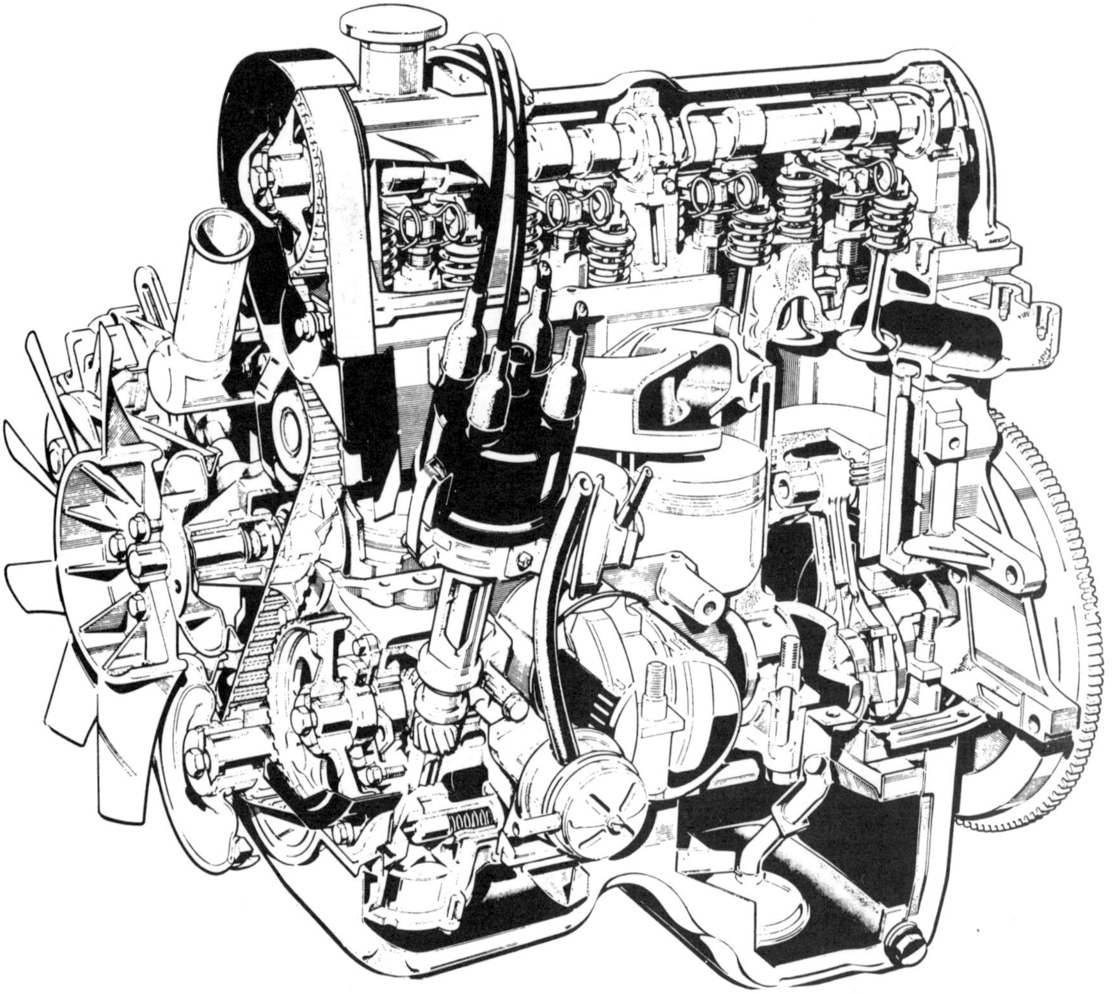

FIG 1:3 Part section through engine

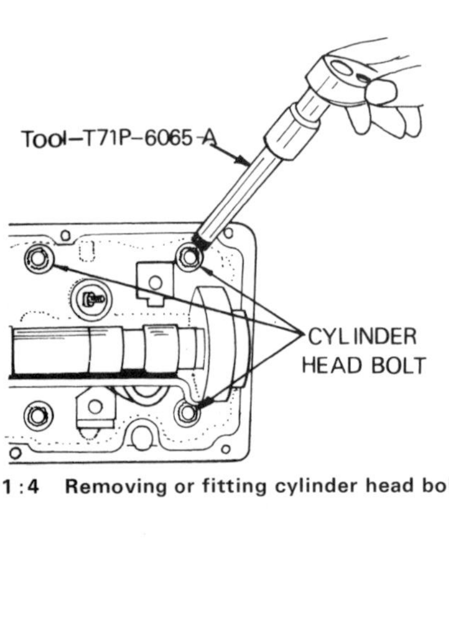

FIG 1:4 Removing or fitting cylinder head bolts

Fit the radiator splash shields, the air cleaner and couple up the crankcase ventilation hose. Replace the hood. Exploded and part sectional views of the engine are given in **FIGS 1:2** and **1:3**.

1:3 Removing and refitting the cylinder head

These operation can be carried out with the engine in or out of the car, so these instructions should be read in conjunction with the description given for removing the engine in **Section 1:2**.

Disconnect the battery, drain the cooling system and remove and air cleaner assembly.

Unbolt and remove the valve gear cover, remove the two manifolds, noting that it is not necessary to remove the carburetter unless work on this is also intended.

Remove the cover for the camshaft drive belt, being careful not to lose the rubber grommets from the screws, loosen the belt tensioner and remove the belt. Remove the water outlet elbow from the cylinder head.

The ten cylinder head retaining bolts are of a special pattern with splined countersunk holes in a cylindrical head and a special tool is needed for their removal. See **FIG 1:4**. Remove the bolts and lift off the cylinder head and camshaft from the block.

Refitting the head:

Although this is basically the removal procedure in reverse it may be of assistance to detail the operation and mention some of the points requiring particular attention.

Make sure that everything is clean and in good condition then place a new head gasket on the cylinder block using the two guide pins shown in **FIG 1:5**.

To avoid any possibility of the valves fouling the pistons it is important to set up the engine before replacing the cylinder head. Turn the camshaft into the position for No. 1 at TDC on the firing stroke i.e. with both valves closed. Turn the crankshaft to bring No. 1 piston to TDC and the distributor in the position shown in **FIG 1:6**.

Place the cylinder head in position and after screwing in the bolts finger tight, tighten them up in three stages

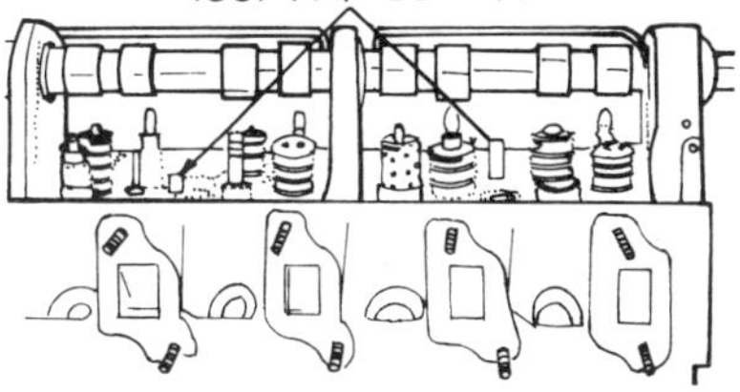

FIG 1:5 Showing guide pins for locating cylinder head

and in the order shown in **FIG 1:7**, the first stage is to 14-29 lb ft, the second to 36-50 lb ft and finally to 65-80 lb ft after running the engine for 20 minutes.

Make sure that one end of the belt tensioner spring is engaged in the groove in the anchor stud behind the pin of the back plate. Rotate the tensioner in a clockwise direction as far as possible, then tighten the adjustment bolt.

Align the timing marks as in **FIG 1:6** and position the belt on the sprockets. Loosen the tensioner adjustment bolt, rotate the crankshaft two whole turns to eliminate

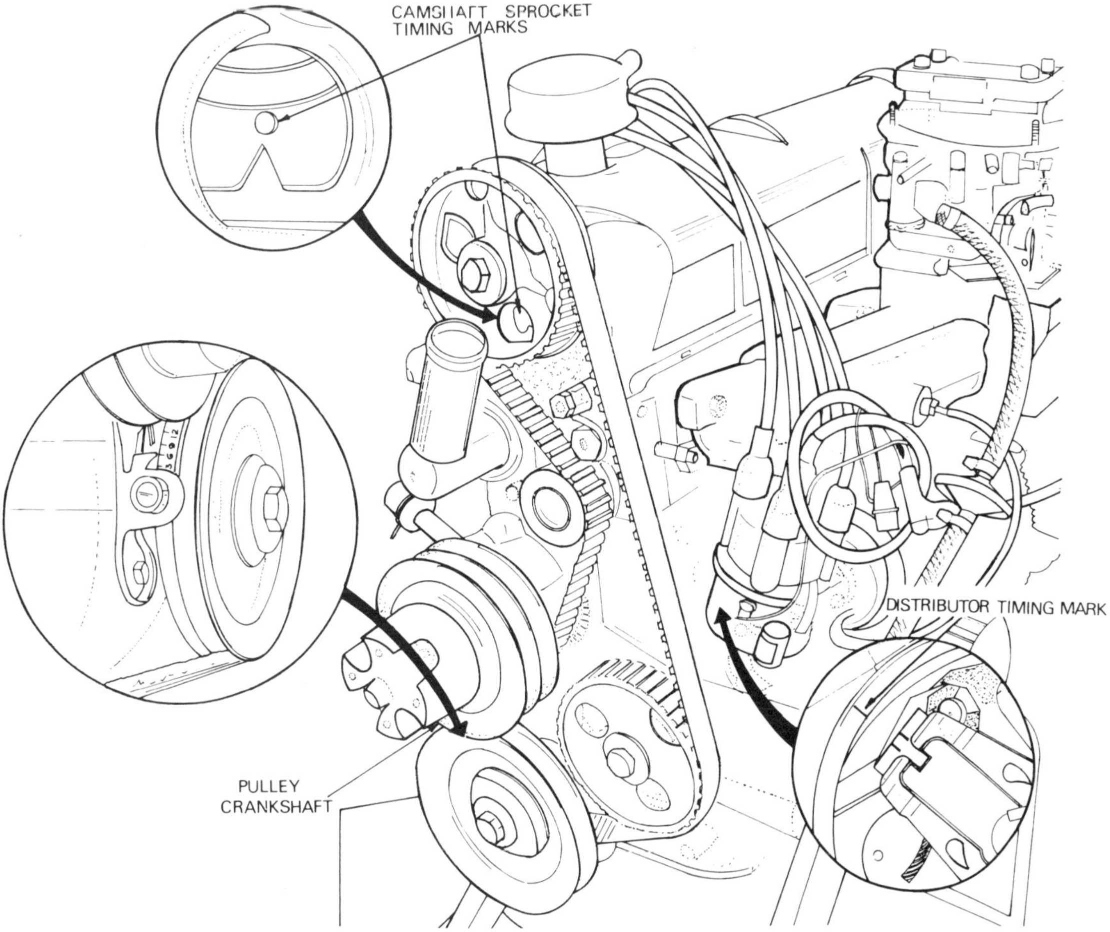

FIG 1:6 Showing the engine timing marks

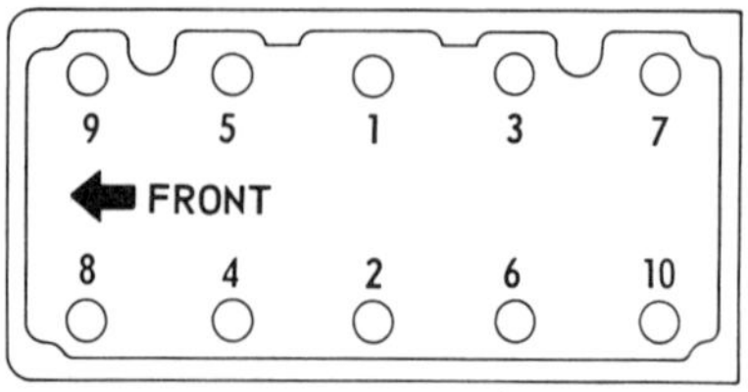

FIG 1:7 Sequence for tightening cylinder head bolts. See text for details

any slack in the belt and allow the tensioner to move tightly against the belt. Tighten the adjustment and pivot bolts and make a further check on the timing marks.

Fit the cover over the camshaft drive belt, insert the retaining screws and grommets and tighten to 10 lb ft.

Fit the washer outlet elbow with a new gasket, tighten the attaching screws to 10 lb ft and connect the water hose.

Fit a new intake manifold gasket then fit the manifold assembly and tighten the nuts to 12-15 lb ft. The exhaust manifold is fitted with a film of graphite grease on the mating surfaces and the nuts tightened to 12-15 lb ft. Use a new gasket when fitting the inlet pipe.

Adjust the valve clearances to .008 and .010 inch for inlet and exhaust valves respectively. Fit a new gasket and the valve gear cover.

Fit the air cleaner and the crankcase ventilation hose. Fill the cooling system.

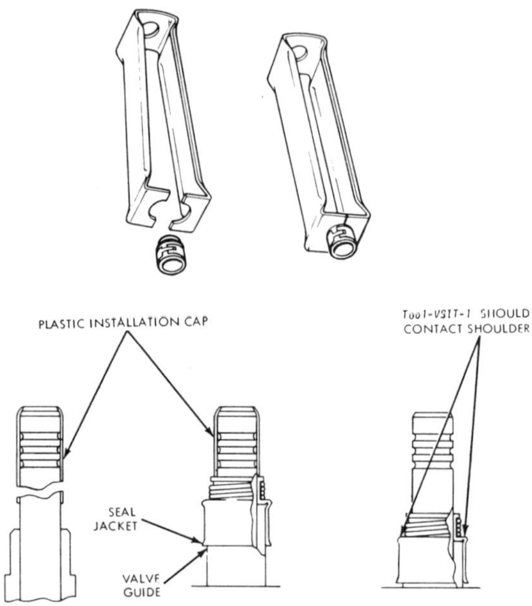

FIG 1:8 Fitting valve stem seals

Left. With valve in position fit plastic cap over end of valve stem Centre. Press seal carefully over cap and push down until jacket touches top of valve guide Right. Remove cap and use tool VSIT-1, to locate seal on valve guide Top. Tool VSIT-1

1:4 Servicing the cylinder head

Clean the cylinder head assembly and then remove the water pipe connection and take out the thermostat.

Remove the rocker arms. This is best done by turning the camshaft to bring the lowest part of the cam against the rocker arm, removing the retaining spring and then depressing the valve spring sufficiently to enable the rocker arm to be withdrawn.

Remove the bolt securing the camshaft sprocket then slide the sprocket and the belt guide plate off the shaft. Remove the camshaft thrust plate from the rear of the cylinder head and then carefully slide the camshaft out to the rear.

Remove the sparking plugs. Loosen the locknuts and remove the rocker adjusting screws or pivot posts.

In order to avoid damage to the valve seats it is best to remove all carbon deposits from the combustion chambers and valve heads before removing the valves with a blunt screwdriver blade or wire brush and taking care not to scratch the gasket surface.

Compress the valve springs with any suitable compressor and take out the retainer locks, retainers, springs and seals. Remove the valves from the head and either mark or store them so as to ensure their return to their original positions when reassembling.

The camshaft bearings should only be removed if it is intended to renew them. This is easily done with the special service tool. Replacement is also simple, but make sure that the oil hole in the bearing lines up with the one in the bearing bracket.

Examine the valve seats and check the condition of the valve stems in the guides. If wear is slight the valves may be ground in onto their seats or recut if necessary, but badly worn seats, stems or guides will necessitate valve and guide replacement. A range of oversize valves is available for which the guides can be reamed out to fit.

When all parts have been inspected, passed or renewed, reassembly can be started in the reverse order.

First refit the valves in their original places, smearing them well with oil first and then fit a new stem seal on each with the service tool as shown in **FIG 1:8**. Fit the valve spring and retainers, compress the springs and fit the retainer locks.

Measure the assembled height of the valve spring from the surface of the cylinder head spring pad to the underside of the spring retainers. The dimension should be 1.417 inch and if it is greater than this a spacer or spacers should be inserted between the spring pad and the spring as necessary.

Oil the camshaft bearings and slide the camshaft into position and complete the installation by reversing the removal procedure.

Refit the ball headed pivot posts and oil retainer caps, pressing the latter into position with the service tool if available, then depress each valve in turn with a spring compressor and fit each rocker in place, retaining it by means of its spring. See **FIG 1:9** which shows clearly the arrangment of the valve operating gear and the gap for setting valve clearances.

Setting valve clearances:

These are set with the engine cold and are adjusted by varying the height of the post by means of the upper nut and locking in position with the lower nut.

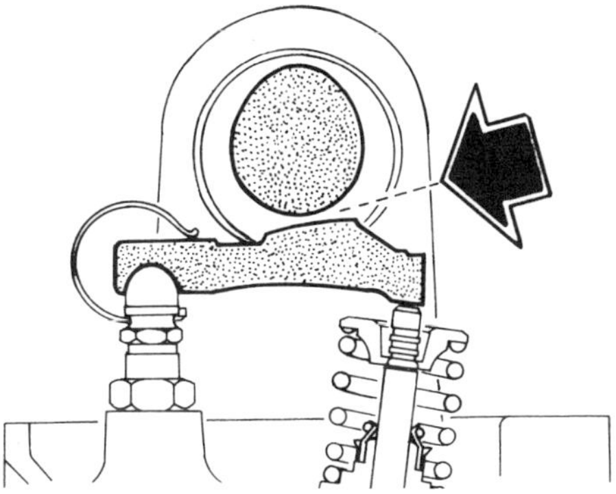

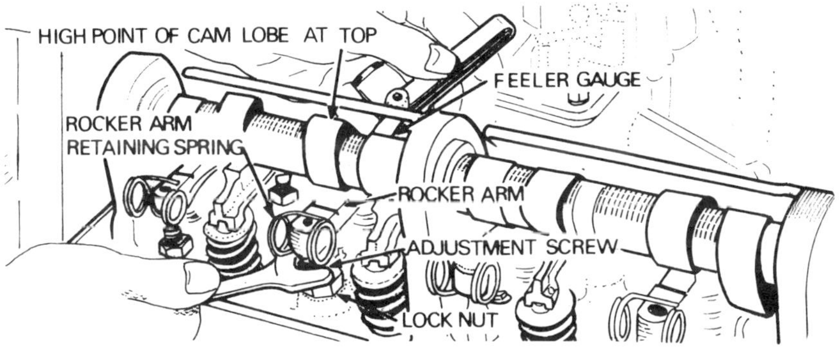

FIG 1 :9 Adjusting valve clearances

Turn the camshaft until the cam of the valve to be adjusted is in the vertical position as shown and insert the requisite feeler gauge as indicated by the arrow. The correct clearances are .008 inch for an inlet valve and .010 for an exhaust valve and the setting is correct when the feeler gauge can just be slid in and out.

1 :5 The timing gear

Removal:

First remove the alternator drive belt and then unbolt and remove the crankshaft pulley. Turn the engine until No. 1 is at TDC as indicated by the timing marks (see **FIG 1 :6**). Unscrew the three bolts securing the cover over the camshaft drive belt and lift off the cover.

Loosen the belt tensioner adjustment bolt and press the roller as far out as possible to relieve the tension on the belt. Tighten up the bolt and remove the belt and take great care not to allow any rotation of either the camshaft or crankshaft until the belt is replaced, otherwise the timing will be lost and damage may be caused through valves fouling the pistons.

Camshaft end play:

This can be measured with a feeler gauge or a dial indicator while levering the shaft to and fro with a large screwdriver. The correct clearance should be between .001 and .004 inch, and if necessary this dimension can be obtained by changing the thrust washer at the rear of the cylinder head after removing the camshaft as described in **Section 1 :4**.

Renewing shaft oil seals:

The seals on the crankshaft, camshaft or auxiliary shafts are all renewed in the same manner after the drive sprocket has been removed. Normally this can be slid off, but in some cases a puller may be required.

Fit the service tool over the end of the shaft as shown in the upper illustration in **FIG 1 :10** to remove the seal and use the appropriate service tool to fit the new seal as shown in the lower illustration. When refitting the sprocket on the crankshaft, slide on the sprocket guide plate and then the sprocket with the large chamfer towards the engine. Follow with the pulley, washer and bolt, tightening the bolt to 39-43 lb ft.

Auxiliary shaft:

After removing the sprocket, remove the fuel pump and the distributor and then the auxiliary shaft cover by unscrewing the three retaining bolts.

Take out the two securing screws and lift out the shaft thrust plate. Withdraw the auxiliary shaft from the block. If the bearing is worn or damaged it can be pulled out with the service extractor tool.

The new bearing is driven in with a special service tool after seeing that the two oil holes in the bearing are in line with those in the block.

Slide the shaft carefully into position and fit the thrust plate to retain it. Fit the cover with a new gasket and tighten the three bolts to 32-36 lb ft. Measure the shaft end float and ensure that it is between .002 and .007 inch.

Fit the fuel pump with a new gasket. Fit the distributor.

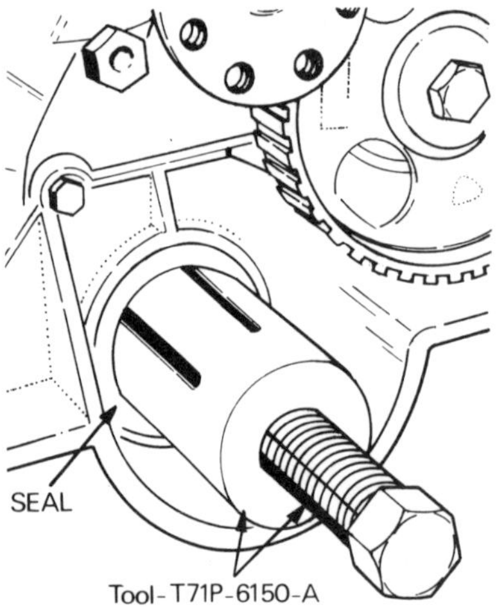

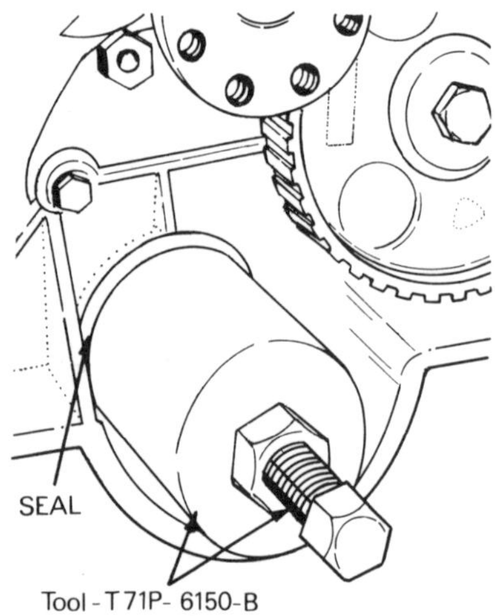

FIG 1:10 Removing (top) or installing (bottom) crankshaft oil seal

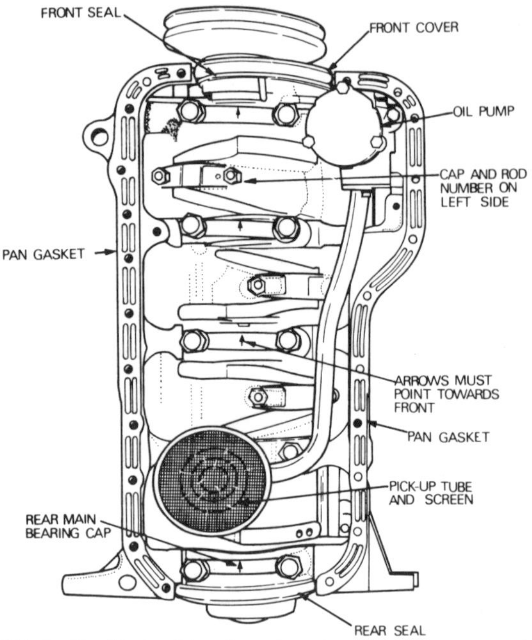

FIG 1:11 Underside of engine showing oil pump and pan gaskets and seals

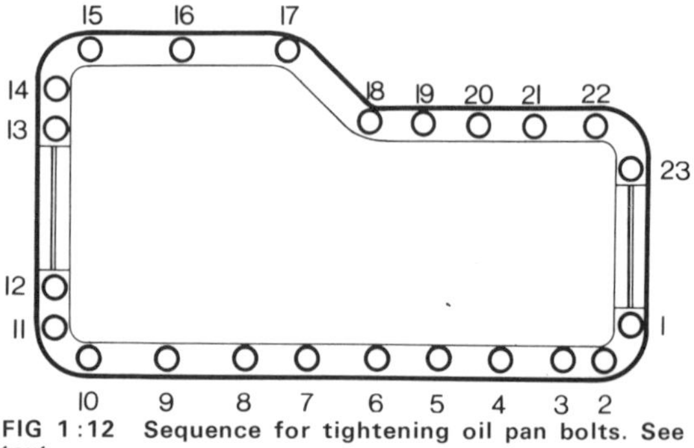

FIG 1:12 Sequence for tightening oil pan bolts. See text

Fit the sprocket on the auxiliary shaft, confirm that the timing marks are lined up as shown and then fit the rubber belt. Release the belt tensioner and give the crankshaft two complete turns, bringing the timing marks into their original positions and taking up any slack in the belt. Recheck the timing and tighten the tensioner attachment and pivot bolts.

Fit the timing belt cover and tighten the three securing bolts to 6-13 lb ft.

1:6 The oil pan and pump

The oil pan can be removed without taking the engine out of the car if necessary and the procedure for this is as follows:

Raise the car or run it over a pit. Remove the dipstick and drain the crankcase. Remove the starter. Disconnect the right and left engine mount retaining nuts at the underbody bracket.

Remove the flywheel or the front cover of the converter housing and then raise the engine slightly and take out the capscrews securing the oil pan.

Loosen the capscrews securing the front crossmember on each side, making sure that the crossmember is still retained by a few threads.

Disconnect the oil pick-up tube from the pump and the cylinder block—see **FIG 1:11**—and allow it to rest in the pan, which should now be moved out to the left at the rear and eased out between the engine and the crossmember.

Refitting the pan:

Clean all parts thoroughly, coat the surfaces of the block and gasket with a suitable sealer and stick the two parts of the oil pan gasket on the block.

Position the oil pan front seal on the cylinder front cover, making sure that the ends of the seal are in contact with the gaskets.

Similarly fit the rear seal on the rear main bearing cap and coat all joints with sealer.

Manoeuvre the oil pan into position, having first laid the oil pick-up tube and screen along the bottom of the pan. Attach the oil pick-up tube, fit the pan retaining screws and tighten them in three stages as follows: Refer to **FIG 1:12**.

Start with bolt No. 1 and tighten all bolts in numerical order to 1 to $1\frac{1}{2}$ lb ft.

Starting with bolt No. 13 tighten them all in rotation to $4\frac{1}{2}$ to 6 lb ft.

At the completion of the operation the engine should be started and run for about 20 minutes and the bolts retorqued to $4\frac{1}{2}$ to 6 lb ft.

Fit the crossmember to the frame and tighten to 25-30 lb ft. Lower the engine and tighten the engine mounting nuts.

Refit the flywheel or the converter housing front cover. Fit the starter. Fill up with the oil as specified, start the engine and check for leaks.

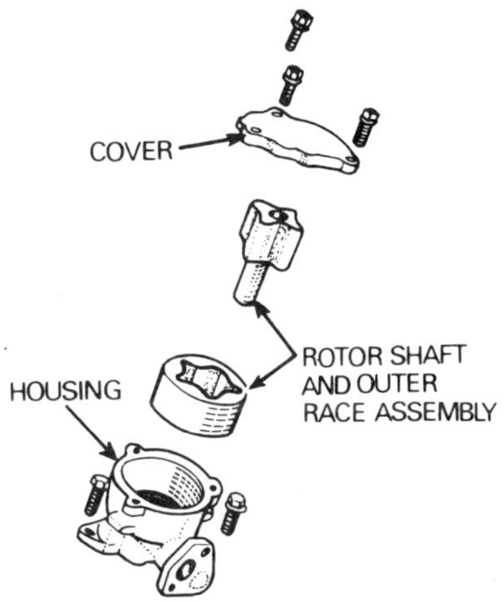

FIG 1:13 Components of oil pump

Oil pump:

This is attached by two bolts and is shown dismantled in **FIG 1:13**.

The pump is driven by a short shaft from the end of the distributor shaft and comprises a four lobe rotor turning within the five lobe centre of a ring which in turn rotates inside the circular pump body. A spring loaded relief valve is included to ensure that if pressure should build up in excess of that set by the spring, the excess oil is returned to the sump.

To inspect the pump, having removed the union securing the pick up tube and strainer, remove the three screws holding the two halves of the pump together. Separate them and withdraw the rotor and shaft from the upper half, thoroughly clean all the parts and carefully extract the ring.

Check for obvious signs of wear or damage noting that the outer ring, shaft and rotor are replaceable only as an assembly. The cover should be renewed if its mating surface is worn or scored.

Refer to **FIG 1:14** and measure the clearance between the outer ring and the housing, this should be between .005 and .011 inch. The clearance, shown in **FIG 1:15** between the rotor and the end cover (end play) should be .001 to .004 inch and if these clearances are exceeded the components should be renewed.

Be sure when reassembling that the identification marks both face towards the bottom of the pump.

Always use a new gasket when refitting the pump and note that the securing bolts are tightened to 12-15 lb ft.

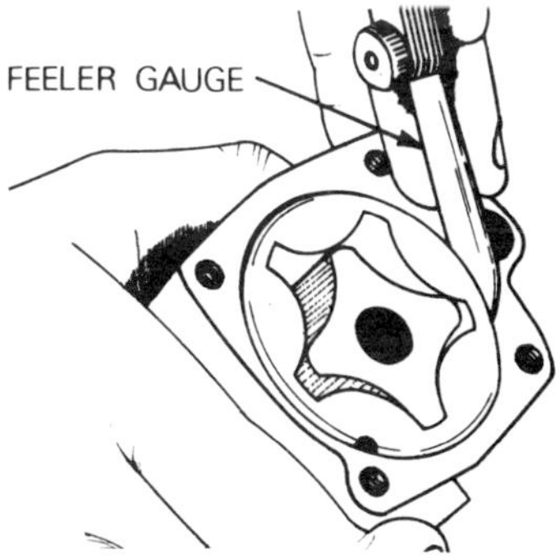

FIG 1:14 Measuring clearance between outer race and housing

Oil filter:

When removing the oil filter always place a drip pan underneath before unscrewing it from the adapter fitting in an anti-clockwise direction.

Clean the mating surfaces before fitting the new filter and apply a smear of engine oil.

Screw the filter on to the adapter until the gasket contacts the cylinder block and then give it an extra half turn. Do not over-tighten.

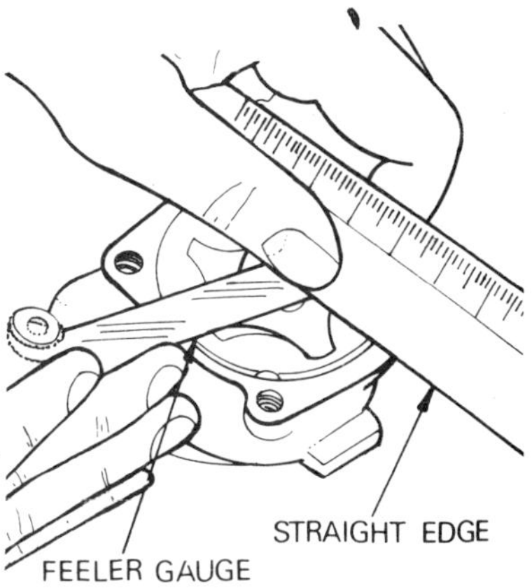

FIG 1:15 Measuring rotor end play

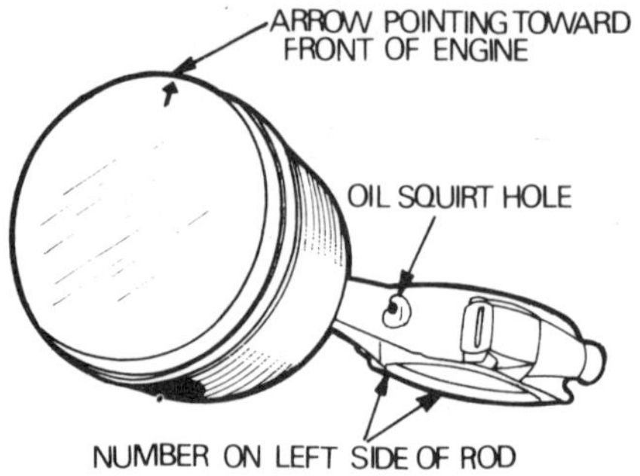

FIG 1:16 Correct fitting of piston and connecting rod

1:7 Pistons and connecting rods

Removal:

Before the piston assembly can be removed from the engine it is necessary to remove the cylinder head as described in **Section 1:3**, and also the oil pan, **Section 1:6**, as the pistons cannot be pulled out of the bottom of the engine past the crankshaft, but must pass out at the top of the bores.

Remove the oil pump assembly from the bottom of the block and at the upper end carefully remove the ring of carbon deposit round the top of the bore(s) from which the piston is to be withdrawn.

Each connecting rod and cap is marked with the number of the cylinder to which it is fitted, and it is essential to ensure that they are returned to the same cylinder and the same direction when reassembling. Unbolt and remove the connecting rod cap, push the piston assembly out through the top of the bores and replace the cap for security. It will be seen that the identifying markings are on the left hand side from 1 to 4 beginning at the front of the engine and that an arrow or a notch on the top of the piston points towards the front. This can be seen in **FIG 1:16**.

Examine the fit of the piston pin in the piston bores. If there is excessive play in any direction, both piston and pin should be renewed as a matched pair.

Check that the rings are a close but free fit in the ring grooves and renew any that are broken.

Check the bearing inserts and the bearing bore in the connecting rod and when refitting make sure that the tangs in the bearing inserts register with the slots provided.

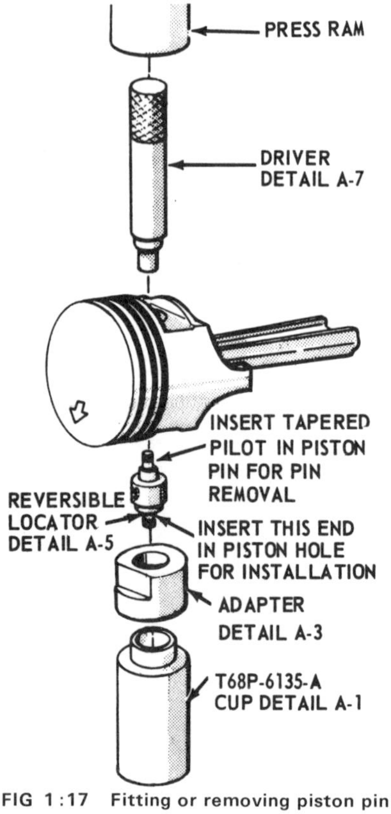

FIG 1:17 Fitting or removing piston pin

Piston pins:

Make a note of the colour of the paint spot in the piston crown and on the end face of the piston pin, it will be either red, blue or yellow. The colour identifies the different tolerance grades as detailed in Technical Data. Pistons and piston pins are precisely matched as units and in each case should be renewed as an assembly. The pin is a clearance fit in the piston bore but in the small end bore it is an interference fit which means the upper end of the connecting rod must be heated to a temperature between 260 and 300°C to expand the bore sufficiently to admit the pin. Furthermore, apart from the requirement of special heating appliance it is essential that the special service tool and arbor press is used to extract the pin and for the 2 litre models to press the pin into its correct location as shown in **FIG 1:17**. It must be done properly at the first attempt as it cannot be adjusted after the assembly has cooled.

Under these circumstances it is not recommended that the operator attempts to separate the assemblies but entrusts this work to a Ford service garage to separate, to renew the components as required and to assemble them accordingly.

Piston rings:

Before fitting a new ring to a piston it is important to check the gap between the two ends is according to specification. This is .019 to .021 inch for the compression rings and .016 to .055 for the oil control ring.

The gap may be measured with a feeler gauge after the ring has been pushed squarely down into its own bore, preferably on top of an old piston to ensure correct positioning. If the gap is less than specified a little metal can be removed with a fine file to bring the gap within the limits.

It is also important to see that the ring gaps are correctly spaced around the circumference of the piston and the manufacturers have issued the diagram given in **FIG 1:18** for guidance in this respect.

Ring side clearance in its groove may be checked by sliding the appropriate feeler gauge around the whole circumference of the ring. The gauge should pass freely without any binding, but if binding does occur the piston should be renewed.

Installation:

After applying a smear of engine oil over all running surfaces, insert the big end of the connecting rod into the top of the cylinder bore, checking that the numbers on the rod and the cap correspond and that the positions of the oil hole and the mark on the piston head are correct, see **FIG 1:16**. See that the ring gaps are correctly located then fit a ring compressor on the piston and press it down into its bore, guiding the connecting rod to avoid damage in contact with the crankshaft journals.

Smear the bearing surfaces with oil, turn the crankshaft throw to the bottom of the stroke and then push the piston fully down until the connecting rod bearing seats on the crankshaft journal. Fit the cap and tighten the nuts to a torque of 29 to 34 lb ft.

Instructions for ensuring the correct fit on the big end bearings are given in the next section on the crankshaft.

1:8 Servicing the crankshaft

Refer to **FIG 1:22**. Remove the main bearing caps, ensuring that they are identified for later refitting, and lift out the crankshaft. Clean the shaft thoroughly and examine for signs of excessive wear or damage. Make sure that all the oil ways are clear.

Measure the main bearing and big end bearing journals for roundness and note that the maximum permissible ovality is .0004 inch and if this figure is exceeded the journals should be reground.

The main and connecting rod bearing journals may be one of two sizes: standard or 10 thousandths undersize. If all MAIN journals are undersize they are coded by a white slash on the front crankshaft counterweight (**FIG 1:19**). If all ROD journals are undersize they are coded by a white dot on the front crankshaft counterweight (**FIG 1:20**). If both MAIN and ROD journals are undersize there will be both a white slash and a white dot on the counterweight.

Reference must be made to Technical Data regarding the tolerance limits of the main bearing bores, crankshaft journals and crankpins. Apart from the white marks that, as already mentioned, denote that the crankshaft journals and crankpins have been ground undersize, further colour markings of either red or blue denote the tolerance grades. Blue denotes a **minimum** size within the tolerance grade and red a **maximum** size within the tolerance grade.

With regard to the main bearing parent bores in the cylinder block, colour spots are not used but the initial letter of the colour (r) or (b) is stamped on the machined gasket face (sump end). In those instances where the letters (r) or (b) are followed by the letters 'OS', the parent bores are of .4 mm (.0157 inch) oversize.

When all the main bearing journals of the crankshaft are within the same tolerance range, the single red or blue colour mark will be found on the crankshaft web behind the spigot bearing. When the main journals vary within the tolerance ranges the red and blue marks will be found on the narrow side of the webs at the rear of the respective journal. The exception is No. 5 journal when the spot appears on the web in front of the journal.

When all the big end crankpins are within the same tolerance grade, the single red or blue spot will be found on the web behind No. 3 crankpin journal. Where the

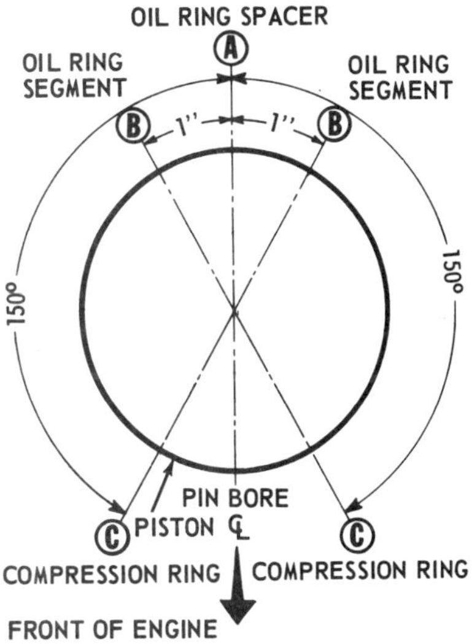

FIG 1:18 Spacing the piston ring gaps

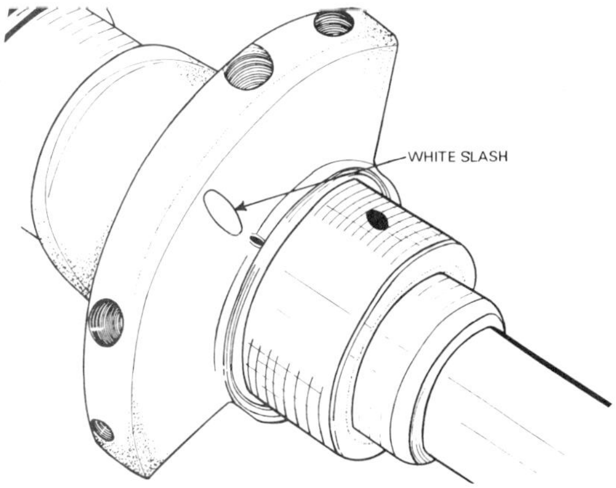

FIG 1:19 Main journals undersize. White slash

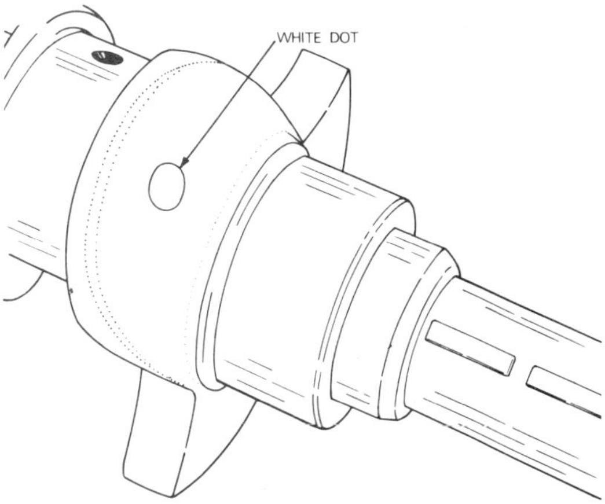

FIG 1:20 Rod journals undersize. White dot

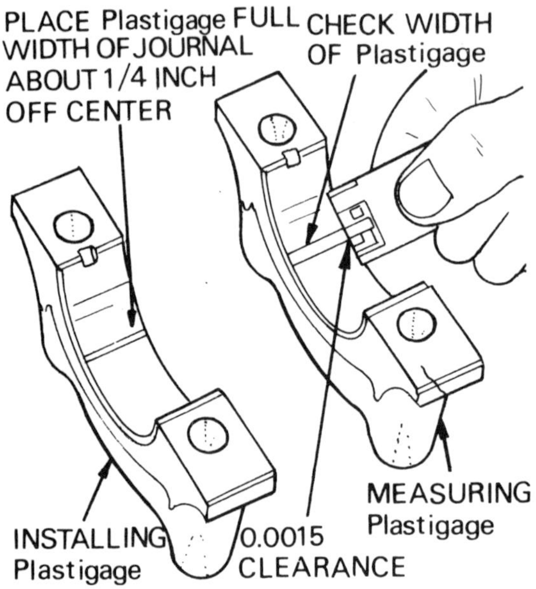

FIG 1:21 Measuring bearing clearance with Plastigage

crankpin journals vary within the tolerance ranges the red and blue marks will be found on the web immediately behind the respective crankpin.

Renewing bearings:

It is possible to renew main bearings with the engine still in the car, and this is done one bearing at a time. Remove the appropriate main bearing cap, insert the upper bearing removal tool in the journal oil hole and turn the crankshaft slowly in the normal direction to force the bearing insert out of the block.

See that the journals are clean and smooth, check the position of the four thrust washers on the centre main bearing, lubricate the upper bearing with heavy engine oil and place its plain end over the shaft on the locking tang side of the block and partially install the bearing so that the tool can be inserted in the journal oil hole. Rotate the crankshaft slowly backwards until the bearing tang is seated. Remove the tool.

Selection of the bearing for proper clearance will be according to the following procedures applicable to the operation being carried out with the engine on the bench and to the appropriate red or blue marking on the connecting rod and bearing liner. The oversize liners are marked accordingly on their outer face.

To measure the actual bearing clearance, which should be .001 to .0015 for big ends and .0005 to .0015 for main bearings, place a piece of Plastigage on the bearing surface across the full width of the bearing cap and about $\frac{1}{4}$ inch off centre as shown in **FIG 1:21**. Fit the cap and tighten the bolts to 29-34 lb ft for big-end bearings or 65-75 lb ft for main bearings. On no account should the crankshaft be turned during this operation.

Remove the cap and check the width of the Plastigage on the scale provided. The widest reading gives the minimum clearance and the narrowest point shows maximum clearance. The difference between the two will show the taper.

When replacing standard bearings with new bearings it is good practice to fit the bearings to the minimum specified and if this condition is not obtained with a standard bearing, it is permissible to try one half of a .001 or .002 inch undersize in combination with a standard size to obtain the proper clearance.

If .002 inch undersize main bearings are used on more than one journal be sure that they are all fitted on the cylinder block side of the bearing. If a combination of .002 inch undersize and standard bearings does not bring the clearance within the specified limits, the journal must be reground and undersize bearings fitted.

After the bearing has been fitted, apply a light coat of engine oil to both journal and bearings, fit the cap and tighten the nuts as specified.

A ball bearing for the clutch spigot is pressed into the rear end of the crankshaft. The outer race is a press fit into the crankshaft and if examination shows excessive wear or damage, it must be extracted and a new bearing fitted.

Crankshaft end play:

This is adjusted by a selection of thrust washers which are fitted on each side of the centre main bearing. These washers are in two halves, an upper and a lower half, and must always be renewed complete. If new washers are being fitted, make sure that they are installed on the rear side of the bearing cap.

In order accurately to measure the crankshaft end play, all components except the crankshaft and bearings should be removed from the block. Press the crankshaft towards the two ends of the block by levering with a screwdriver, measure the movement either with a feeler gauge or a dial indicator and compare this figure with the specified dimension of .003 to .001.

If the end play is not within these limits remove the centre main bearing cap and install new thrust washers as necessary. Refit the bearing cap and recheck.

Rear seal:

If this is to be renewed with the engine still in the car, it is necessary first to remove the gearbox, clutch and flywheel or the automatic transmission, converter and flywheel. The seal may then be removed with a sheet metal screw as shown in **FIG 1:23**.

A new seal is fitted by pressing it into place using the special service tool.

1:9 The flywheel

On cars fitted with automatic transmission, remove the transmission and converter housing. With a manual shift gearbox remove the gearbox, clutch pressure plate and disc.

Remove the flywheel securing bolts and lift off after marking the parts to ensure correct replacement.

Refitting is carried out in the reverse order, not forgetting to smear the bolts with an oil resistant sealer. The bolts are tightened in diagonal sequence to a torque of 47-51 lb ft.

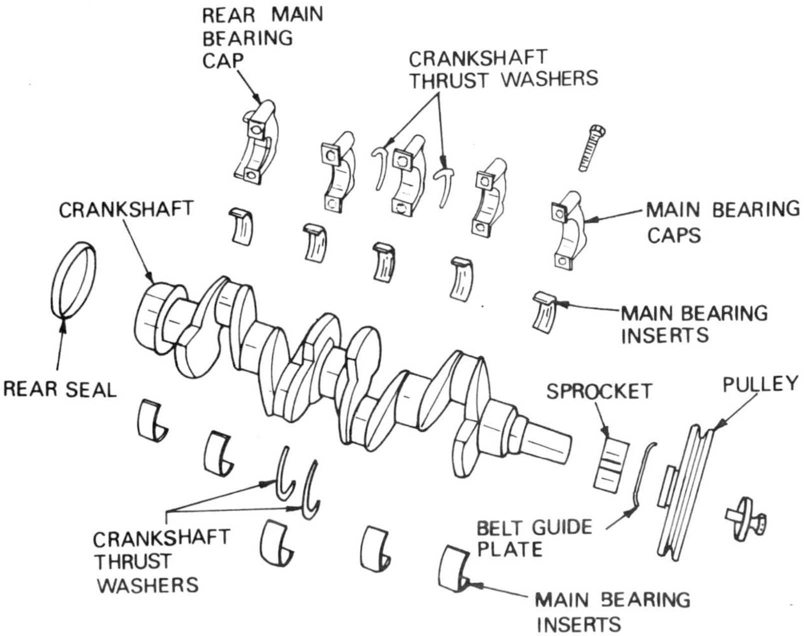

FIG 1:22 The crankshaft and related components

Runout:

Flywheel face runout is checked with a dial indicator in the normal manner, but when turning the flywheel make sure that it is either fully forward or rearward so that crankshaft end play will not be included in the measurements for runout which should not exceed .025 inch on its outside diameter or .005 on the clutch face.

If the runout on the clutch face is too great the flywheel should be detached and the mating surfaces of flywheel and crankshaft flange checked for condition, and if this appears in order check the runout on the crankshaft flange.

Replace the flywheel or machine the crankshaft flywheel mounting face sufficiently to true up the surface.

On automatic transmissions set the dial indicator with its point resting on the face of the ring gear close to the teeth. Remove the sparking plugs.

Rotate the flywheel one complete turn, taking care as before not to let crankshaft end play affect the reading, and note the TIR or total indicator reading. If this exceeds .025 inch the flywheel and ring gear must be renewed.

1:10 Emission control system

Ventilation of the crankcase is effected by the vacuum created in the inlet manifold all the time the engine is running. Reference to **FIG 1:24** will show that a portion of the fresh air entering the air cleaner by-passes the carburetter to be directed to the oil filler cap through the primary vent hose.

The air then passes around the overhead valve cover and crankcase, and then through the oil separator on the lefthand side of the engine and its ventilation control valve, through the secondary vent hose and so into the inlet manifold and the engine where it takes part in the normal combustion sequence.

The exhaust emission control system is composed of the following items: a distributor with a dual diaphragm vacuum unit, a carburetter specially calibrated for use with the control system and a deceleration valve.

The deceleration valve is designed to supply the engine with a greater air-fuel mixture volume during deceleration and so produce a lower hydro carbon content in the exhaust gases.

The dual-diaphragm distributor is also brought into operation at these times by having the ignition timing retarded as a result of decreased vacuum in the inlet manifold.

Removal:

Disconnect the inlet hose from the air cleaner and oil filler cap, also the carbon canister hose from the air cleaner. Remove the air cleaner.

While holding the crankcase vent hose at the oil separator pull out the regulator valve from the separator.

Disconnect the hose from the inlet manifold and the hose from the regulator valve.

Refitting will be a reversal of the above procedure.

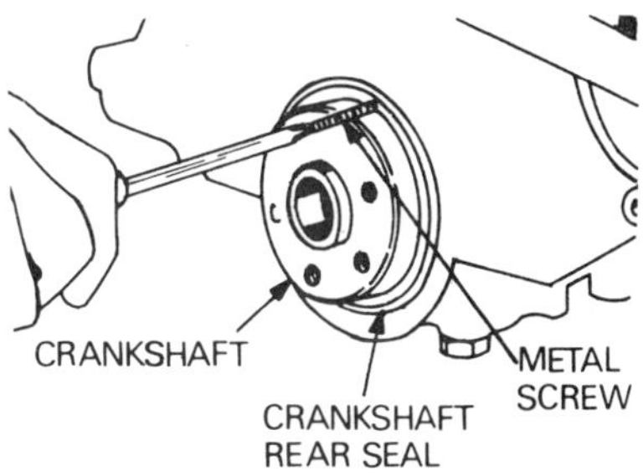

FIG 1:23 Removing crankshaft rear seal

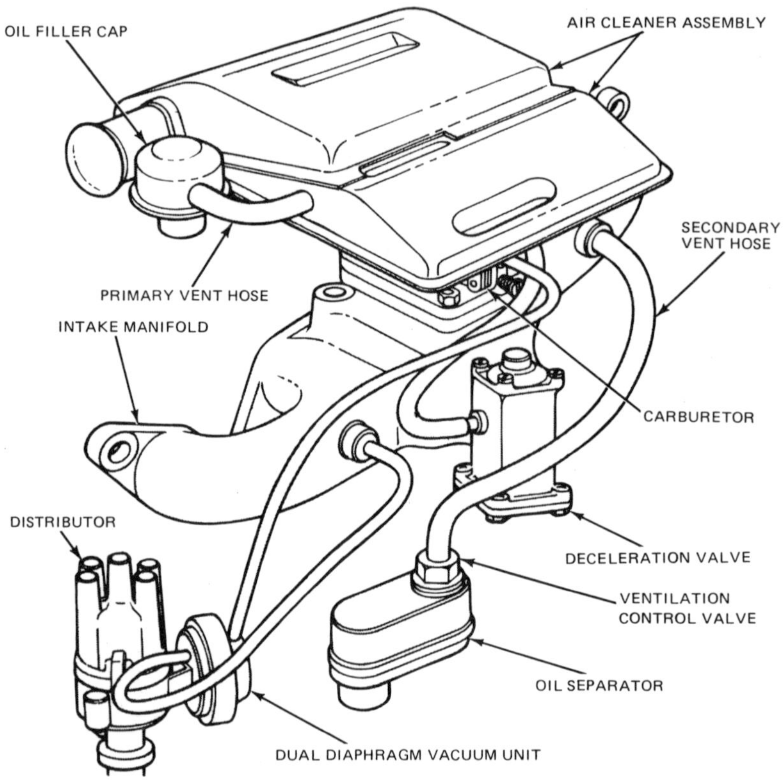

FIG 1:24 The crankcase ventilation system

Testing:

This is best performed with an official testing set, but as this may not be available the following procedure may be adapted.

A faulty system may often be indicated by a rough engine idle, and this condition should not be compensated by disconnecting the system or attempting to adjust the carburetter. To confirm that the condition is caused by the ventilation system, remove the regulator valve and in its place fit one that is known to function correctly.

If the idle is now satisfactory use the new regulator valve and clean the various hoses, fittings, etc.

If the poor idle persists the regulator valve is clearly not the cause, so the rest of the system must be examined particularly for restriction at the inlet manifold or carburetter spacer. If this check reveals no fault, further engine component diagnosis will have to be made to find the malfunction.

1:11 Reassembling the engine

Before commencing this operation make sure that all the parts have been cleaned, inspected and passed for re-use or renewed. Have a complete set of new joints, seals and gaskets available and see that where oilways have been opened up for inspection any seals or plugs are securely installed.

Fit the correct size upper main bearing inserts with the tang in its slot, fit the lower inserts in their caps. Fit the two upper crankshaft thrust washers on each side of the centre journal in the cylinder block (**FIG 1:22**). If only one pair of new thrust washers is being used they should be fitted at the rear of the journal.

Carefully lower the crankshaft into position, having well oiled all running surfaces, fit the four outer bearing caps in their original locations and the arrows pointing to the front of the engine and tighten the cap bolts to 65-75 lb ft.

Place the other two (lower) thrust washers on each side of the centre main bearing cap, tighten the bolts and check the crankshaft end play as described in **Section 1:8**. If necessary fit new thrust plates.

Lubricate the pistons, rings and cylinder bores and install the piston and connecting rod assemblies into their respective bores. The numbers on the rods and caps must be on the left hand side and the arrow on the piston head to the front.

Check the big end bearings and fit each to the crankshaft journal, tightening the bolts to a torque of 29-34 lb ft. Check the connecting rod side clearance on each journal, this should be between .004 and .010 inch.

Bolt the flywheel to the crankshaft flange with a torque of 47-51 lb ft and check the run out as described in **Section 1:9**.

Clean the cylinder front cover and the gasket face of the cylinder block. Fit a new crankshaft front oil seal in the cover. Apply an oil resistant sealer to both surfaces and fit the front cover using a new gasket and tighten the bolts to 6-9 lb ft.

Prime the oil pump by filling the inlet screen with engine oil. Insert the drive shaft into the pump and rotate until the oil issues from the outlet connection. Fit the pump with a new gasket and tighten the securing screws to a torque of 12-15 lb ft.

Refit the oil pan as described in **Section 1 : 6**.

Fit the clutch pilot bushing and the engine rear cover plate. Bolt on the flywheel and check according to **Section 1 : 9**.

On Manual transmission models use the special service tool or dummy shaft to locate the clutch disc. Fit the pressure plate and tighten the attaching bolts to 22-27 lb ft.

Fit the fuel pump.

Turn the crankshaft to bring No. 1 at TDC on the firing stroke. Position the distributor and intermediate drive shaft into the block with the rotor pointing to the segment for No. 1 cylinder and the contact breaker points open. Fit the mounting clamp. Make sure that the oil pump intermediate drive is fully seated in the oil pump, noting that some movement of the shaft may be required to secure full engagement.

Fit the oil filter.

Clean the top of the block and the cylinder head, fit the guide studs and lay the gasket in position. Carefully lower the cylinder head over the guides and fit two bolts at each end of the head to hold it in place, remove the guides and fit the remaining bolts.

The cylinder head bolts must be tightened as instructed in **Section 1 : 3** and after the engine has been started and run for a few minutes to get it warm they should be retorqued to 80 lb ft. When the bolts have been tightened in this manner it should not be necessary to re-tighten them after extended operation.

Lightly oil the rocker gear and position the valve rocker arms, securing them to the adjustment studs with the retaining clips. Adjust the valve clearance.

Clean and position the new gasket for the valve cover, ensuring that each gasket tab engages the slot provided in the cover. Fit the cover and see that the gasket seats evenly all round. The screws securing the cover must be tightened in the following 4 stages:

1	6 rear screws from back to front	4-6 lb ft
2	2 vertical screws in the front	1-2 lb ft
3	2 lateral screws	4-6 lb ft
4	2 vertical screws in the front	4-6 lb ft

Fit the sparking plugs, the distributor cap and the ignition cables.

Smear a film of graphite grease on the manifold joint surfaces. Fit the exhaust manifold and tighten the nuts diagonally to 12-15 lb ft. Fit the exhaust manifold shroud and tighten the two nuts to 5-8 lb ft.

Using a new gasket fit the inlet manifold and tighten the nuts to 12-15 lb ft. Fit the carburetter and gasket.

Fit the crankcase ventilation oil separator on the cylinder block and connect the hose to the union on the inlet manifold.

Fit the deceleration valve on the inlet manifold and connect the hoses to their respective ports. Connect the distributor vacuum hoses to their respective ports on the inlet manifold.

Install the oil pressure transmitting unit.

Fitting the camshaft drive belt. Ensure that one end of the belt tensioner spring engages the groove in the anchor stud behind the pin of the back plate, then turn the tensioner clockwise as far as possible and firmly tighten the adjustment bolt. Align the timing marks as shown in **FIG 1 : 6** and fit the drive belt on the sprockets. Loosen the tensioner adjustment bolt, rotate the engine two complete turns to remove any slack in the belt and allow the tensioner to move firmly against the belt. Tighten the adjustment and pivot bolts to 34 lb ft and recheck the timing marks.

Fit the water outlet elbow and thermostat. Fit the water pump. Fit the alternator and its mounting brackets, adjusting the belt until there is about $\frac{1}{2}$ inch movement in the centre.

Fit the oil pan drain plug and fill with a recommended grade of engine oil.

The engine is now ready for installation in the car. This operation is described in **Section 1 : 2**.

1 :12 Fault diagnosis

(a) Engine will not start

1 Defective coil
2 Faulty capacitor in distributor
3 Dirty or incorrectly set contact breaker points
4 Ignition wires loose, insulation faulty
5 Water on ignition cables
6 Discharged battery or terminals
7 Faulty or jammed starter
8 Plug leads wrongly connected
9 Vapour lock in fuel pipe
10 Defective fuel pump
11 Over or under choking
12 Blocked fuel filter or jets
13 Leaking valves
14 Sticking valves
15 Valve timing incorrect
16 Ignition timing incorrect

(b) Engine stalls

1 Check 1, 2, 3, 4, 5, 10, 11, 12, 13 and 14 in (a)
2 Defective or incorrectly set sparking plugs
3 Ignition incorrectly set
4 Weak mixture
5 Water in fuel system
6 Fuel tank vent blocked
7 Incorrect valve clearances

(c) Engine idles badly

1 Check 2 and 7 in (b)
2 Air leak at manifold joints
3 Carburetter out of adjustment
4 Air leak in carburetter
5 Over rich mixture
6 Worn piston rings
7 Worn valve stems or guides
8 Weak valve springs
9 Fault in crankcase ventilation system

(d) Engine misfires

1 Check 1, 2, 3, 4, 5, 8,10, 12, 13, 14 and 16 in (a) and 2, 3, 4 and 7 in (b)
2 Weak or broken valve springs

(e) Engine overheats

(See **Chapter 4**).

(f) Compression low

1 Check 13 and 14 in (a), 6 and 7 in (c) and 2 in (d)
2 Worn piston ring grooves
3 Scored or worn cylinder bores

(g) Engine lacks power

1 Check 3, 10,11, 12, 13, 14, 15 and 16 in (a), 2, 3,4, and 7 in (b), 6 and 7 in (c) and 2 in (d). Also check (e) and (b)
2 Leaking joint washers
3 Fouled sparking plugs
4 Automatic ignition advance faulty

(h) Burnt valves or seats

1 Check 13 and 14 in (a), 7 in (b) and 2 in (d). Also check (e)
2 Excessive carbon around valve seats

(j) Sticking valves

1 Check 2 in (d)
2 Bent valve stem
3 Scored valve stem or guide
4 Incorrect valve clearance

(k) Excessive cylinder wear

1 Check 11 in (a) and see **Chapter 4**
2 Lack of oil
3 Dirty oil
4 Piston rings gummed up or broken
5 Badly fitting piston rings
6 Bent connecting rod

(l) Excessive oil consumption

1 Check 6 and 7 in (c) and check (k)
2 Ring gaps too wide
3 Oil holes in piston blocked
4 Scored cylinders
5 Oil level too high
6 External oil leaks
7 Valve stem oil seals defective

(m) Crankshaft or connecting rod bearing failure

1 Check 2 in (k)
2 Restricted oilways
3 Worn journals or crankpins
4 Loose bearing caps
5 Extremely low oil pressure
6 Bent connecting rod

(n) Poor water circulation

(See **Chapter 4**)

(o) High fuel consumption

(See **Chapter 2**)

(p) Engine vibration

1 Loose alternator bolts
2 Engine mounting rubbers loose or defective
3 Exhaust pipe mountings defective
4 Fan blades out of balance
5 Misfiring due to mixture, ignition or mechanical fault

CHAPTER 2

THE FUEL SYSTEM

2:1 Description

Some engines in this series are equipped with an approved system of crankcase ventilation and exhaust emission control and any modification may render the operator liable to an infringement of Government specification.

The carburetters on engines manufactured for use in the U.S. are equipped with idle fuel mixture adjustment limiters to keep emissions within specified limits. Under no circumstances may these limiters or their stops be modified. If, for any reason, the limiters have been removed, any fuel mixture adjustments must be made with an approved exhaust gas analyser.

Another feature of the system is the decel (deceleration) valve the purpose of which is to meter to the engine an additional supply of fuel and air during engine deceleration periods to permit more complete combustion at these times.

The fuel tank is located in the luggage compartment with a flush fitting pressure and vacuum sensitive filler cap as part of a fuel evaporative emission system. This is designed to limit the emission of fuel vapour or raw fuel into the atmosphere. It comprises: the fuel tank, pressure and vacuum sensitive filler cap, a .040 inch restrictor in the vapour line and a vapour absorbing charcoal canister. These may be seen in diagrammatic form in **FIG 2:1**.

The filler cap incorporates two valves, one to release excess pressure in the tank if the vapour line becomes blocked, and a vacuum relief valve to admit air to the tank as fuel is consumed.

As the level of fuel in the tank rises vapours are discharged to the atmosphere through the fill control tube and the annular space between the inner filler tube and the outer neck.

When the fuel level covers the fill control tube, vapours can no longer escape and the filler tube begins to fill up. So a vapour lock is created by the .040 inch restrictor and neither vapour nor fuel can flow through the vapour line to the charcoal canister.

The level of fuel in the tank is controlled by the level of the fill control tube which is positioned to maintain an expansion volume of approximately 10% of the tank capacity.

Under conditions of thermal expansion, vapour is forced through the restrictor to be absorbed in the charcoal canister mounted in the engine compartment. Vapours

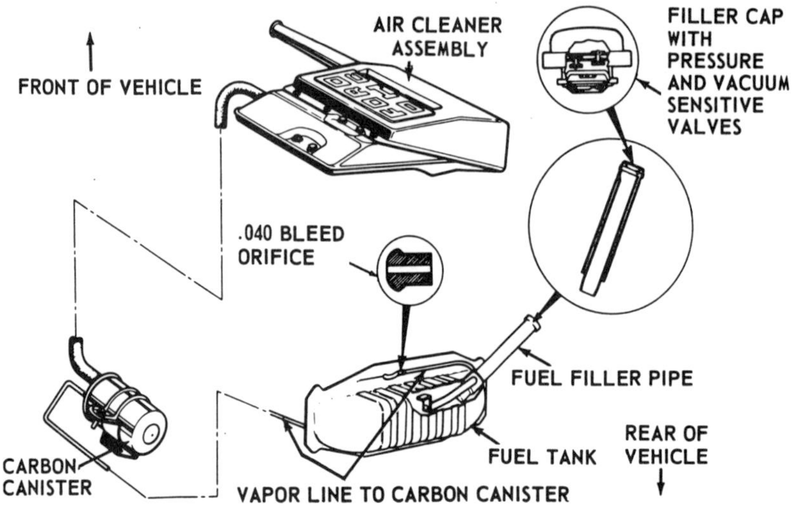

FIG 2:1 The fuel evaporative emission control system

absorbed by the charcoal are extracted by the flow of air through the canister into the air filter when the engine is started.

The carburetter fitted to these cars may be either a Motorcraft Model 5200 or a Weber 32/36 DFAV. They are both identical in operation, being two stage, two venturi carburetters in which the larger secondary is brought into operation by a mechanical linkage.

The primary stage includes a curb idle system, accelerator pump, idle transfer, main metering and power enrichment systems. On the secondary side, which draws its fuel supply from a common float chamber, there is a transfer system, main metering and power system. Fuel enrichment for cold starting is by means of an automatic choke operated by a thermally controlled spring located in a housing connected in the engine cooling system.

Throttle plate opening is sequential, the primary throttle opening first and bringing in the secondary throttle by means of a lever linkage with both throttles reaching the fully open position together.

The carburetter fitted to some of the 1300, 1600 range, is a single venturi downdraught, incorporating the usual embodiments, such as, idling, main, power valve and diaphragm type accelerator pump systems. Cold starting is by a fully automatic choke system that is attached to the upper body casting. It is operated by a thermal clock type spring that reacts to water temperature circulating through the engine.

Detachable upper and lower body castings form the carburetter unit, apart from the choke the upper body incorporates the float chamber cover, float pivot brackets, fuel inlet connection tube, gauze filter, needle valve assembly, air intake, choke plate, the main and idling jets, power valve system and discharge nozzle. The lower body incorporates the float chamber, throttle barrel and integral venturi, throttle plate spindle and lever, idling discharge orifice and progression slot, adjustment screws, distributor vacuum connection and the choke linkage.

Adjustments for slow running are provided for by volume control and throttle stop screws. Float setting, choke plate pull down, fast idle and accelerator pump stroke can be adjusted by bending tabs and linkage rods. However, the bending of linkage rods should not be necessary as these are accurately adjusted during assembly.

An exploded view of a typical Ford downdraught carburetter with a single venturi is shown in **FIG 2:2**. The identification number of the carburetter is stamped on the float chamber.

2:2 The fuel pump

This is a mechanical unit located on the lefthand side of the engine and actuated by a rod driven by an eccentric on the auxiliary shaft. The pump is permanently sealed and in the event of failure to operate satisfactorily it must be renewed. See **FIG 2:3**.

Testing:

Before commencing to test the pump make sure that the disposable in-line fuel filter is serviceable. If in any doubt, change the filter. These tests are made with the pump fitted to the engine and at normal working temperature.

Remove the air cleaner assembly and, taking great care to avoid spillage on a hot engine, disconnect the supply line at the carburetter. Connect a pressure gauge, restrictor and flexible hose between the filter and the carburetter as shown diagrammatically in **FIG 2:4**.

Run the engine at the specified idle speed, 750 rev/min for manual transmissions, 650 for automatic, and vent the system into the jar by opening the restrictor for a moment. Close the restrictor, allow the pressure to stabilize and note the reading. The pressure should be between 4 and 5 lb/sq inch and a reading outside these limits indicates a defective pump which should be renewed.

If the pressure test is satisfactory make the capacity (volume) test as follows:—

With the engine at idle speed open the restrictor and allow the fuel to discharge into the jar for 43 seconds. In this time at least one pint of fuel should have been delivered.

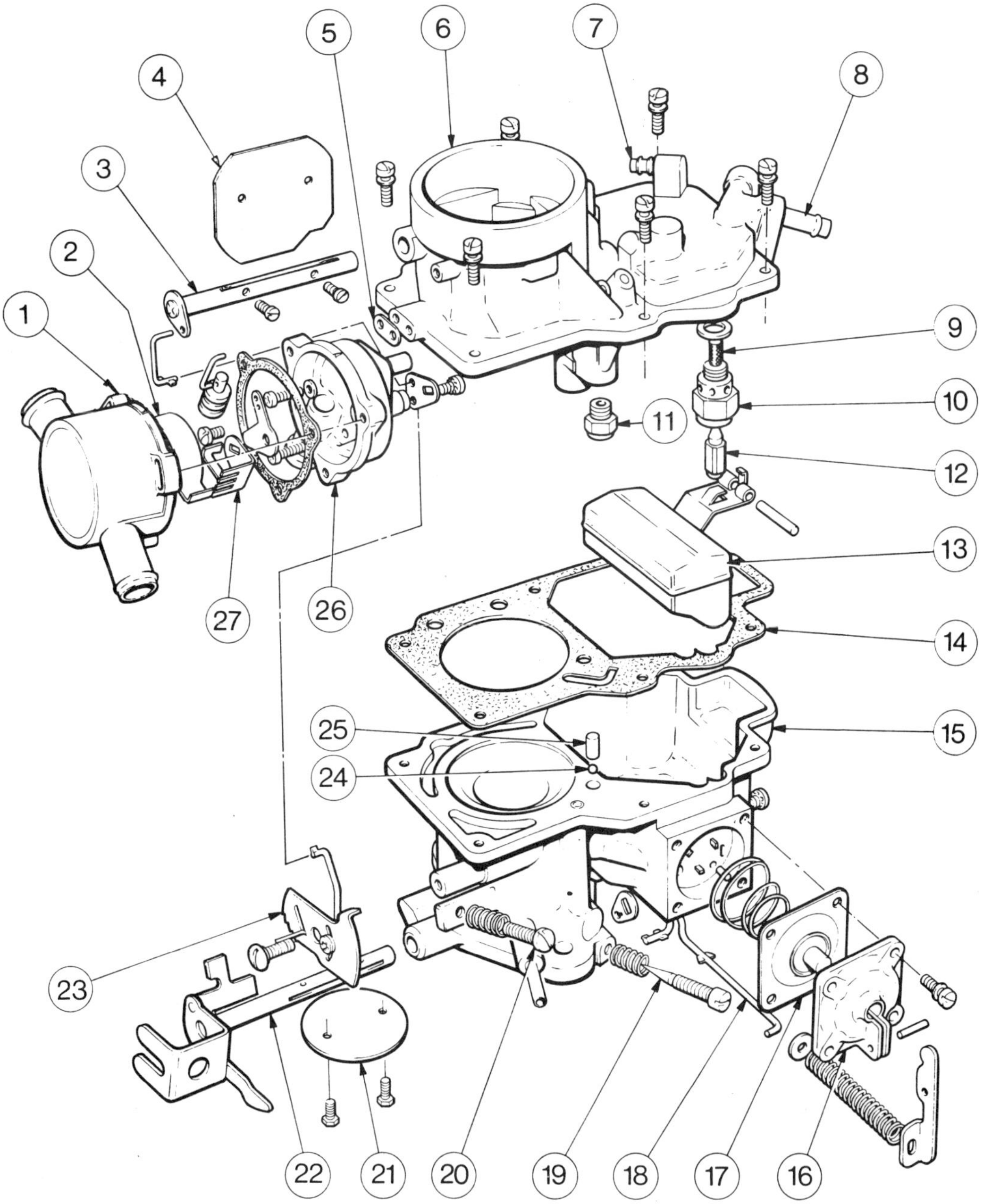

FIG 2:2 Exploded view of typical Ford downdraught carburetter with automatic choke

Key to Fig 2:2 1 Bi-metal spring and water housing 2 Bi-metal spring 3 Choke spindle 4 Choke plate 5 Gasket 6 Upper body 7 External vent 8 Fuel inlet 9 Filter 10 Needle valve housing 11 Main jet 12 Needle valve 13 Float 14 Gasket 15 Lower body 16 Accelerator pump cover 17 Pump diaphragm 18 Pump rod 19 Volume control screw 20 Throttle stop screw 21 Throttle plate 22 Throttle spindle 23 Fast idle cam 24 and 25 Discharge ball and weight 26 Autochoke housing 27 Spring operated lever

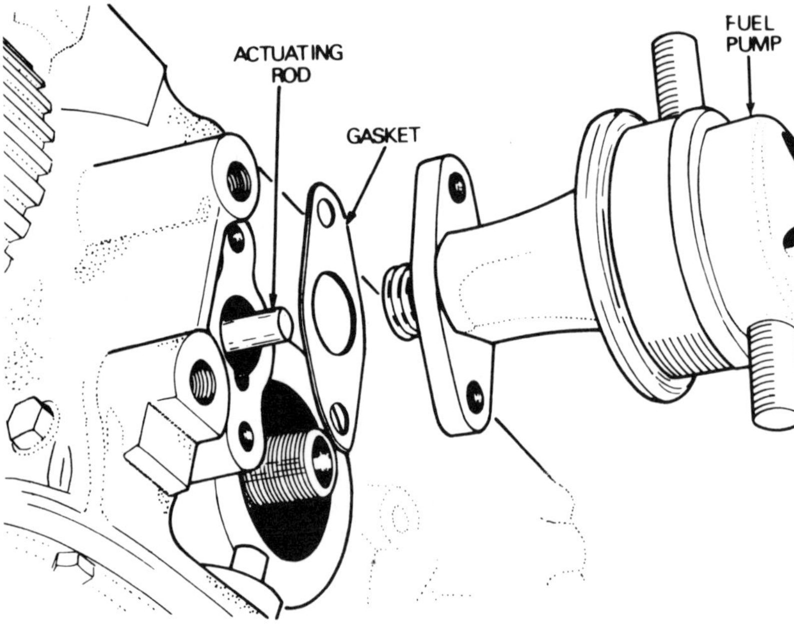

FIG 2:3 The fuel pump and actuating rod

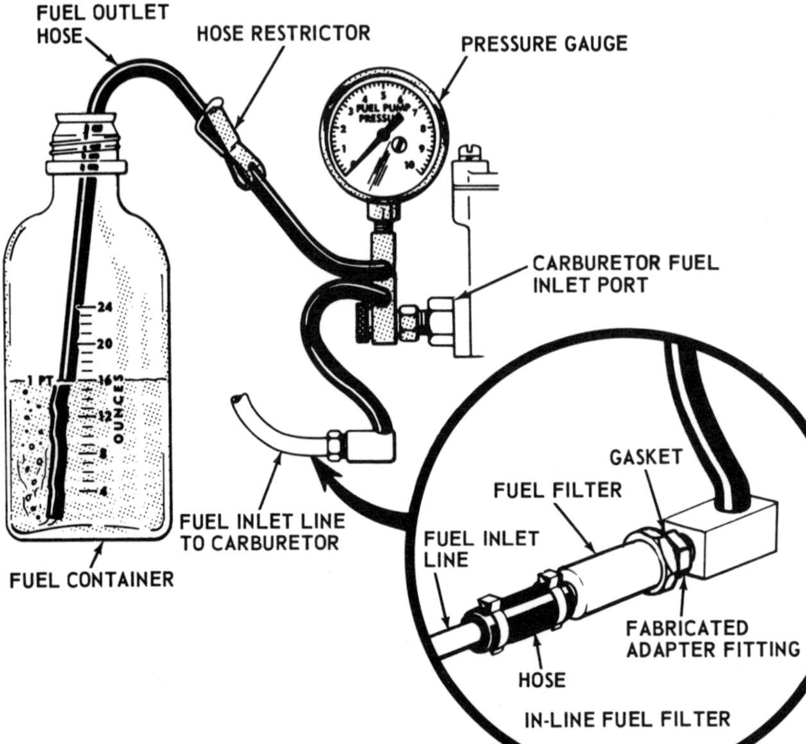

FIG 2:4 Testing the fuel pump

Failure to reach this amount may be due to a restriction in the supply from the car's tank or a blocked vent, and this can be checked by repeating the test using an external fuel supply.

Removing the pump:

Disconnect the two fuel hoses from the pump unions.

Unscrew the two retaining bolts and lift off the pump and gasket. The gasket should be discarded and a new one obtained for refitting.

Remove the actuating rod.

Before reinstalling the pump, make sure that all jointing material is removed from the two faces and prepare the new gasket with an oil resistant sealer on both sides.

Fit the actuating rod, place the new gasket in position and fit the pump, progressively tightening the bolts to 12-15 lb ft.

Reconnect the two fuel hoses using new clamps if available.

Start the engine and check for leaks.

2:3 The fuel tank

This is mounted in an upright position in the luggage compartment and held by four retaining bolts. See **FIG 2:5**.

Removal:

Drain the fuel from the tank by siphoning into a suitable container and loosen the lower clamp securing the flexible hose to the neck of the tank.

Disconnect the fuel supply line and the vapour line, then remove the four bolts and partly lower the tank to give access for the removal of the wire from the fuel gauge tank unit. Remove the tank and unscrew the sender unit.

Replacement of the tank is carried out in the reverse order. Note that a new gasket should be used on the sender unit which is installed with the float hanging downwards.

After filling the tank the operation of the fuel gauge should be checked, but remember that the gauge takes about half a minute to reach a true reading.

2:4 The Weber 32/36 DFAV carburetter

This particular type of Weber carburetter is fitted to the 2000 OHC model but the foregoing instructions will suffice for the Weber carburetters fitted to other models. Refer to Technical Data for the reference numbers and jet sizes.

Removal:

Remove the air cleaner, this is described fully later in this chapter, and disconnect the fuel supply hose. Disconnect the vacuum hose from the carburetter. Disconnect the operating linkage from the throttle control shaft.

Drain sufficient coolant from the cooling system so that the hoses may be removed from the automatic choke without spillage.

Remove the four securing nuts from the flange studs with their washers and lift off the carburetter and gasket. Discard the old gasket and clean the joint surfaces.

Refitting will be a reversal of the above operation.

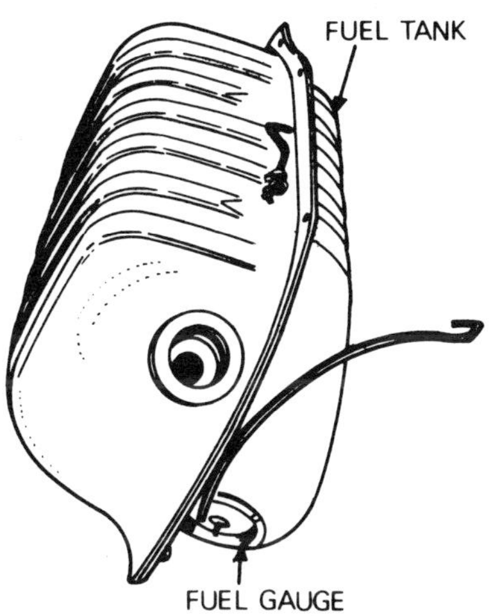

FIG 2:5 The fuel tank

2:5 Dismantling the carburetter

The components of the carburetter are shown in **FIG 2:6** and reference to this illustration will assist in the following operations.

Bowl cover:

Remove the fuel inlet filter plug and filter, then remove the retaining screws and washers from the bowl cover (air horn).

Remove the retaining clips from the choke rod and lift off the cover (**FIG 2:7**). Remove the choke rod seal plug and seal.

Remove the float shaft, float and needle valve. Remove the three vacuum diaphragm screws and the diaphragm.

Automatic choke:

Remove the screw securing the water housing and lift off the cover and gasket. Take out the screws securing housing for the thermostatic spring and remove the ring, housing and gasket.

Remove the three screws from the choke housing and slide it off the main body—see **FIG 2:8**, disengaging the fast idle rod. Note the location of the long screw, and do not forget the O-ring for the vacuum passage.

Remove the nut and locking washer from the choke shaft, noting the position of the fast idle cam spring, shown also in **FIG 2:8**.

Remove the loop of the spring from the choke lever then withdraw the choke lever and the spring. Remove the spring retainer. Remove the washer, choke shaft, lever and Teflon bearing.

Remove the fast idle lever and shaft retaining screw, bush and spring washer. Remove the lever and flat spacer, adjusting screw and spring.

Remove the three screws and lift off the choke diaphragm cover. Remove the return spring and the diaphragm and rod assembly. Take out the diaphragm plug and adjusting screw from the cover.

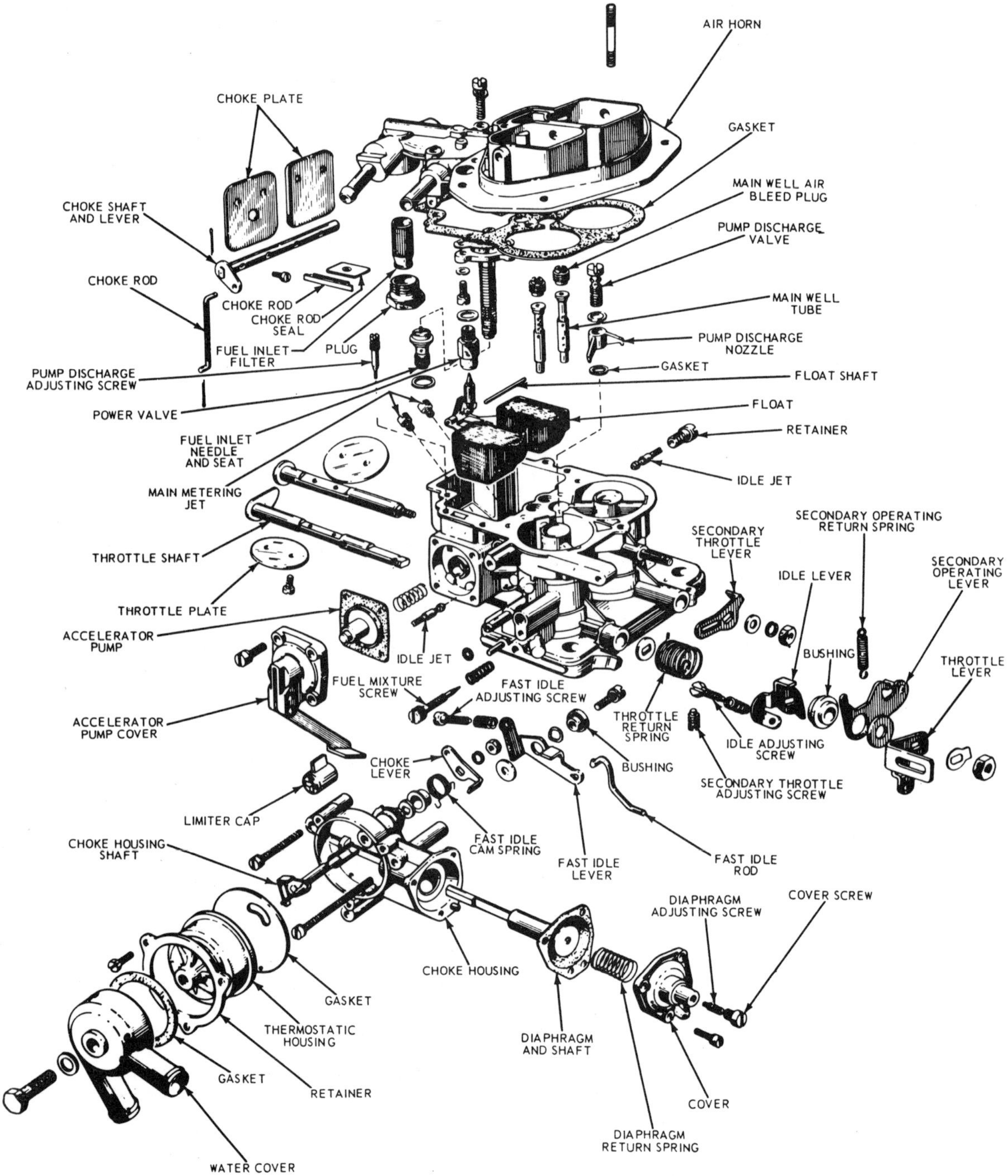

FIG 2:6 Components of the carburetter

Accelerator pump:

Remove four screws and lift off the pump cover assembly, lift out the diaphragm assembly and the return spring.

Remove the pump discharge valve assembly also the discharge nozzle and two gaskets. Remove the pump channel plug screw.

Main body:

Carefully note the sizes of the items about to be dismantled in order to ensure correct replacement.

Remove the primary and secondary main well air bleed plugs and tubes. Remove the main metering jets.

Remove the power valve and gasket. Remove the primary and secondary idle jet retainer plugs and the jets which are located on the sides of the main body. The location of the various jets can be seen in **FIG 2:9**.

Turn the idle limiter cap in to the stop and remove it. Count the number of turns required to lightly seat the idle adjustment needle to the nearest $\frac{1}{16}$ of a turn, then remove the needle and spring.

Remove the secondary operating lever return spring.

Remove the nut for the primary throttle lever, the lock-washer, lever and flat washer. Remove the secondary operating lever assembly and lever bushing.

Note how the primary throttle return spring is hooked over the idle adjusting lever and the carburetter body, then remove the idle adjusting lever spring and shaft washer. Remove the idle speed screw and spring from the idle adjusting lever.

Remove the secondary throttle lever nut, washers and lever. Remove the secondary idle adjusting screw.

Reassembling the carburetter:

This is a reversal of the dismantling procedure but mention will be made of a few points requiring attention.

When installing the idle mixture adjusting needle and spring, turn it in until it bottoms lightly and then turn it back exactly the number of turns recorded when dismantling. Fit a new limiter cap on the idle mixture needle with its stop tab against the lean side of the stop on the body.

Be very careful to see that the correct size of jet or tube is fitted in each location.

Fit the accelerator pump discharge nozzle with a gasket on both top and bottom.

When fitting the pump diaphragm gasket it will be of assistance to hold the operating lever open. Tighten the four cover screws in rotation.

Automatic choke:

First insert the diaphragm adjusting screw so that the threads are flush with the inside of the cover. See **FIG 2:10**. Fit the adjusting screw plug.

Install the diaphragm and rod assembly, fit the return spring and cover and the three securing screws.

Fit the fast idle adjusting screw and spring, then the flat spacer and adjusting lever. Fit the spring washer, bushing screw and lock washer.

Install the Teflon bushing at the thread end of the choke housing shaft and carefully insert the shaft into the bore.

Fit the choke shaft washer, spring retainer, fast idle cam spring and choke lever with the loop of the spring over the arm of the lever. Fit the lock washer and nut.

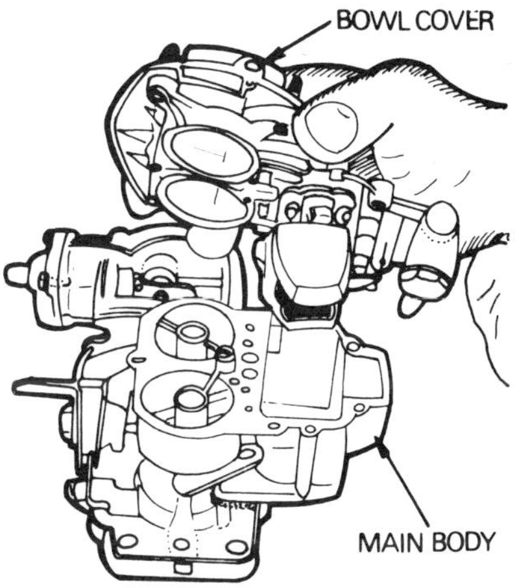

FIG 2:7 Removing the bowl cover

Fit the O-ring on the vacuum passage. Fit the bent end of the fast idle rod in the fast idle adjusting lever and the other end in the primary throttle operating lever.

Fit the three screws for the choke housing and note the position of the long screw.

Place the thermostatic housing and gasket in position with the index mark correctly aligned, fit the retaining ring and tighten the three screws.

Fit the choke water housing and gasket and the retaining screw.

Bowl cover:

Fit the needle seat and gasket. Install the vacuum diaphragm by depressing the spring and, with the screws just finger tight, hold the stem so that the diaphragm is horizontal then tighten the screws evenly.

Fit the float, shaft and needle and adjust the level as described later in **Section 2:6**.

Fit the choke rod seal and plug, insert the choke rod and hook it into the choke lever. Fit the retaining clip.

Screw down the cover, fit the filter with the open end inwards and the plug.

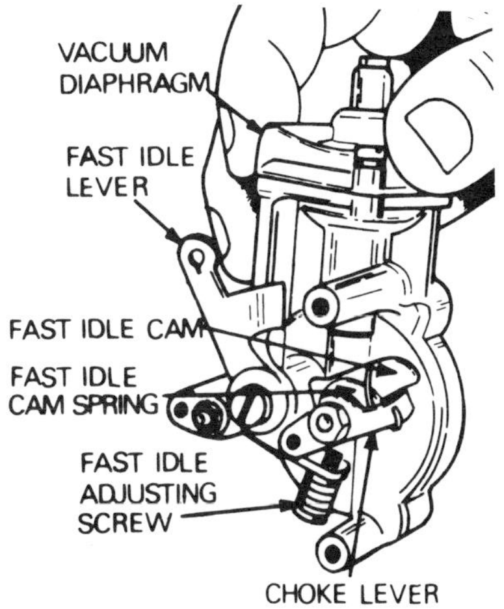

FIG 2:8 Removing the automatic choke

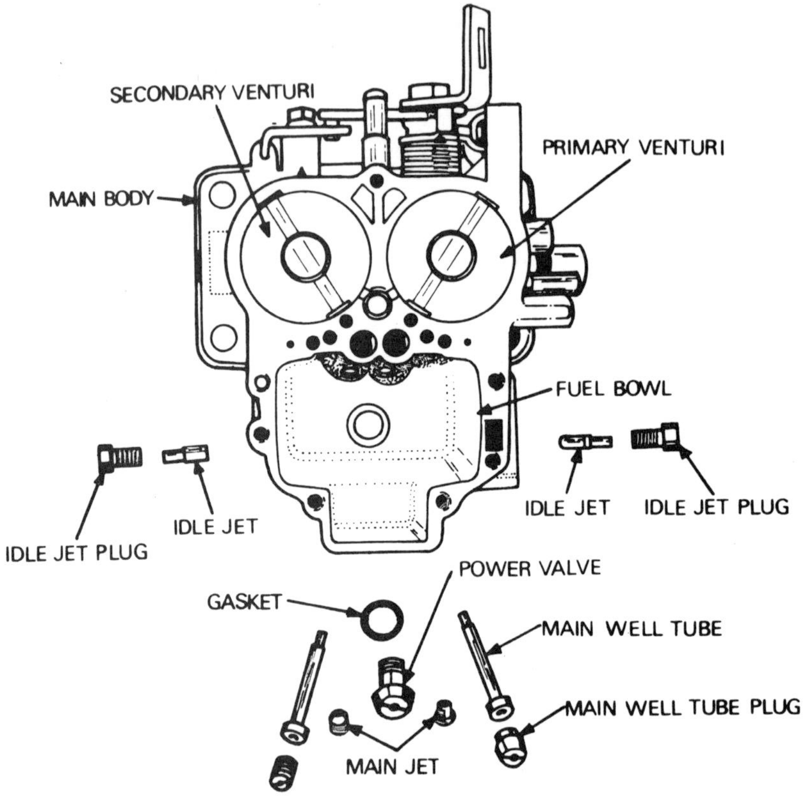

FIG 2:9 Vertical view showing location of jets

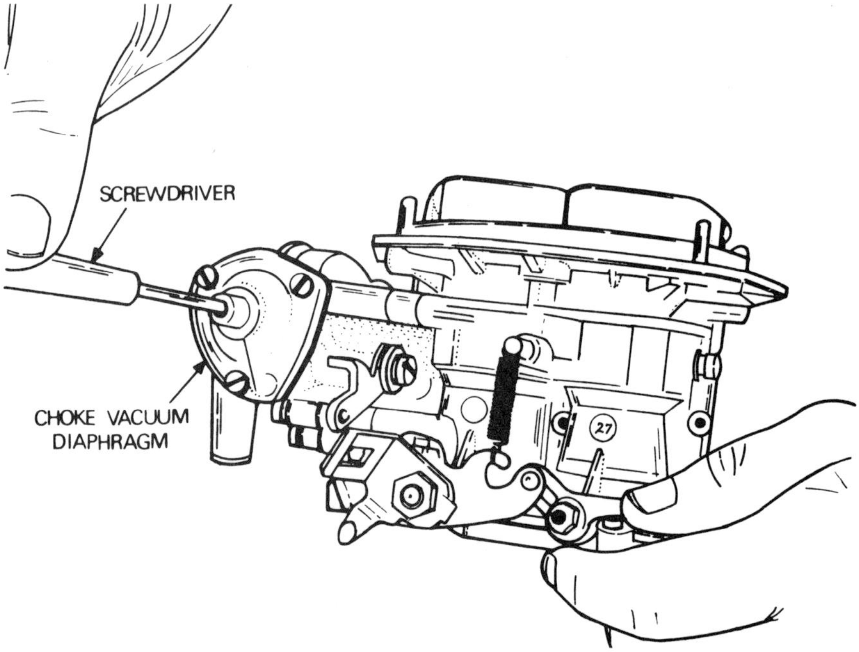

FIG 2:10 Adjusting the diaphragm of the automatic choke

2:6 Carburetter adjustments

Idle speed and fuel mixture:

Bring the engine to full working temperature after ensuring that the ignition timing is correct. Fit an accurate tachometer. On manual transmission cars the gear must be in Neutral, with automatic transmission the selector must be in Drive.

With the air cleaner in position, adjust the curb idle to 750 rev/min for manual or 650 for automatic transmissions with the idle adjustment screw.

Turn the idle mixture adjusting screw inwards to obtain the smoothest possible idle within the range of the idle limiter, which as mentioned earlier must not be disturbed in any way.

Fast idle cam clearance (see FIG 2:11):

Insert a $\frac{5}{32}$ inch drill between the lower edge of the choke plate and the wall of the bore.

Hold the fast idle screw on the second step of the cam, and measure the clearance between the tang on the choke lever and the arm of the fast idle cam. This dimension should be between .01 and .03 inch and the choke lever tang should be bent up or down as necessary to obtain this dimension.

Choke plate vacuum pull down:

Remove the three screws and the ring retaining the thermostatic spring cover. Do **not** remove the screw to the water cover, but pull the water cover and spring cover out of the way as shown in **FIG 2:12** and with a screwdriver push the diaphragm stem back against its stop.

Place a .26 inch rod between the lower edge of the choke plate and the wall of the bore and remove any slack from the linkage by pressing with the finger on the upper edge of the choke plate.

Adjust the clearance by removing the plug from the diaphragm and turning the adjusting screw in or out as necessary.

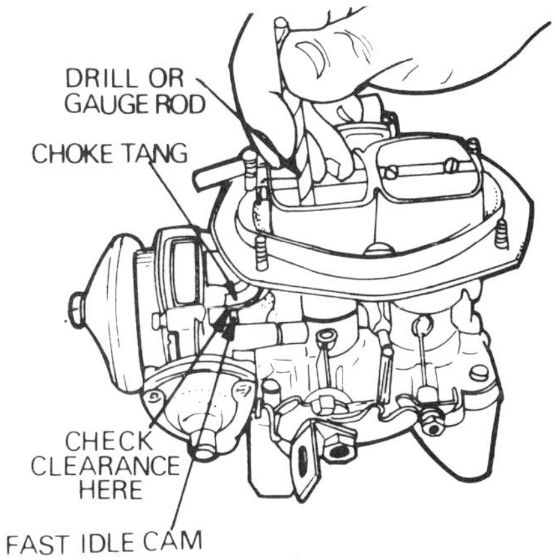

FIG 2:11 Fast idle cam clearance

Dechoke clearance:

With the throttle lever held fully open, take up any slack in the choke linkage by pressing with a finger on the top edge of the choke plate and measure the clearance between its lower edge and the bore wall.

This should be .320 inch and can be set if necessary by bending the tab on the fast idle lever where it touches the fast idle cam.

Fast idle:

This adjustment also must be made with a hot engine. Position the fast idle screw on the second step of the cam against the shoulder of the first step and adjust the engine speed to 1800 rev/min by turning the adjusting screw as required.

Float level setting:

Hold the bowl cover assembly upside down so that the float tang rests lightly on the spring loaded needle valve and note that the distance between the top of the float

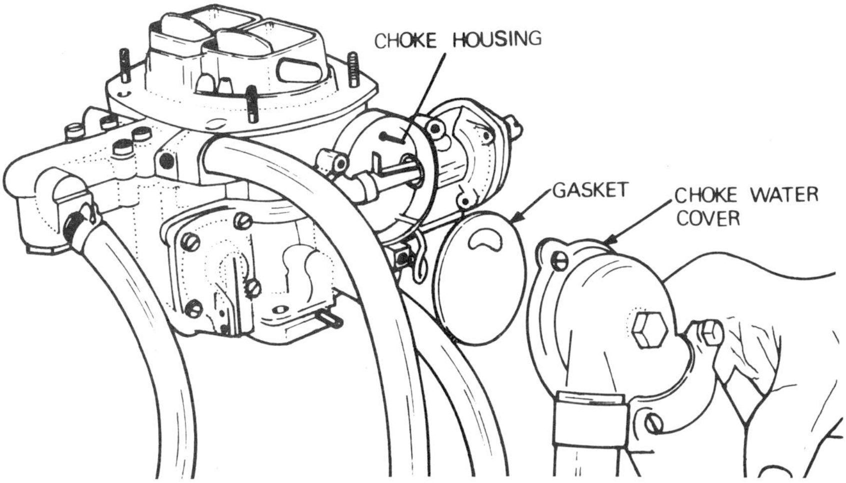

FIG 2:12 Removing choke spring cover

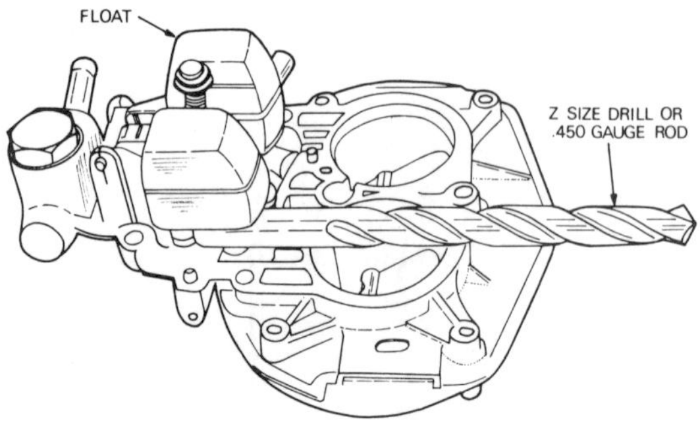

FIG 2:13 Setting the float level

and the under surface of the cover should be .45 inch. This is shown by the insertion of a Z size drill as in **FIG 2:13**.

If it is necessary to adjust the clearance, carefully bend the float tang up or down as required.

Now hold the cover assembly in its normal position and measure the distance between the under surface of the cover and the lowest point of the float. This should be 1.9 inches and may be obtained by bending the drop tang as necessary.

Choke spring:

The correct setting for the cover to the thermostatic spring is $\frac{1}{8}$ inch on the weak (anti-clockwise) side of the index mark. A small scribed line or punch mark may be made to indicate the correct location.

To adjust when necessary, remove the air cleaner, loosen the three choke cover screws and rotate the cover as required. Do not remove the water cover.

Secondary throttle stop screw (See FIG 2:14):

Screw back the stop screw until the secondary throttle seats fully in its bore.

From this point turn the screw in until it just touches the tab on the secondary throttle lever and then give it $\frac{1}{4}$ turn in addition.

Deceleration valve adjustment:

With a hot engine connect up a tachometer and, by means of a T piece, connect a vacuum gauge in the line between the carburetter and the decel valve.

Raise the engine speed to 3000 rev/min for two seconds and release the throttle completely, noting the time taken for the reading on the vacuum gauge to drop to zero.

For engines with manual transmission this time should be between $2\frac{1}{2}$ and $3\frac{1}{2}$ seconds. With automatic it should be $1\frac{1}{2}$ to $3\frac{1}{2}$ seconds.

If the valve needs to be adjusted, remove the coloured cap (when fitted) for access to the central nylon adjuster. To increase the timing the adjuster is turned outwards, while to increase the time interval it must be screwed in until the correct timing is obtained.

When the nylon adjuster is flush with the threaded collar the maximum permissible adjustment is one turn in or 9 turns outward. If the specified timing cannot be obtained within these limits a new deceleration valve should be installed.

2:7 The Motorcraft carburetter type 5200 2-V

As mentioned earlier, this is for practical purposes the same as the Weber carburetter and the information given in **Sections 2:4, 2:5** and **2:6** is applicable.

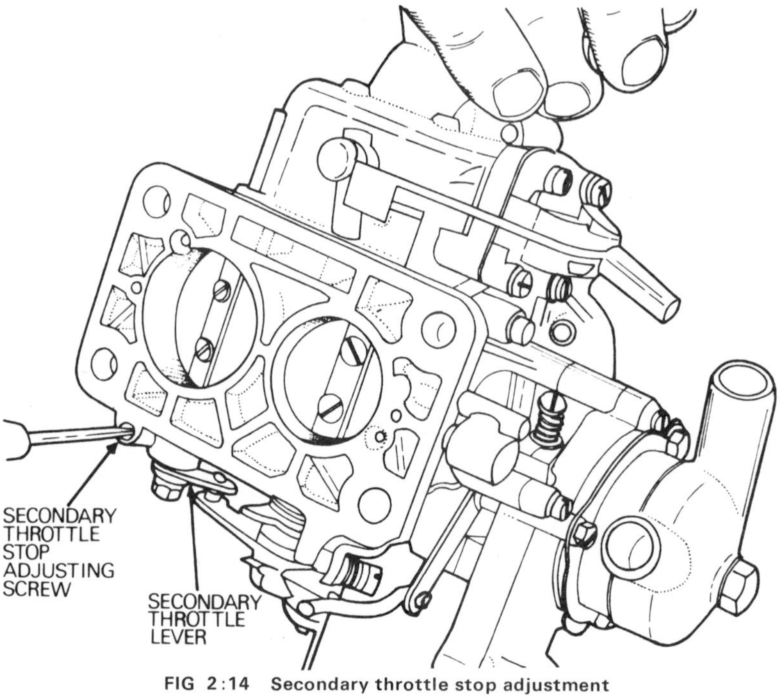

FIG 2:14 Secondary throttle stop adjustment

2:8 Ford downdraught carburetter

An exploded view of the Ford carburetter with automatic control is shown in **FIG 2:2**.

The automatic control of the choke is effected partly by a bi-metallic coil 2 heated from the cylinder head, and partly by a piston under the influence of intake depression. The closed head canister 1 with water from the cylinder head circulating, supports a bi-metal coil the free end of which engages a three-position slotted lever 27 controlling the choke plate 4 and spindle 3 through a short link.

The same shaft supports, within the housing, a second two-position lever linked with a piston and cylinder assembly sensing the intake depression. The coil, when the engine is cold, closes the choke plate but opens it gradually as the coolant temperature rises. Depression of the accelerator pedal with the choke in the closed position, lowers the pressure in the intake and this, communicated to the piston, overcomes the force of the coil and opens the choke plate.

A spring-loaded power valve in the main jet supporting stub is held closed by manifold depression at part engine load, fuel being supplied only by the main jet. At full throttle, the depression is virtually destroyed and the power valve opens to admit extra fuel via a supplementary jet into the emulsion tube.

Dismantling and inspection:

Remove the fuel pipe to the carburetter, the vacuum control pipe to the distributor, the vent pipe and the throttle control linkages, disconnect the water hoses, loosen and remove the three screws attaching the thermal head to the choke control and ease the end of the bi-metal coil free of the linkage. The thermal head may then be tied out of the way without disturbing the water connections. Unbolt and remove the carburetter from the inlet manifold and transfer to the bench.

Commence dismantling by removing the six screws securing the upper body 6, to the lower and lift carefully, unlatching the choke link. Remove complete with gasket 14. Extract the accelerator pump discharge ball valve and weight 24 and 25, and store in a safe place.

Withdraw the float arm pivot and remove the float 13. Extract the needle valve assembly 10, unscrewing the housing from the upper body. Carefully extract the small gauze filter 9, then unscrew and remove the main jet 11.

To remove the choke plate and spindle 3 and 4, remove the two screws securing the plate to the spindle and ease the plate from the slot in the spindle. Remove the spindle from the body.

Remove the screw securing the thermostatic spring lever from its shaft (see **FIG 2:15**), remove the spring lever, piston lever, link and piston from the housing, loosen and remove the screws securing the housing to the body and remove the housing. Carefully extract the ptfe bush and dismantle the choke and throttle linkage behind.

To dismantle the accelerator pump, release the four screws securing the pump to the lower body and remove complete with operating arm, spring lever, diaphragm and diaphragm return spring. Dismantle the components.

Remove the screws securing the throttle plate to its spindle, withdraw the spindle and remove the valve plate. Thoroughly clean all parts and examine for wear or damage.

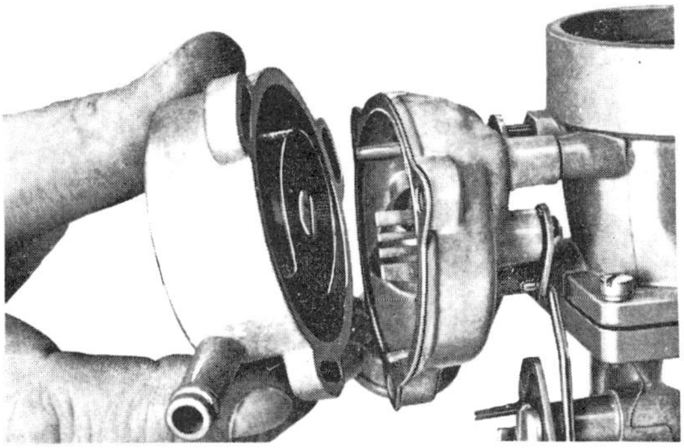

FIG 2:15 Fitting the autochoke cover

Reassembly and installation:

Reassembly is a simple reversal of the dismantling sequence followed by certain adjustments to ensure maximum performance when installed.

During assembly, pay particular attention to the following points. First, check that both the choke and the throttle plates on their shafts are free to turn without fouling the sides of the throats in which they are located.

When assembling the automatic choke control, see that the coil tongue is inserted in the centre slot of the lever and that the index mark on the rim of the water housing coincides with the centre mark on the body (see **FIG 2:15**).

When fitting the upper body, check that the link between choke and throttle levers is properly located. If this is over centre, the choke is inoperative. Hold the choke lever in the closed position when tightening the retaining screws.

Do not operate the throttle linkage with the upper body removed unless the ball valve and weight have been extracted. Operation may cause these to be ejected from their seating and lost or,

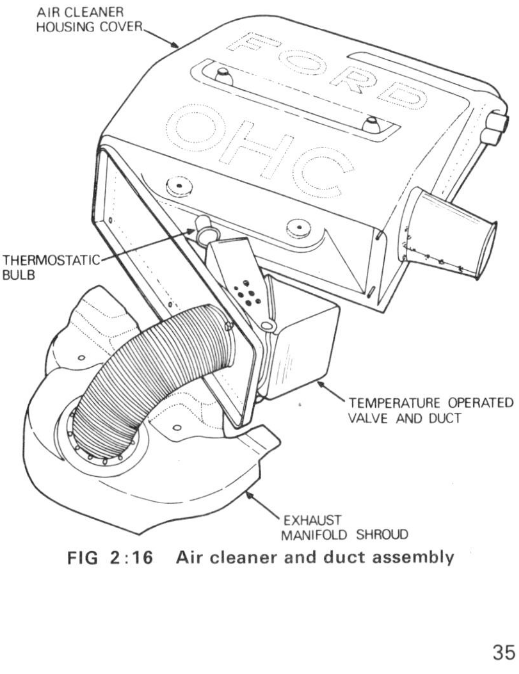

FIG 2:16 Air cleaner and duct assembly

should the carburetter be in place on the engine, fall into the venturi and possibly the engine intake. This would cause serious damage.

After the carburetter has been reassembled, reinstall it in position on the inlet manifold and reconnect the fuel pipe, vent pipe and control linkages. On the automatic models, reconnect the water hoses or, should the thermal head have been unscrewed from the body at dismantling,

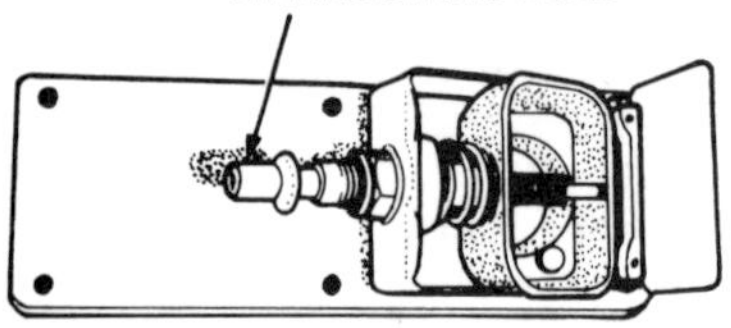

FIG 2:17 **Thermostatic valve assembly**

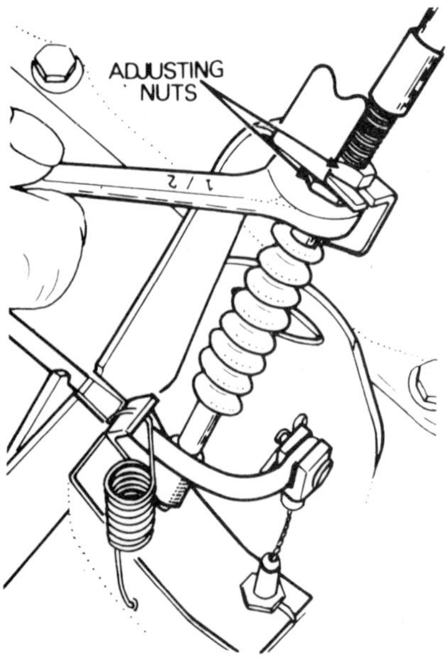

FIG 2:18 **Accelerator cable adjustment**

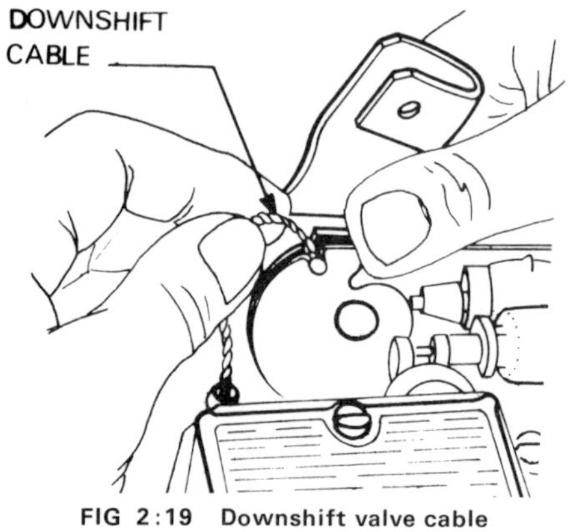

FIG 2:19 **Downshift valve cable**

replace the thermal head. Reconnect the vacuum lines to the pipe (seen below 20 in **FIG 2:2**). Tuning can now be carried out before installing the air filter.

Tuning for slow-running:

With the engine warmed up and the throttle stop set to give an engine speed of 1000 rev/min, adjust the slow-running volume control screw 19 (see **FIG 2:2**) until the engine begins to hunt. Turn back $\frac{1}{8}$ of a turn. Reduce the engine speed to about 700 rev/min, the normal warm engine idling speed, and check that each time the throttle is opened suddenly, the engine responds. Check that the engine speed increases to about 1800 rev/min on the fast-idling cam.

2:9 Air cleaner system

This is shown in **FIG 2:16** and has a more important role than is often the case. A temperature operated valve is included which not only provides the engine with an air supply at optimum temperature (90°C-100°F) at all times, but also assists the vehicle to meet Federal regulations with regard to exhaust emissions.

Operation:

While the engine is warming up air is drawn through the hot air intake over a thermostatic bulb and into the air cleaner. **FIG 2:17**. This air comes from around the exhaust manifold and soon heats up and at about 90°F causes the thermostatic bulb to start closing the valve to the hot air intake and allow air from the under-hood area to pass to the engine in varying ratio until at about 110°F the hot air intake is fully closed.

Testing:

Under normal conditions at an ambient temperature of 85°F or less and the engine cold, the flap valve should be in the open position, shutting off the cold air intake. If the valve is not open, check for excessive wear or breakage of the valve in the duct. As the duct and valve flap are not serviced separately a new assembly will be required if these conditions are present.

Remove the assembly from the car and immerse in water so that the thermostatic bulb is completely covered. Raise the water temperature to 85°F and observe the valve position after 5 minutes. It should still be open.

Increase the temperature to 110 and again observe the valve position after 5 minutes. The valve should now be fully closed.

If the valve does not operate as specified and no binding or damage is present the bulb should be renewed.

Servicing:

The filter element is removed for renewal by unscrewing the five retaining nuts on the housing cover and lifting it off.

For access to the bulb, remove the duct and valve assembly from the air cleaner housing (**FIG 2:17**). Remove the bulb using a suitable wrench on the flats provided.

Remove the metal shims from the old bulb and fit them on the new one, but do **not** under any circumstances adjust the size of the shim pack.

Use a soft setting sealer when refitting the bulb and use the correct wrench, never use pliers or grips on the bulb as this may affect the calibration. Check the operation of the new assembly as described.

2:10 Throttle pedal adjustment

The correct positioning of the accelerator pedal when automatic transmission is fitted is most important and it should be adjusted as follows:

Disconnect the accelerator cable at the bellcrank ball joint and then adjust the bolt under the instrument panel to obtain a distance of $4\frac{1}{2}$ inches between the top face of the pedal and the floor.

Set the engine idle speed to specification.

Adjust the cable—see **FIG 2:18**—until it just slides on to the bellcrank ball joint and connect the cable to the joint.

Check to make sure that the carburetter throttle plates reach the fully open position when the pedal is fully depressed and that it returns freely to the idle position when the pedal is released.

Downshift valve control cable:

This determines the gearshift points on an automatic transmission and also actuates the kick-down mechanism. Adjustment of this control will be described in **Chapter 7** but removal of the cable if required is as follows:

Disconnect the cable at the bellcrank assembly, loosen the nut retaining the cable to the bracket and remove the cable.

Raise the car and drain the transmission. Remove the transmission oil pan.

Rotate the cam and disconnect the cable as shown in **FIG 2:19**, then unscrew the cable from the transmission casing and remove.

To fit a new cable, screw it tightly into the transmission case. Rotate the cam and connect the cable. Refit the oil pan.

Lower the car. Position the cable in the bracket and fit the retaining nut.

Connect the cable to the bellcrank assembly. Fill the transmission with the specified fluid and then carry out a pressure check and adjust the control cable as required.

2:11 Fault diagnosis

(a) Leakage or insufficient fuel delivered

1 Tank air vent restricted
2 Fuel pipes blocked
3 Air leaks at pipe connections
4 Pump or carburetter filter blocked
5 Pump gasket faulty
6 Pump diaphragm defective
7 Pump valves sticking or seating badly
8 Fuel vapourizing in pipes due to heat

(b) Excessive fuel consumption

1 Carburetter needs adjusting
2 Fuel leakage
3 Sticking choke control
4 Dirty air cleaner
5 Excessive engine temperature
6 Automatic choke not returning to open position
7 Float level too high, float punctured
8 Brakes binding
9 Tyres under inflated
10 Idle speed too high
11 Car overloaded
12 Excessive use of low gears

(c) Idle speed too high

1 Rich mixture, wrong jets
2 Controls sticking
3 Idle adjustment incorrect
4 Worn throttle plate(s)

(d) Poor idling

1 Air leaks at manifold gaskets
2 Defective servo or distributor vacuum hoses
3 Worn carburetter bushes, spindles or controls

(e) No fuel delivery

1 Float needle stuck
2 Tank vent blocked
3 Obstructed pipe lines
4 Pump diaphragm defective, broken spring
5 Pump inlet valve stuck open
6 Air leak on suction side of pump
7 Blocked filters

NOTES

CHAPTER 3

THE IGNITION SYSTEM

3:1 The ignition system

This is a conventional arrangement of coil, battery and distributor. A resistance wire is included in the circuit between the switch and the coil to ensure that while full battery voltage is available for starting, the actual running voltage is reduced with the aim of increasing component life.

The distributor is mounted on the left hand side of the engine and is driven by skew gear from the auxiliary shaft, rotating in a clockwise direction. On the North America 2000 models, in conjunction with the Imco system of exhaust emission control a dual vacuum capsule is fitted. The outer or primary diaphragm uses the carburetter vacuum to advance the ignition timing during normal road-load operation, but not during deceleration or idle.

The inner or secondary diaphragm is actuated by the vacuum in the inlet manifold and provides additional retardation of the spark during periods of closed throttle operation, as at idle or deceleration. By this means the emission of exhaust hydrocarbons is reduced at these times.

3:2 Removing and refitting the distributor

Remove the distributor cap and disconnect the vacuum lines from the advance capsule.

In order to simplify reinstallation the engine should be turned until the crankshaft pulley is at the specified timing mark, the timing marks being clearly shown in **FIG 3:1**, refer also to Technical Data. To check that No. 1 is on the compression stroke, remove the oil filler cap and note that the two cam lobes are both up i.e. in the fully closed position the distributor rotor should now be pointing at the No. 1 mark on the distributor body.

Remove the LT wire and loosen the clamping bolt. The distributor may now be lifted out perhaps bringing with it the hexagonal shaft that drives the oil pump.

Refitting:

Ensure first that the crankshaft is in the position described above.

If the oil pump drive shaft was withdrawn with the distributor, coat one end of the shaft with heavy grease

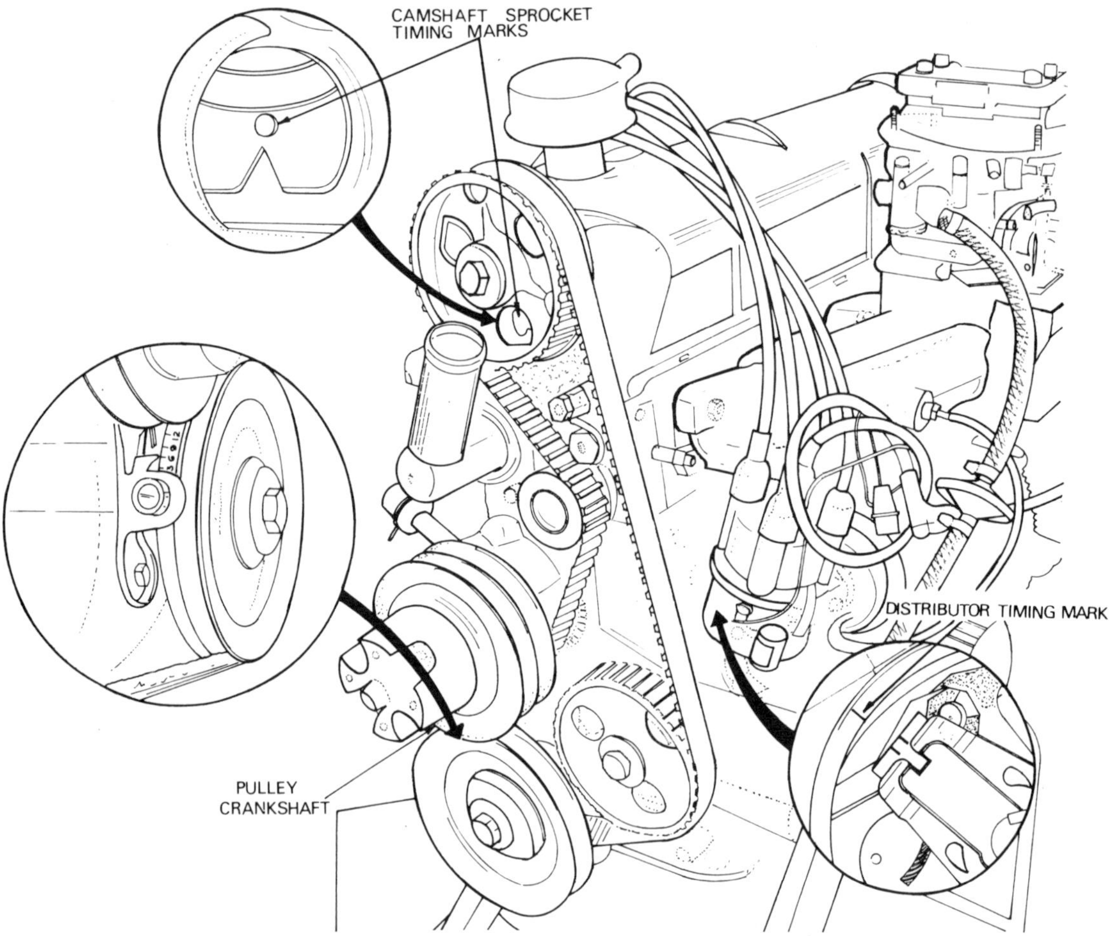

FIG 3:1 The timing marks

to hold it in position and insert the greased end into the recess in the distributor drive shaft.

Insert the distributor, ensuring that the rotor is lined up with the No. 1 mark when in position, and that the oil pump shaft is firmly located in the pump.

Fit the distributor clamp bolt and the distributor cap.

3:3 Dismantling the distributor

One of two makes of distributor will be installed, either a Bosch or Fords own make under the trade name of Motorcraft. The part numbers applicable to the OHC variants of the Capri are listed in Technical Data and reference should be made to the type applicable before ordering spares.

The following instructions for dismantling are a generalization of the two makes but little, if any, difficulty should be encountered with this simple dismantling operation. The important points to remember are to replace the primary and secondary springs in the exact position from which they were removed. If the drive gear is removed, take note that the locking pin hole is slightly offset and the locating holes in the shaft and gear must align perfectly before fitting the locking pin.

Refer to **FIG 3:2**. Disconnect the condenser lead from the contact breaker. Undo the retaining screw and remove the condenser assembly.

Remove the two diaphragm retaining screws and the clip securing the diaphragm rod to the breaker plate then lift off the diaphragm assembly.

Undo the securing screw and remove the contact breaker points.

The screws which hold the clips for the distributor cap also hold the advance plate in position. Remove these, and with a screwdriver inserted through the diaphragm mounting hole lever out the advance plate from the housing.

Remove the felt lubrication pad from the top of the cam under the rotor, extract the snap ring and washer.

Refer to **FIG 3:3** and remove the primary and secondary advance springs. Lift the cam off the shaft and remove the weights.

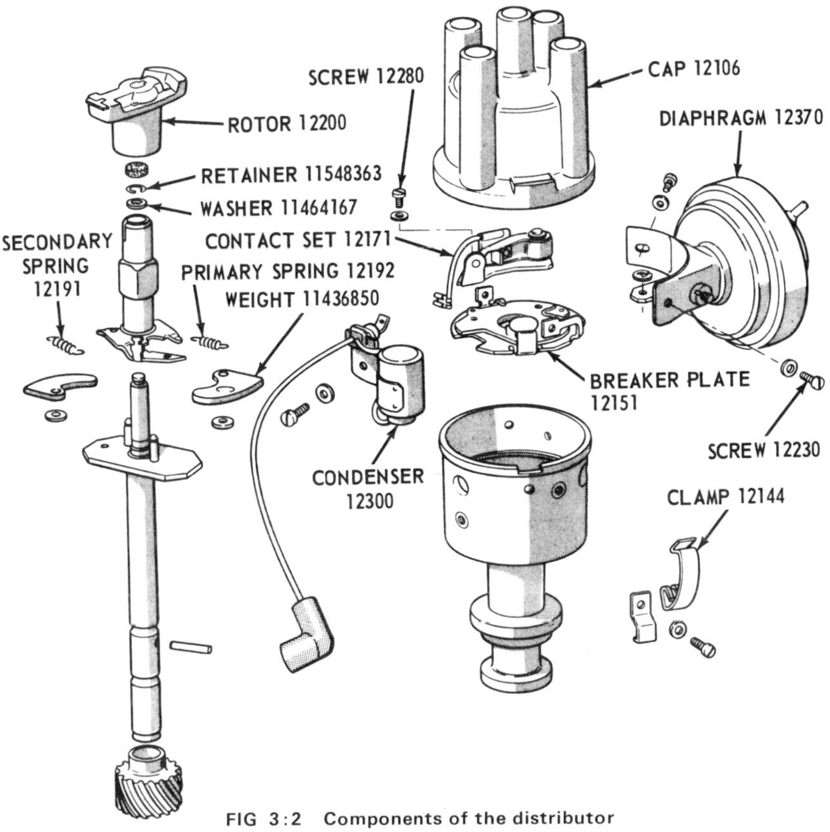

FIG 3:2 Components of the distributor

Assembly:

Smear the pivot pins with oil and fit the weights. Move the weights into position, lubricate the shaft and fit the cam. Refit the two advances springs.

Fit the advance plate in position and replace the clip and plate securing screws.

Push the condenser wire and grommet through the hole in the body and refit the condenser retaining screw.

Place the contact breaker joints in position and fit the wire lead and securing screw.

Hook the diaphragm rod over the pin in the advance plate. Tighten up the diaphragm mounting screws and fit the snap ring on the advance plate pin. Adjust the breaker points as described in **Section 3:4**.

3:4 Setting the points

Remove the distributor cap and turn the engine until the rubbing block of the contact breaker is on a high point of the cam and the points are at their maximum opening.

Refer to **FIG 3:4** loosen the contact breaker lock screw slightly, insert a .025 inch feeler gauge (Bosch distributors between .020 and .025 inch) between the joints and open or close the gap to the correct dimension by inserting the blade of a screwdriver between the bosses on the advance plate and the notch in the breaker joint base as shown.

Tighten up the lock screw and recheck the gap.

Renewing the points:

Remove the distributor cap and the rotor and then disconnect the wire to the breaker point assembly from the terminal for the coil wire.

Refer to **FIG 3:5**, remove the single retaining screw and lift out the contact breaker assembly.

If the condenser is also to be renewed, remove the screw attaching the condenser to the distributor body, ease the rubber grommet out of its hole and disconnect the ignition wire at the coil.

Re-install the condenser by threading the blade terminal for the coil wire into the distributor and fit the grommet in place. Fit the coil securing screw and connect the ignition wire to the coil.

Position the contact breaker assembly as shown and fit the retaining lockscrew. Reconnect the wire to the coil wire blade terminal.

Adjust the points as described earlier in this Section, fit the rotor and cap. Check the ignition timing and adjust if necessary.

3:5 Timing the ignition

The firing order on these engines is 1-3-4-2 and the static setting for ignition timing the various OHC engines and the distributor types is shown in Technical Data.

Ignition timing is best carried out using a stroboscopic timing lamp but in the absence of this or to obtain a preliminary setting the following method may be used.

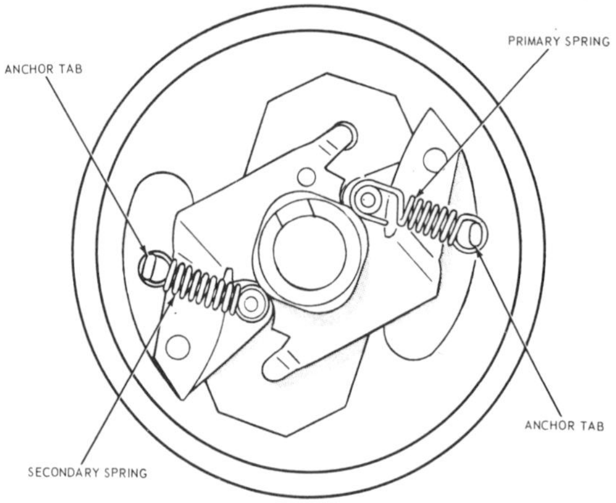

FIG 3:3 The mechanical advance assembly

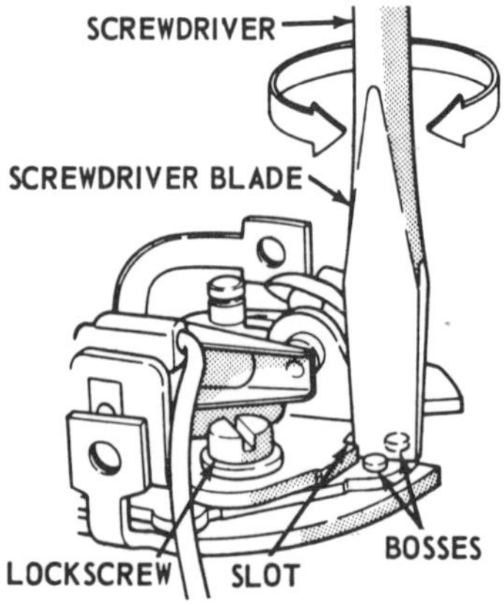

FIG 3:4 Adjusting the contact breaker points

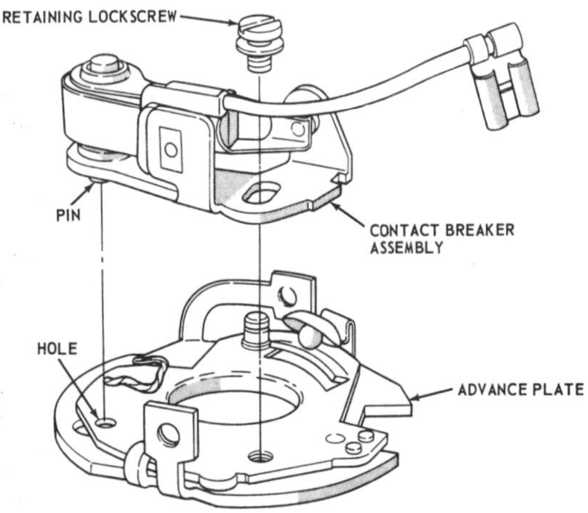

FIG 3:5 Removing or fitting contact breaker

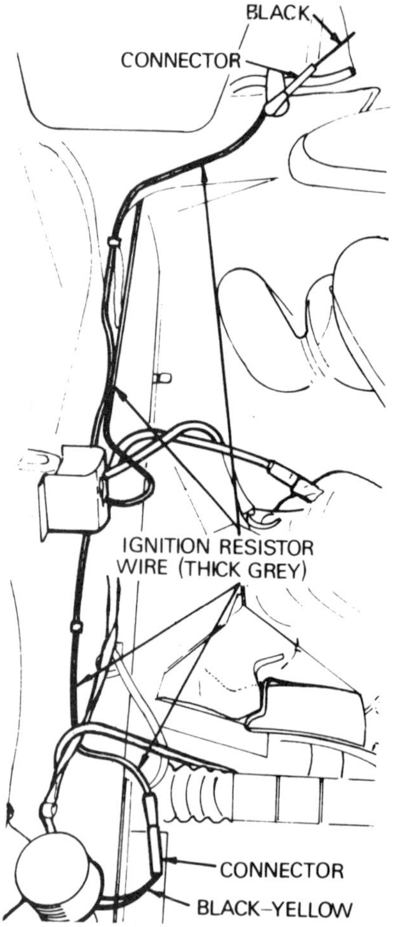

FIG 3:6 Location of ignition resistance wire

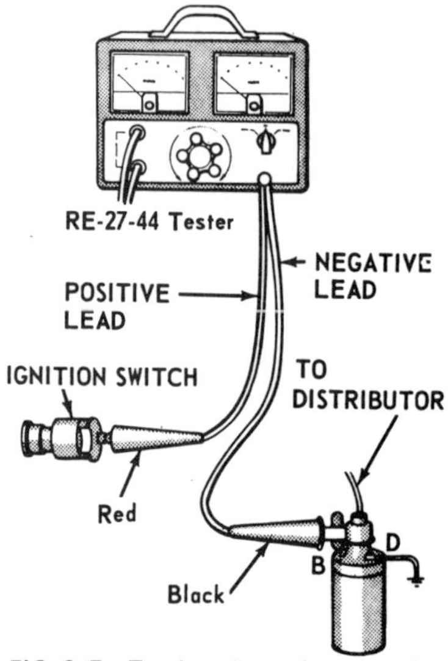

FIG 3:7 Testing the resistance wire

First ensure that the contact breaker point gap is correct, then rotate the engine until the crankshaft pulley is in line with the specified initial advance setting.

Remove the distributor cap, loosen the distributor clamp, bolt and rotate the distributor body by hand until the points are just opening to fire No. 1 cylinder (according to the position of the rotor).

A more accurate way to determine the moment at which the joints open is to connect a 12 volt bulb between the low tension terminal on the distributor housing and earth. Then with the ignition switched on, the bulb will light up as the points open when the distributor is rotated. At this point tighten the clamp bolt, give the engine two full revolutions and check that the bulb lights up as the timing marks coincide.

Stroboscopic timing:

Clean and if necessary mark the timing indicators with a touch of white paint. Disconnect the plug the vacuum pipes. Wire up the stroboscopic lamp to No. 1 cylinder in accordance with the makers instructions and connect a reliable tachometer.

Start the engine and reduce the speed to 600 rev/min to ensure that the centrifugal advance is not operating.

Loosen the distributor clamp bolt and rotate the distributor body as required to bring the timing marks into alignment and then tighten the clamp. It maybe noted that clockwise rotation of the distributor retards the ignition.

To check that the centrifugal advance mechanism is functioning correctly, accelerate the engine to about 2000 rev/min and observe the apparent position of the timing marks. If the timing advances, as shown on the timing scale, the mechanism is in order.

Vacuum retard check (North American models):

Connect the inlet manifold vacuum line to the inner diaphragm side of the vacuum capsule and reset the carburetter to the normal idle speed i.e. 750 for manual transmission or 650 for automatic in Drivegear.

The initial timing should retard approximately to the maximum specified i.e. 0—3.5 or —2.5 respectively, if the initial timing is correct. If it is out of calibration it will be necessary to renew the dual diaphragm unit as it is non-adjustable.

3:6 Ignition resistance wire

The function of this device has already been mentioned and in cases where the engine will start but will not run with the switch in the running position check the resistance wire. It is routed along the right hand fender apron as shown in **FIG 3:6**.

Connect the leads from a voltmeter as shown in the diagram (**FIG 3:7**) leaving the coil battery and distributor leads connected.

Connect a wire from the distributor terminal on the coil to a good earthing point. Turn off all lights and accessories.

Switch on the ignition and note the voltmeter reading. A reading between 4.5 and 6.6 bolts is satisfactory, but if it is outside these limits a new resistance wire must be fitted.

Note that under no circumstances should the resistance wire be spliced or replaced by any wire other than a service replacement. Do not coil or loop any surplus wire as excessive heat may be generated and cause the main harness to overheat.

Disconnect one end of the resistance wire from the black/yellow coil wire at the right hand fender apron and the other end from the short black wire at the bulkhead. Remove the resistance wire and fit a new wire in the reverse order.

3:7 Sparking plugs

The plug type recommended for use in these engines is the Autolite BRF 32 with a gap setting of .023 to .027 inch. The cable used for high tension leads is the internal resistance type with a resistance value of 5000 to 9000 ohms per foot.

When removing a sparking plug, loosen it first by one or two turns and then brush or blow out any accumulated debris from around the plug before removing it.

Examination of the firing end of the plugs and the condition of the electrodes will give a good idea of the running conditions in the engine.

Normally the deposit on the plug will be a thin powdery coating of light tan or grey. A fluffy black deposit is usually caused by too rich a fuel mixture or weak ignition, whereas an excessively weak mixture will usually be indicated by a white blistered look caused by overheating.

Wet black deposits are due to oil entering the combustion chambers usually past worn valves and guides, bores, pistons or piston rings. The cure for this is obviously an engine overhaul, but a hotter plug may provide a temporary relief.

The plugs when merely fouled and not excessively eroded, may be cleaned on a sand blast machine and then examined for cracked insulation or other signs of wear or damage. It is false economy to use old sparking plugs and a new set should be fitted every 10,000 miles.

3:8 High tension cables

As mentioned earlier these are of the resistance type and it is important when renewing cables to ensure that the cable is not only the same type, but also the same length as the original.

Remove the cable from each sparking plug by grasping, twisting, and then pulling the moulded cap of the wire only. Do **not** pull on the wire because the wire connection inside the cap may become separated or the weatherseal damaged.

When fitting the cables into the distributor cap, see that they are pushed fully into their sockets and securely fastened. Make sure also that the sparking plug connectors are pressed fully home on the insulators.

3:9 Fault diagnosis

(a) Engine will not fire

1 Battery discharged
2 Contact breaker points dirty, pitted or wrongly set
3 Distributor cap dirty or cracked
4 Rotor arm not in contact with cap electrode
5 Faulty cable or loose connection in LT circuit
6 Rotor arm cracked or tracking
7 Faulty ignition coil
8 Broken contact breaker spring
9 Contact breaker points stuck open
10 Defective ignition switch
11 Plug leads wrongly connected
12 Excessive moisture on H.T. cables

(b) Engine misfires

1 Check 2, 3, 5, and 12 in (a)
2 Weak contact breaker spring
3 H.T. cables cracked or perished
4 Sparking plug loose
5 Sparking plug insulation cracked or wrongly set
6 Faulty ignition timing
7 Excessive wear in distributor

(c) Engine lacks power

1 Check 2 and 3 in (a). Check (b)
2 Retarded ignition timing
3 Advance mechanism defective
4 Vacuum pipe loose or broken
5 Sparking plugs defective
6 Sparking plug leads loose or broken

CHAPTER 4

THE COOLING SYSTEM

4:1 Description

The pressurized cooling system has a circulating pump and fan assembly bolted to the front face of the cylinder block, driven by a belt from the crankshaft pulley. This belt also drives the alternator, which is adjustable on its mounting to regulate the belt tension.

The coolant is circulated from the bottom of the radiator through the pump and into the cylinder block. After passing round the engine the coolant reaches the thermostat at the front of the cylinder head. At temperatures below about 85°C (185°F) this will be closed and the coolant is directed back to the engine by way of the by-pass tube. Above this temperature the thermostat valve starts to open and the coolant passes to the top of the radiator, down through the tubes where it is cooled by the air flow and so back to the water pump.

The temperature of the cooling water is measured electrically by a sender unit in the water jacket which is coupled to a gauge on the instrument panel. In order to raise the boiling point of the coolant and permit the engine to operate at a higher temperature the system is pressurized to 13 lb/sq inch at which point the valve in the filler cap opens to prevent any further increase.

The system is illustrated diagrammatically in **FIG 4:1** which also shows how the water in the heater circuit passes through the automatic choke housing in the carburetter after leaving the cylinder head.

The use of an anti-freeze solution is recommended at all times and is normally added in production with a tag attached to the radiator as a reminder. This is Long Life Antifreeze which meets Ford specification M97B18-C and is in a 50 per cent solution. It is not necessary to drain the system in summer as the mixture should be quite satisfactory for up to two years when it should be emptied and refilled with a fresh solution.

4:2 Removing the radiator

Remove the filler cap and the upper and lower splash shields.

Drain off the coolant liquid by opening the drain plugs which are located underneath the radiator and cylinder block (see **FIG 4:2**). As the coolant will normally contain antifreeze it should be collected in a clean container and retained for further use.

Slacken off the clamps and disconnect the upper and lower radiator hoses. Remove the securing screws and lift out the radiator assembly. Remove the overflow hose from the base of the filler neck.

Installation:

Fit the drain plug and overflow hose, also the drain plug in the cylinder block.

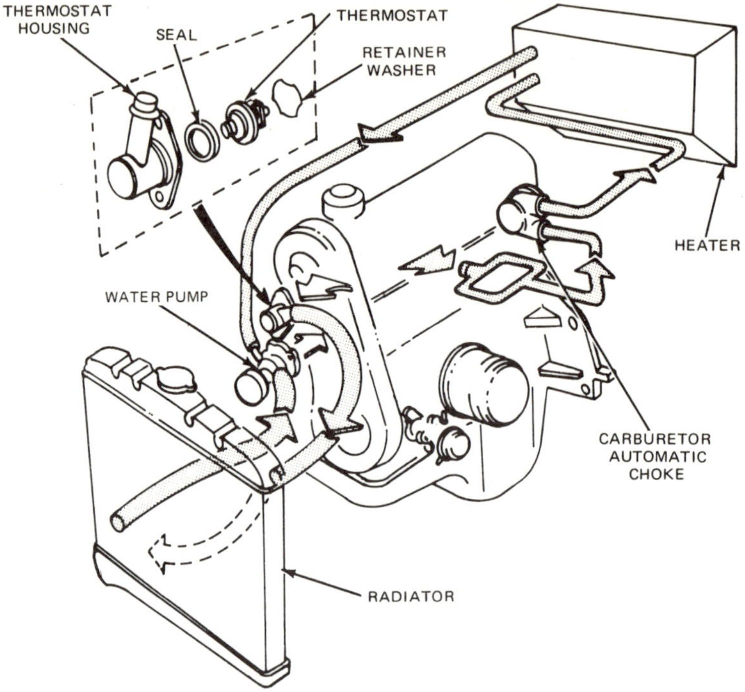

FIG 4:1 Schematic layout of cooling system

Fit the radiator is position and tighten the securing screws. Replace the top and bottom hoses and tighten the clamps.

Refill the cooling system and run the engine for a few minutes without the filler cap in order to clear any air locks. Top up the radiator as required and replace the filler cap. Run the engine up to normal working temperature and inspect for leaks.

Fit the upper and lower splash shields.

It may be noted that certain cars with automatic transmission will have an oil cooler included in the radiator assembly. This will need to be disconnected and the pipes plugged to prevent oil spillage. As some oil is likely to be lost in the operation the transmission level should be checked.

4:3 The thermostat

The thermostat is housed under the outlet elbow at the front end of the cylinder head. To remove it, partially drain the cooling system so that the level is below the thermostat and then detach the hose from the elbow.

Remove the two securing bolts and pull the housing away from the engine. Extract the retaining washer, thermostat and gasket. See **FIG 4:3**.

Testing:

Suspend the thermostat in a suitable container of water so that it does not touch the sides or bottom and gradually heat the water.

Suspend an accurate thermometer similarly in the water and observe the readings.

The thermostat valve should commence to open at 185° to 192°F (85° to 89°C) and be fully open at 210° to 216°F (99° to 102°C).

If it should fail to operate within these limits the thermostat must be renewed as no servicing is possible.

Refitting:

This is a reversal of the removal procedure, not forgetting to check the installation after running the engine for a few minutes.

4:4 The water pump

Servicing the water pump is not an operation recommended to the average owner/driver, and if trouble is experienced he is strongly advised to fit a new pump as follows:

Drain the cooling system as described in **Section 4:2** and disconnect the hoses from the pump.

Slacken the alternator mounting bolts, pivot the alternator towards the engine and remove the driving belt.

It is possible on some models to remove the pump without removing the radiator but if it does prove at all difficult remove the radiator as described in **Section 4:2**.

Remove the fan retaining bolts and lift off the fan, spacer and pulley. Remove the cover over the camshaft drive belt, then unscrew the mounting bolts and lift off the water pump as shown in **FIG 4:4**.

Refitting is a reversal of the above procedure, after cleaning the joint faces and using a new gasket.

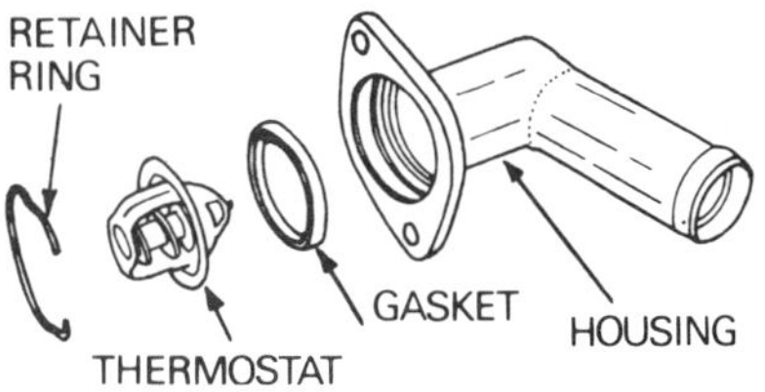

FIG 4:3 Thermostat and housing

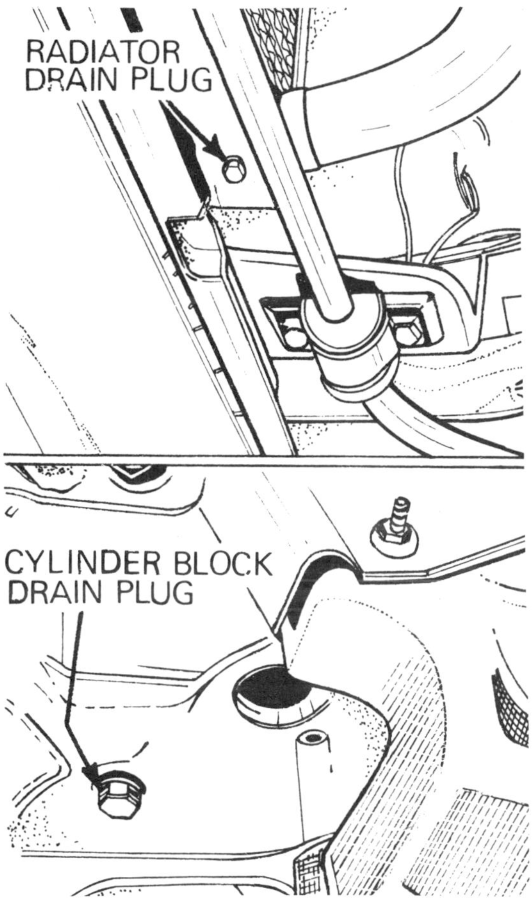

FIG 4:2 Showing location of drain plugs

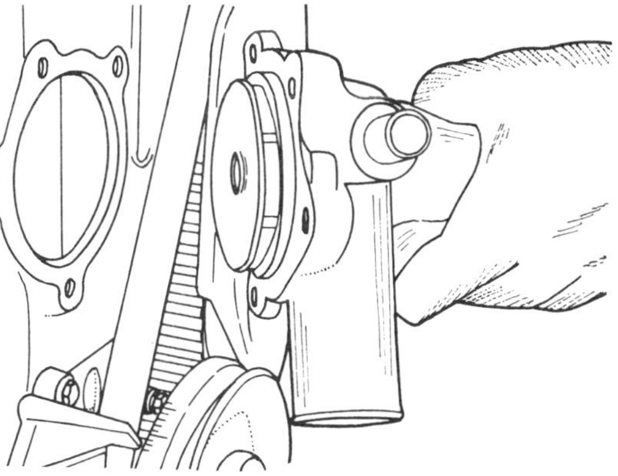
FIG 4:4 Removing the pump

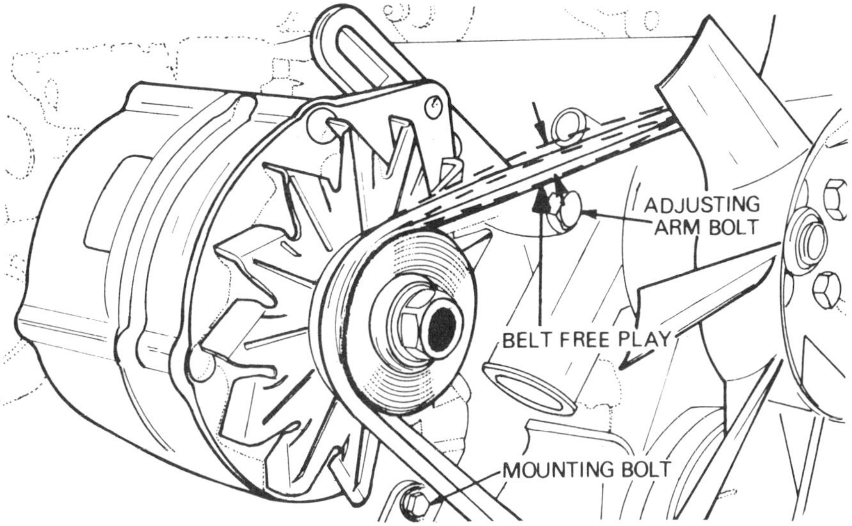

FIG 4:5 Adjusting belt tension

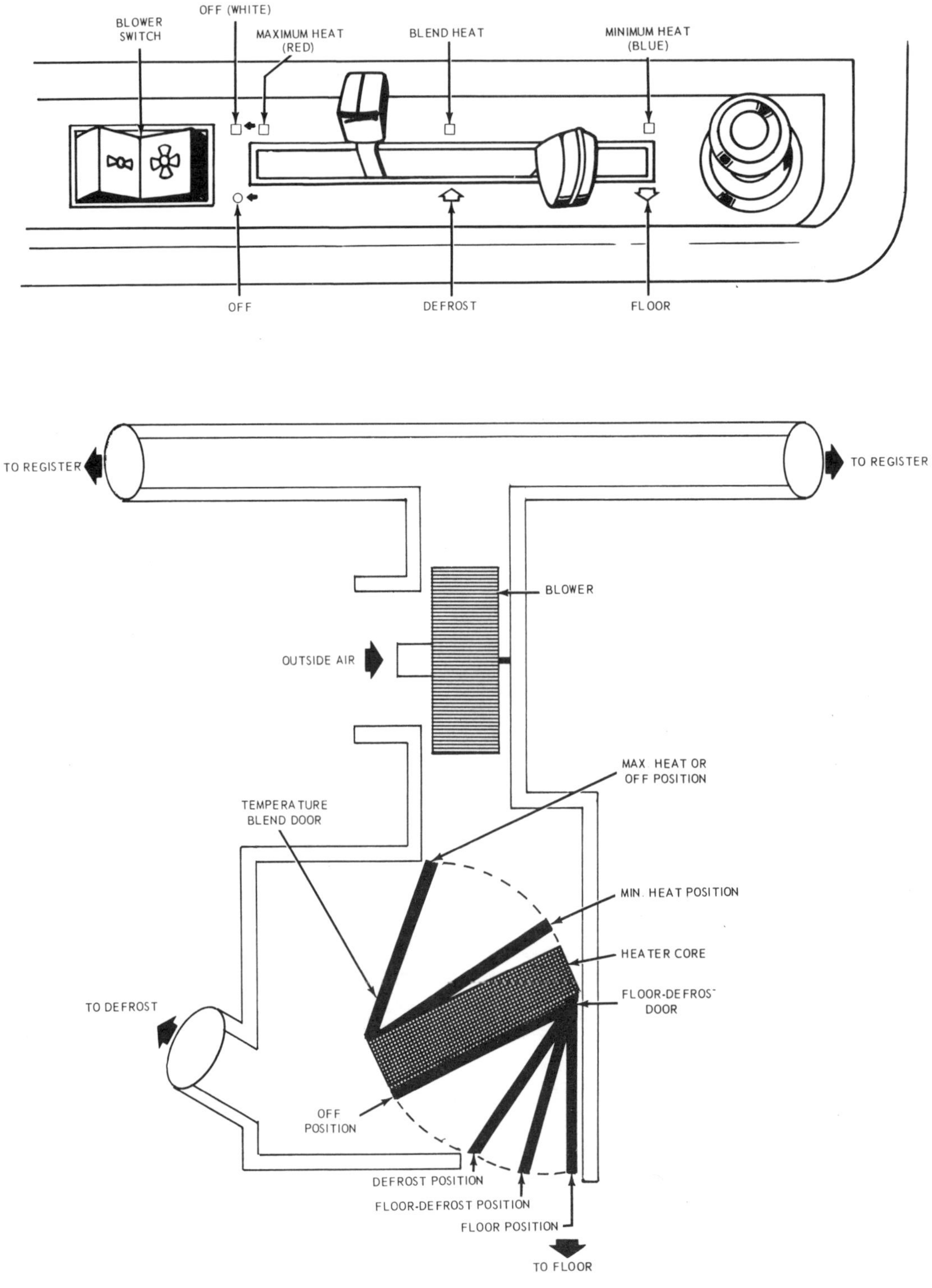

FIG 4:6 The heater system layout and controls

4:5 The drive belt

The tension on the drive belt should be checked at regular intervals as a loose or slipping belt may cause overheating and a reduction in the electrical charging rate.

Tension is correct where is .50 inch total up and down movement of the belt at a point half-way between the fan pulley and the alternator, and adjustment is made by loosening the alternator mounting bolts and then pivoting the alternator as necessary to obtain the correct belt movement.

Do not over tighten the belt as this will result in excessive strain and wear on the alternator and water pump bearings. See **FIG 4:5**.

4:6 Car heating system

Description:

A schematic diagram of the heating system and its control panel is given in **FIG 4:6** and its operation is as follows:

The blower draws in outside air through a grille in front of the windshield and it may then take two directions. One passage leads to the two vent registers at either end of the instrument panel, the other outlet is through and/or around the heater core and discharging through the floor and/or defroster nozzles.

The air flow to the panel registers is never heated and is available whenever the car is moving or the fan is operating. The outlet from the vents is controlled by the knob in the centre vane; turning the knob clockwise opens the vent and vice versa.

The temperature and air flow through the heater is controlled by two air doors, each connected by a cable to a control lever on the panel.

Temperature control:

This is regulated by the upper control lever which activates the temperature blend door. It will be seen that in the minimum heat(right—blue square) position the air is diverted around the heater core and is discharged unheated. In the maximum heat (left—red square) position, all the air is directed through the heater core and then out through the outlets (heated). At intermediate positions between the two extremes the ratio of hot air to cold will be in proportion as the lever is moved from one end to the other.

Directional control:

Reference to the illustration will show that setting the lower control lever to the defrost (centre—upward arrow) position closes the door to the floor outlet and directs all the air to the windshield nozzles while moving it to the right downward arrow opens the outlet to the floor vents. It will be seen that even in this latter position some air will still discharge on to the windshield.

With both levers moved fully left all air flow is cut off.

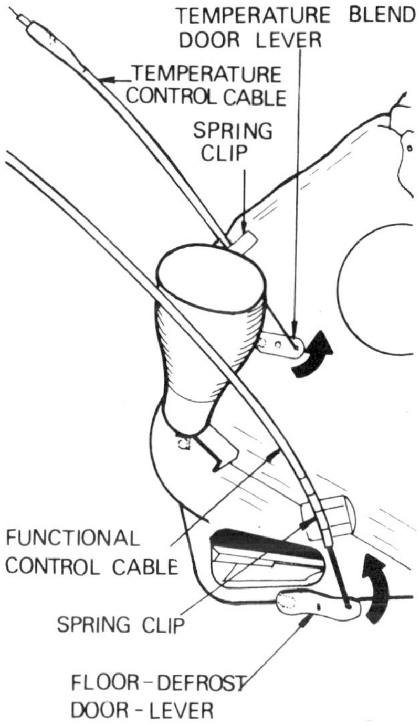

FIG 4:7 Control cable adjustments

Adjustments:

Directional control cable (See **FIG 4:7**):

Move the lower control lever fully to the left and remove the spring clip securing its control cable to the heater.

Move the floor/defrost door upwards to the fully OFF position.

Slide the end of the cable housing to the floor/defrost lever and secure it to the heater with the spring clip.

Temperature control cable:

Move the upper control lever fully left and remove the spring clip securing its cable to the heater.

Position the temperature blend door fully in the MAX HEAT position by rotating the lever to the end of its travel as shown.

Slide the end of the cable housing up to the lever and secure the cable housing to the heater with the spring clip.

Removing the heater (See **FIG 4:8**):

Disconnect the battery and drain the cooling system.

Disconnect the hoses from the two heater core tubes. Remove the coverplate and gasket from around the core tubes at the dash panel (2 screws).

Remove the parcel tray and if a console is fitted, remove it as follows:

Remove the two screws holding the front end of the console to the floor, then lift up the rubber boot on the gear lever and remove the two screws at the rear end.

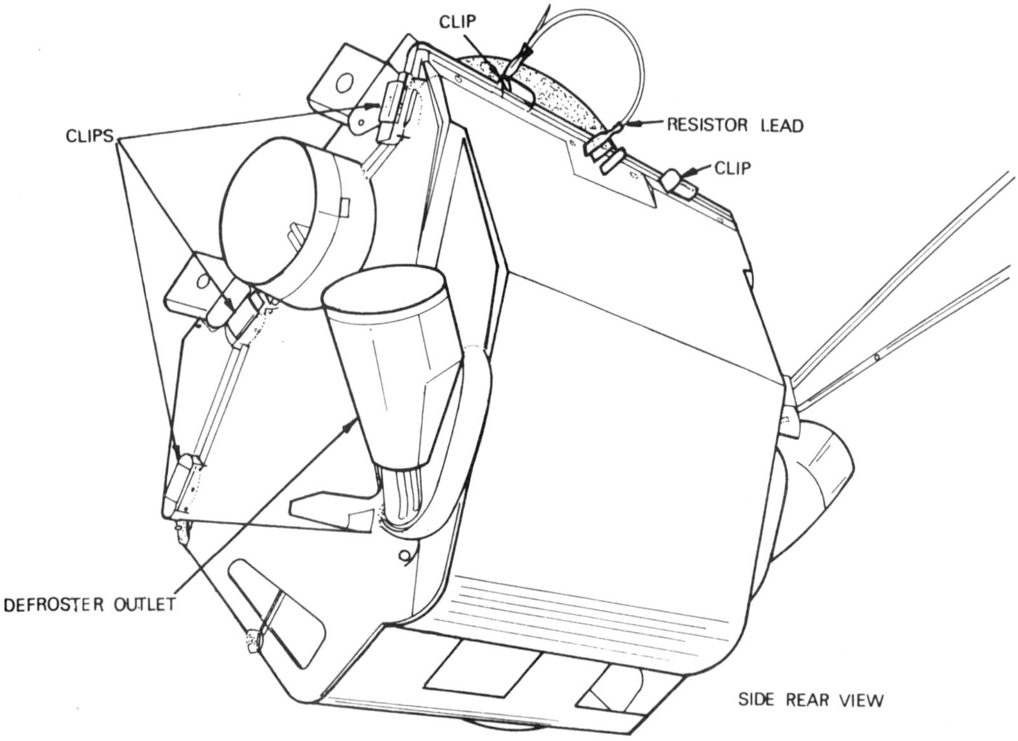

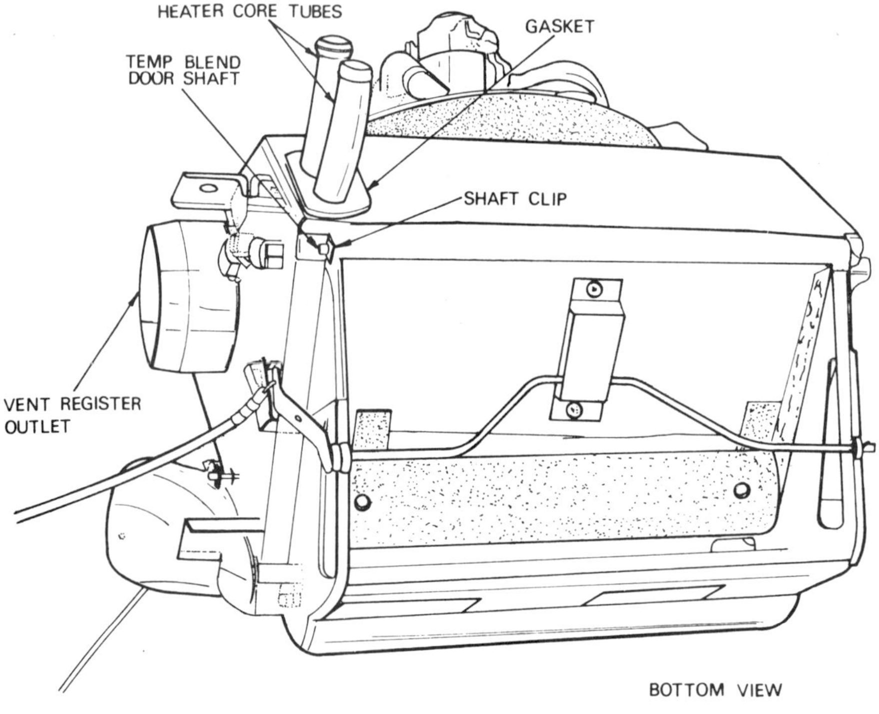

FIG 4:8 The heater assembly

Pry up the rear panel and remove two screws. Carefully pry up the clock panel and disconnect two electrical connectors and one bulb. Remove the main screw at the rear end of the area under the clock panel.

Slide the plastic brace under the handbrake lever towards the front and remove it. Lift out the console.

Remove the retaining clips and disconnect the cables from the control levers.

Disconnect the three wire connectors from the terminals on the heater and disconnect the bullet connector on the other wire.

Disconnect the ducts for the panel and defroster vents from the heater.

Remove the four panel mounting screws and lift out the heater. To obtain access to one screw on the left it may be necessary to remove the windshield wiper motor.

Refitting the heater is carried out in the reverse order, after which the cooling system must be refilled and the operation checked.

Blower motor and fan:

To gain access to these it is necessary first to remove the heater unit as just described, then remove the eight clips holding the two halves of the heater assembly together.

Remove the retaining clips from the shaft of the temperature blend door and remove the shaft.

Remove the core tube gasket. Disconnect the resistor lead and separate the two halves of the assembly.

Disconnect the two motor wires and four retaining clips and withdraw the motor assembly from the upper half of the unit.

Reassemble in the reverse order.

4:7 Fault diagnosis

(a) Internal water leakage

1 Cracked cylinder wall
2 Loose cylinder head bolts.
3 Cracked cylinder head
4 Faulty head gasket
5 Distorted head

(b) Poor circulation

1 Radiator core blocked
2 Engine water passages restricted
3 Low coolant level
4 Loose fan belt
5 Defective thermostat
6 Perished or collapsed radiator hoses
7 Air lock in system

(c) Corrosion

1 Impurities in water
2 Insufficient draining and flushing

(d) Overheating

1 Check (b)
2 Sludge in crankcase
3 Faulty ignition timing
4 Low oil level
5 Tight engine
6 Choked exhaust system
7 Brakes binding
8 Slipping clutch
9 Incorrect timing
10 Weak mixture

NOTES

CHAPTER 5

THE CLUTCH

5:1 Description

The clutch employed on these cars is the single dry plate type with a spring cushioned hub. A diaphragm spring is used to provide the necessary pressure and operation of the release mechanism is by means of a cable linkage.

Different makes and sizes of clutch plate are employed throughout the OHC range. The German 1300 and 1600 models have an L.U.K. 7.5 inch clutch but the 1600 GT is equipped with a Fichtel and Sachs 8.5 inch clutch. British 1600 and 1600 GT models are equipped with a Laycock 7.5 inch and 8.5 inch respectively. The North American 2000 model has a 8.5 inch clutch of unspecified manufacture but it could be of Fords own make. Apart from the number of hub springs in the clutch driven plate which varies with engine capacity, all the makes are operated on the same principle.

The components of the clutch and its associated parts are shown in **FIG 5:1** the clutch pressure plate assembly is bolted to the rear face of the flywheel and consists of a pressed steel cover housing a pressure plate and the diaphragm spring.

The driven plate, or clutch disc is held by the pressure of the spring between the pressure plate and the flywheel and is carried on splines machined on the main drive shaft into the gearbox. Thus, when engaged, the drive is transmitted from the flywheel and pressure plate face to the clutch disc and to the gearbox.

Pressure on the clutch pedal is transmitted to the release bearing by the cable and release lever, which deflects the diaphragm spring and relieves the pressure on the pressure plate, the clutch disc is no longer held and so slows down and stops and disconnects the engine from the gearbox.

5:2 Routine maintenance

The only item to be mentioned under this heading is a regular inspection to ensure that the clutch pedal free travel is as specified. This should also be checked if the clutch should fail to disengage correctly or whenever new clutch parts are fitted. Correct adjustment here is most important as failure to maintain the clearance frequently results in complete clutch failure.

Pull off the rubber boot over the release lever and see that the ball end of the operating cable is well greased.

Loosen the locknut **FIG 5:2** and with the clutch pedal pressed up against its stop on the pedal bracket, turn the adjusting nut as necessary to obtain a clearance of

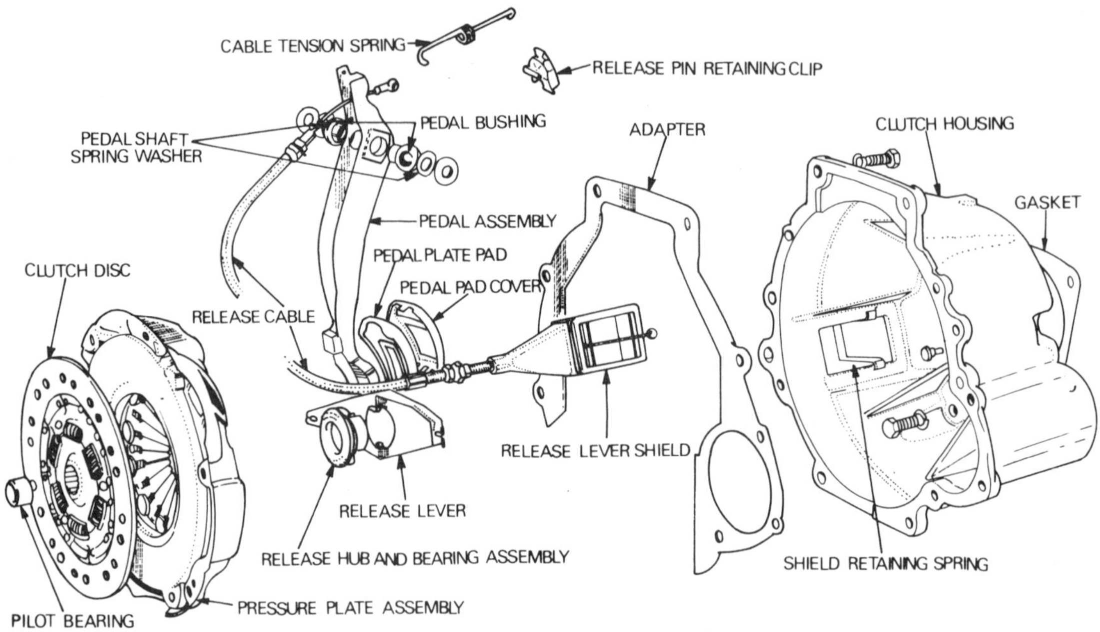

FIG 5:1 Components of a clutch mechanism

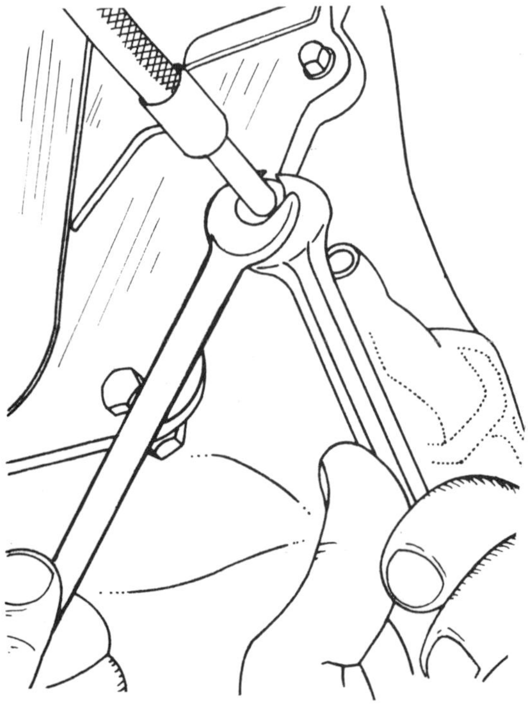

FIG 5:2 Adjusting the clutch cable

between .138 and .144 inch between the nut and the clutch housing as shown in **FIG 5:3** this setting corresponds to free travel at the clutch pedal of .5 to .75 inch.

Tighten the locknut and check that the pedal end of the cable is also well lubricated.

5:3 Removing the clutch

In the event of trouble with the clutch, as there is no provision for servicing or adjustment, the complete assembly should be renewed.

Disconnect the battery and raise the car, supporting it securely.

Identify the flanges of the rear axle pinion and the propeller shaft to ensure correct refitting, remove the four retaining bolts and also the two bolts securing the centre bearing carrier to its bracket, lower the rear end of the shaft and slide the front yoke from the gearbox. Insert a dummy yoke or similar plug into the aperture to prevent the oil running out of the box.

Remove the clip and pull out the speedometer cable from the transmission extension housing. Disconnect the exhaust pipe bracket from the gearbox and swing it clear.

Pull back the rubber boot over the clutch release lever and detach the operating cable.

Unclip the spring retainers shown in **FIG 5:4** and disconnect the shifter rods from the gearbox.

Remove the three securing bolts and move the starter motor to one side.

Remove the six screws securing the clutch housing to the engine and the screws securing the engine rear plate to the front lower portion of the flywheel housing.

Support the gearbox from underneath and remove the four bolts securing the crossmember to the body. Carefully slide the gearbox to the rear, keeping it well supported

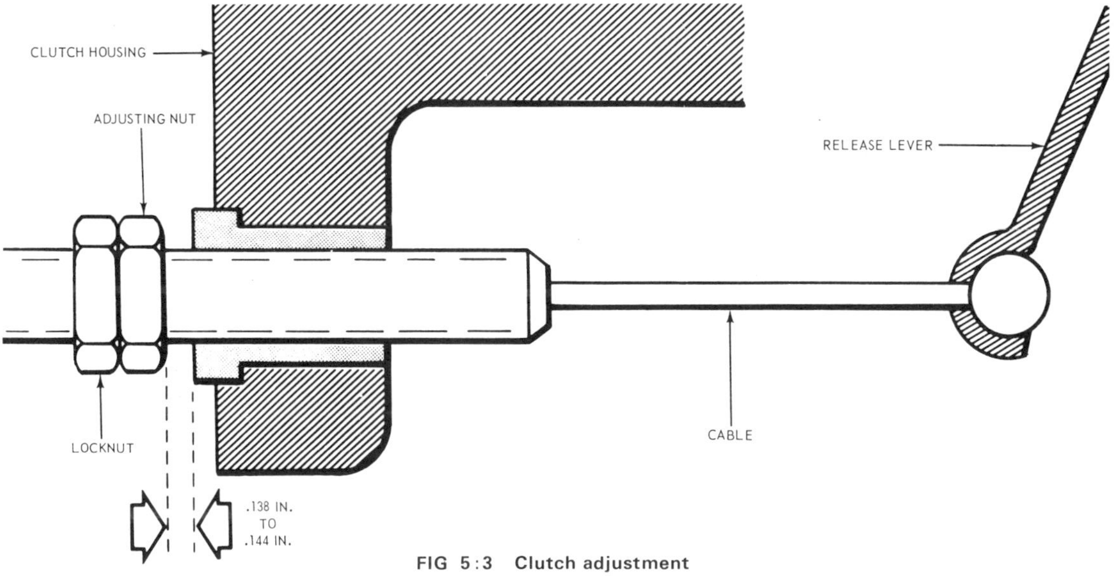

FIG 5:3 Clutch adjustment

and square with the engine, ensuring that its weight is not allowed to hang on the hub of the clutch or considerable damage may result.

Remove the four bolts securing the clutch housing to the transmission.

5:4 Servicing the clutch

Clutch disc and pilot bearing

With the clutch housing removed, slacken the six clutch attaching screws progressively and diagonally and then lift off the disc and pressure plate assembly.

To remove the pilot bearing if required, insert the service puller tool behind the bearing and use a slide hammer to extract the bearing.

The new bearing should be fitted by placing it on the service mandrel tool used in conjunction with a spacer tool and then tapped into place in the crankshaft flange.

Place the clutch disc in position after smearing the splines with a molybdenum grease, noting that the flywheel side of the disc is marked near the centre and the raised centre portion is away from the flywheel. Align the plate with the service mandrel tool shown in **FIG 5:5**.

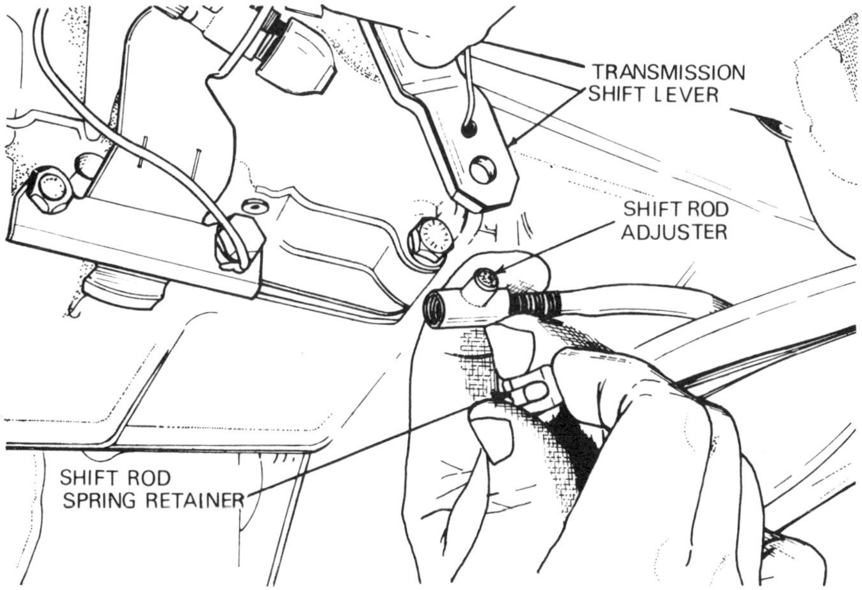

FIG 5:4 Shift rod connection

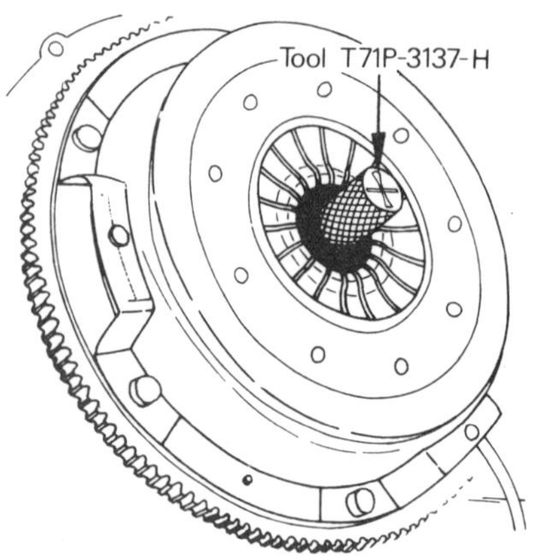

FIG 5:5 **Centralizing the clutch plate**

Refit the pressure plate assembly, locating it on the flywheel dowels. Fit the six securing screws and tighten them to 11-14 lb ft.

Remove the centralizing tool and fit the clutch housing as described in **Section 5:5**.

Clutch release bearing:

After removing the clutch housing, withdraw the release lever from the hub and bearing.

To fit a new bearing first apply a smear of molybdenium grease to the hub and release lever and then engage the lever in the slots in the hub and release bearing assembly.

Pass the release lever through the aperture in the clutch housing and slide the release bearing on to the front bearing retainer. See **FIG 5:6**.

Clutch linings:

The driven plate is serviced as an assembly and it is not recommended that the home operator should attempt to rivet on new linings when replacement is due.

Replacement is necessary when the friction material is worn down almost to the level of the rivets or if oil contamination is evident. Normally, the friction material should stand well proud of the rivets and be smoothly polished. It should be of a light colour, with the grain of the material clearly visible through the surface glaze. A dark brown staining is usually the result of oil or grease finding its way on to the linings and of course the cause should be looked for and rectified. To attempt to salvage the linings by washing is rarely successful and a replacement clutch disc is to be recommended in all these cases.

5:5 Re-installing the clutch

The most important part of this operation is the correct centralization of the clutch disc on the flywheel before the pressure plate assembly is fitted. This has already been described in **Section 5:4** and ensures that the hub of the plate lines up with the pilot bearing in the end of the crankshaft and facilitates the correct entry of the gearbox main shaft.

Having located the driven plate fit the pressure plate assembly on the dowels and tighten the six bolts to 11-14 lb ft.

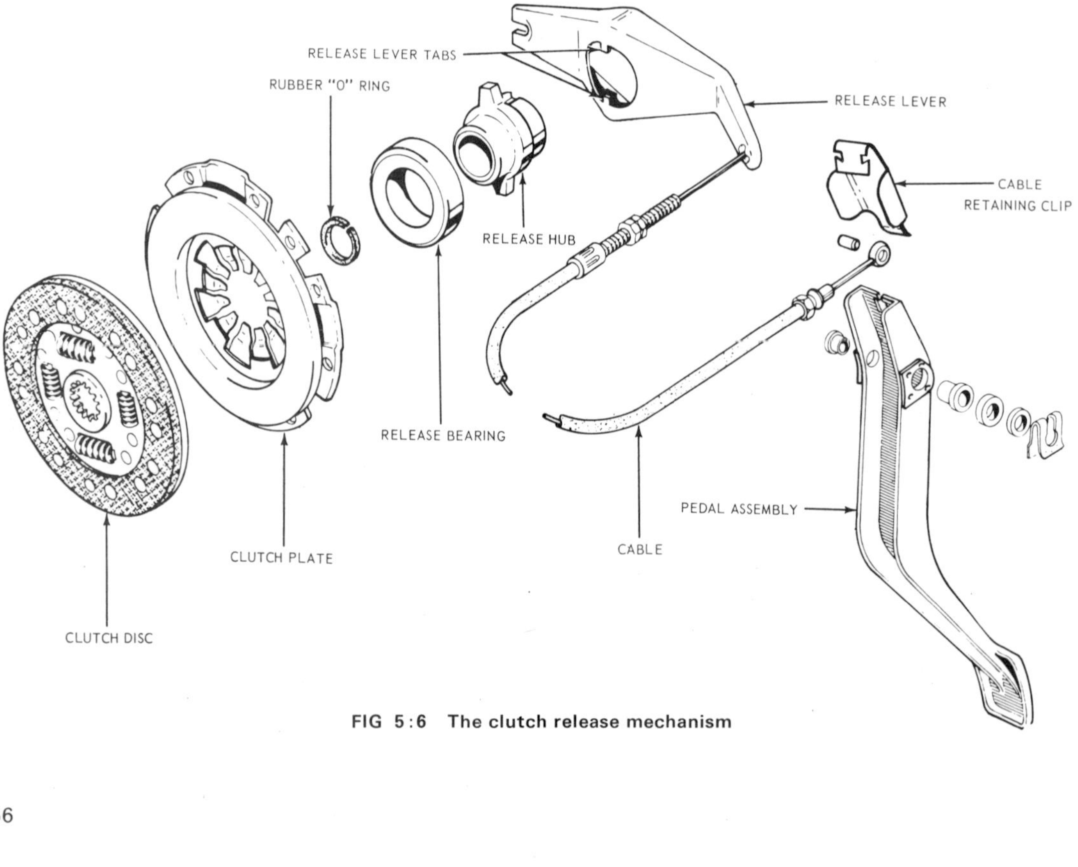

FIG 5:6 **The clutch release mechanism**

Make sure that the adaptor plate is in position on the rear of the engine then move the gearbox and clutch housing carefully into place until the front end of the input shaft enters the hub of the driven plate. Do not let the weight of the gearbox hang on the hub. Push the gearbox fully home. Turning the flywheel a little if necessary to get the splines to mesh. The spigot on the shaft should now be in full engagement with the crankshaft pilot bearing.

Refit the gearbox crossmember to the body, tighten the bolts and remove the transmission support.

Fit the screws securing the clutch housing to the engine. Fit the engine rear plate and secure with the screws.

Fit the starter motor. Fit the gear shift rods, adjust if necessary and secure with clips.

Smear molybdenum grease on the ball end of the clutch operating cable and fit it to the clutch release lever. Fit the rubber boot into the release lever aperture.

Reconnect the exhaust pipe bracket to the gearbox and fit the speedometer cable in the extension housing, retaining it with a clip.

Replace the propeller shaft in the gearbox, line up the marks on the flanges and secure with the four bolts tightened to a torque of 15 to 18 lb ft. Place the centre bearing carrier in position and secure to its bracket with two bolts.

Check the oil level in the gearbox and top up if necessary.

Lower the car and check the gearbox operation.

5:6 Renewing a clutch operating cable

Jack up the front of the car and support it on stands.

Slacken the clutch adjusting nuts, shown in **FIG 5:2** on the clutch housing.

Remove the spring clip securing the clutch cable to the top of the pedal (see **FIG 5:6**) withdraw the pivot pin and pull the cable into the engine compartment.

Move the boot over the clutch release lever and release the cable from the lever. Remove the cable from the car.

Fitting:

Pass the top end of the cable through the engine bulk head and fit it to the top of the pedal. Lubricate and install the pivot pin and secure with the retaining clip.

Connect the lower end of the cable to the release lever, lubricate well and replace the rubber boot.

Adjust the cable as described in **Section 5:2**.

5:7 Fault diagnosis

(a) Dragging clutch

1 Oil on the friction linings
2 Faulty cable
3 Driven plate hub binding on splines
4 Driven plate distorted
5 Warped or damaged pressure plate
6 Broken friction linings

(b) Fierceness or snatch

1 Check 1, 2, 4 and 5 in (a)
2 Worn linings

(c) Slip

1 Check 1 in (a) and 2 in (b)
2 No play in cable adjustment
3 Weak or broken diaphragm spring
4 Outer casing of cable trapped or damaged

(d) Judder

1 Check 1 and 4 in (a)
2 Contact area of linings not evenly distributed
3 Faulty rubber mountings to engine or gearbox

(e) Tick or knock

1 Badly worn splines on driven plates
2 Worn release bearing
3 Faulty pressure plate assembly

NOTES

CHAPTER 6

MANUAL TRANSMISSION

6:1 Description

The manual transmission employed on these cars is a conventional four forward and reverse unit with the four forward gears engaged through block ring type synchromesh. In the interests of silent operation the forward speed gears are helically cut, but the reverse gear on the countershaft has straight cut spur teeth.

One of two types of gearbox are employed throughout the range. This can be either the Ford Type 'C' which is used on some of the Cortina and Taunus models and now also includes the British 1.6 litre OHC Capri; or the Ford 'H' type gearbox which is fitted to the German 1.3 and 1.6 litre GT models and the American 2.0 litre OHC versions.

The 'C' type is the ordinary standard version but the selector locking mechanism has been modified slightly from the original fitted to the Cortina ranges. The 'H' model embraces a standard or heavy duty type, however, the heavy duty versions are fitted exclusively to the big V6 engines. The standard version is identical to the original German Capri transmission which differs slightly from the 'C' model in the gear ratios, selector mechanism and the oil capacity (see **Technical Data**).

Gear selection on the 'C' type is via a lever mounted on the transmission tunnel that operates a single selector rail to which is coupled a fork relay arm, complete with selector forks, through a selector boss and lockplate. The lockplate prevents the simultaneous selection of two different gears.

Gear selection on the 'H' type is by means of a remote control lever mounted on the transmission tunnel which operates three shift levers on the side of the gearbox through the shift rods shown in **FIG 6:1**.

To compensate for manufacturing tolerances and to eliminate excessive end float or backlash in the gears, three of the six snap rings locating the gears are selective and enable close fits to be easily obtained.

6:2 Maintenance and adjustment

After the first 6000 miles the gearbox oil should be drained out and fresh oil of the correct grade poured in through the filler hole on the lefthand side of the casing. When the level is up to the bottom of the filler hole, the plug should be replaced.

At each subsequent 6000 miles the level should be checked and topped up if necessary.

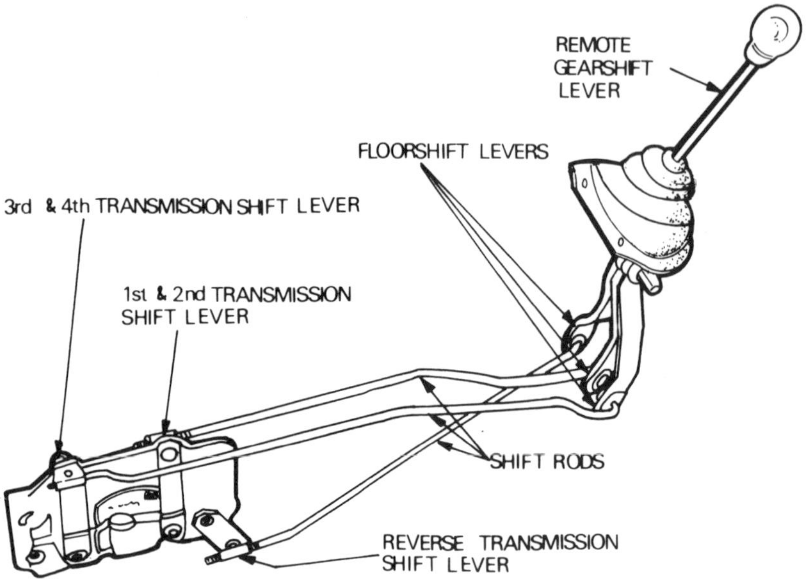

FIG 6:1 The gearshift mechanism

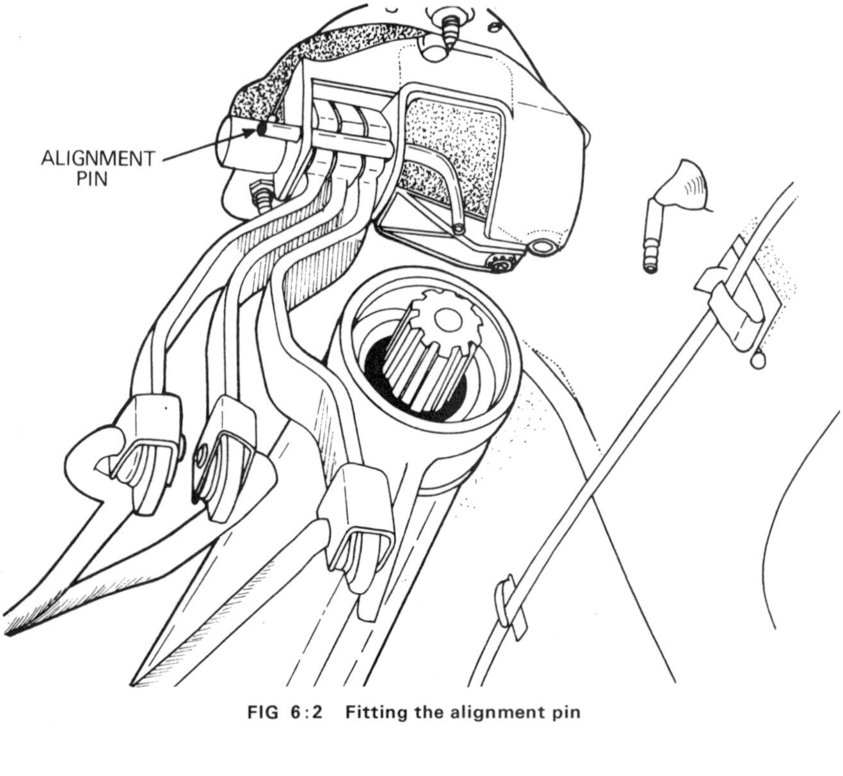

FIG 6:2 Fitting the alignment pin

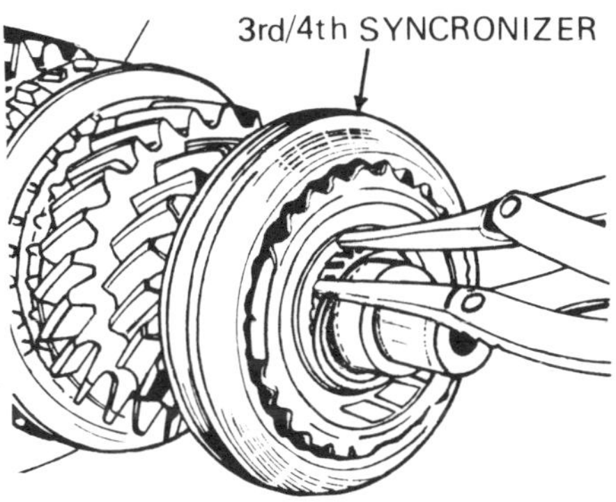

FIG 6:3 Removing 3rd gear snap ring

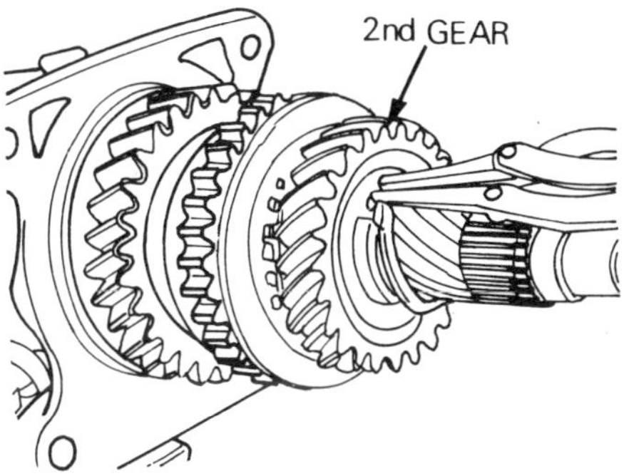

FIG 6:4 Removing 2nd gear snap ring

Adjusting the gearshift linkage ('H' type):

Refer to **FIG 6:2** and fabricate an alignment pin, as shown, out of $\frac{3}{16}$ inch dia wire and $3\frac{1}{2}$ inches long.

Raise the car to give access to the underside and place the gearshift lever in the neutral position.

Remove the spring retainers and disconnect the shifter rods from the transmission shift levers. See **FIG 5:4**.

Insert the alignment pin in the position shown to ensure that the levers are correctly positioned, place all the shift levers on the transmission in the neutral position and then adjust the length of the shifter rods so that they fit easily into the holes in the shift levers. Replace the spring retainers.

Remove the alignment pin, lower the car and check that all gears can be selected.

6:3 Dismantling the transmission

The removal of the gearbox from the car was described in the previous Chapter, **Section 5:3**. Drain the oil from the box. Slide off the clutch release bearing and release fork, take out the four securing screws and carefully remove the clutch housing by tapping it if necessary. Place the gearbox on a suitable stand or fixture.

'H' type:

Undo the seven securing screws and remove the top cover. Lift out the shifter forks, then remove the four securing screws and rotate the extension housing until the end of the countershaft is fully revealed.

Using a dummy countershaft drive out the countershaft from the front, taking great care to ensure that the dummy shaft remains in contact with the countershaft at all times so that the needle bearings do not become dislodged. The gear cluster may be lowered into the bottom of the transmission casing.

Tap the input shaft with a soft mallet and pull it out of the casing. Remove the snap ring securing the input shaft bearing and press off the bearing with the special tool.

Remove the extension housing and output shaft assembly from the case. Remove the cluster gear assembly and if necessary dismantle it by withdrawing the dummy shaft. The needle rollers and spacers may now be removed and it may be necessary to retrieve the thrust washers from the casing.

Drive out the reverse idler gear shaft towards **the rear** of the case.

Remove the snap ring in front of the 3rd/4th gear synchronizer on the output shaft (**FIG 6:3**) and withdraw the assembly.

Remove the 2nd gear snap ring (**FIG 6:4**) and pull off the gear and blocking ring.

Remove the 1st/2nd gear synchronizer sleeve and inserts. Note that the hub is splined to the output shaft and cannot be pressed off.

Unscrew the speedometer drive retainer and remove the driven gear.

Remove the snap ring retaining the output bearing in the extension housing. See **FIG 6:5**. Gently tap the output shaft from the housing.

Press out the speedometer drive gear.

Remove the snap ring in front of the output shaft bearing and press out the bearing. Remove the spacer, pull off the 1st gear and blocking ring and remove the insert spring.

'C' type:

1 The exterior components of a typical type 'C' box are shown in **FIG 6:6** and the internal gears in **FIG 6:7.** With a screwdriver lever the extension housing rear plug 24 in **FIG 6:6** off its seating, unscrew four setscrews and lift off the top cover 1 and gasket 2. If fitted, unscrew the blank plug 7 from the gearbox casing.

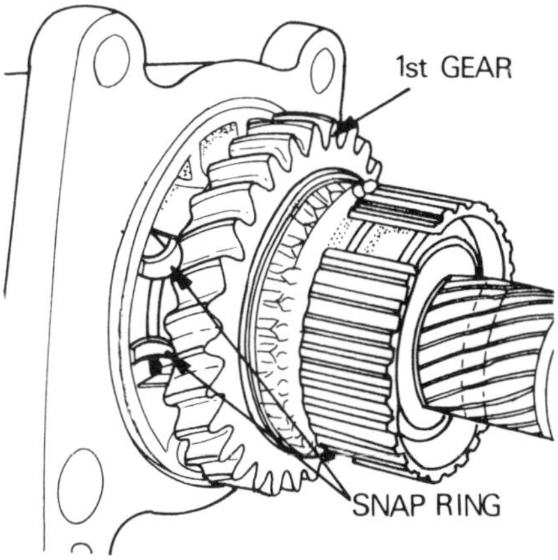

FIG 6:5 Output bearing snap ring location

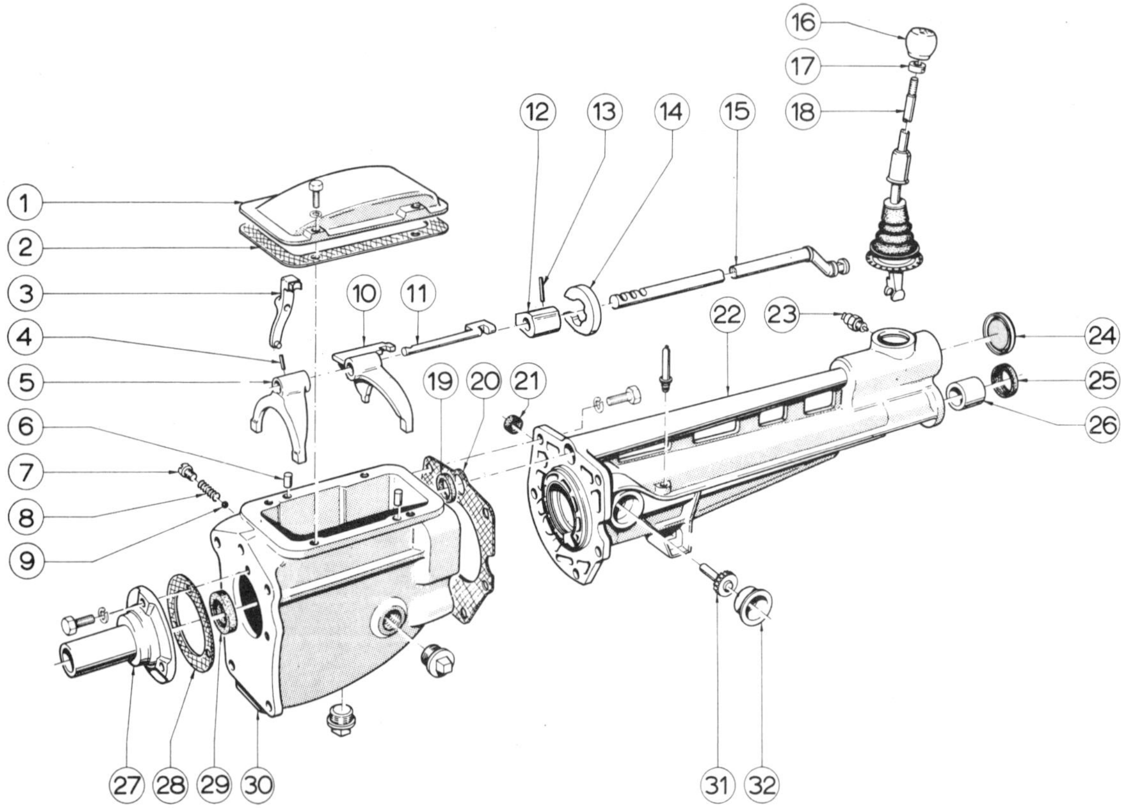

FIG 6 :6 External components of 'C' type box

Key to Fig 6 :6 1 Top cover 2 Gasket 3 Reverse relay arm 4 Spring pin 5 3rd/4th selector fork 6 Locating pin 7 Plug 8 Spring 9 Selector rail detent ball 10 1st/2nd gear selector fork 11 Fork relay arm 12 Selector boss 13 Spring pin 14 Lockplate 15 Selector rail 16 Gearlever knob 17 Locknut 18 Gearlever assembly 19 Oil seal 20 Gasket 21 Oil seal 22 Extension housing 23 Reverse lamp switch 24 Rear plug 25 Oil seal 26 Bush 27 Spigot bearing 28 Gasket 29 Oil seal 30 Casing 31 Speedometer drive gear 32 Retainer plug

2 Using a pin punch, drive out the pin 13 that secures the selector boss 12 to the selector rail 15. Use care to avoid damaging the dog teeth on 1st:2nd synchro hub. Push the hub aside if necessary.

3 Withdraw the selector rail 15 from the rear end and retrieve the boss 12 and the lock mechanism from the gearbox case. To remove the selector forks, push the 1st:2nd and 3rd:4th synchro hubs as far as possible towards the front of the box. Lift out the forks and, if necessary, separate them by removing their respective spring pin 4.

4 Extract the ball 9 and spring 8 from the casing. On later models this selector rod locking mechanism will be fitted in the coverplate instead of the housing.

5 If the extension housing seal 25 and bush 26 are to be renewed, they should be removed at this stage. Using service tool P7657 and adaptor P7657/4, first fully release the centre bolt of the extractor tool then screw the tool into the seal to obtain a secure grip. Tighten the locknut then turn the centre bolt to extract the seal. To withdraw the bush use service tool P7149 (German G2-7941-A).

6 Take out the extension housing securing bolts, free the housing, withdraw it only slightly so that it can be turned to give access to the countershaft assembly.

7 Using a dummy countershaft or service tool P7113 (German G2-7020), from the rear end drift the countershaft forward and out of the box. The dummy shaft must follow through the gear train and remain in constant contact with the countershaft to prevent the needle rollers from falling out of position. Keep the dummy shaft in position in the gear train and lower the assembly into the gearbox.

8 Remove the rear extension housing complete with mainshaft gear train. To do this the 3rd:4th synchro hub must be pushed forward slightly to provide sufficient clearance between the hub and the countershaft gear gear train. Now remove the needle roller bearing 9 and the 4th gear synchronizer sleeve 1 (see **FIG 6 :7**).

9 Take out three setscrews and remove the input shaft seal housing 27 and gasket 28, if necessary, extract the seal 29 from the housing with a screwdriver. Refer to **FIG 6 :7** and remove the large circlip 6b from around the bearing 7, then using a copper drift in contact with

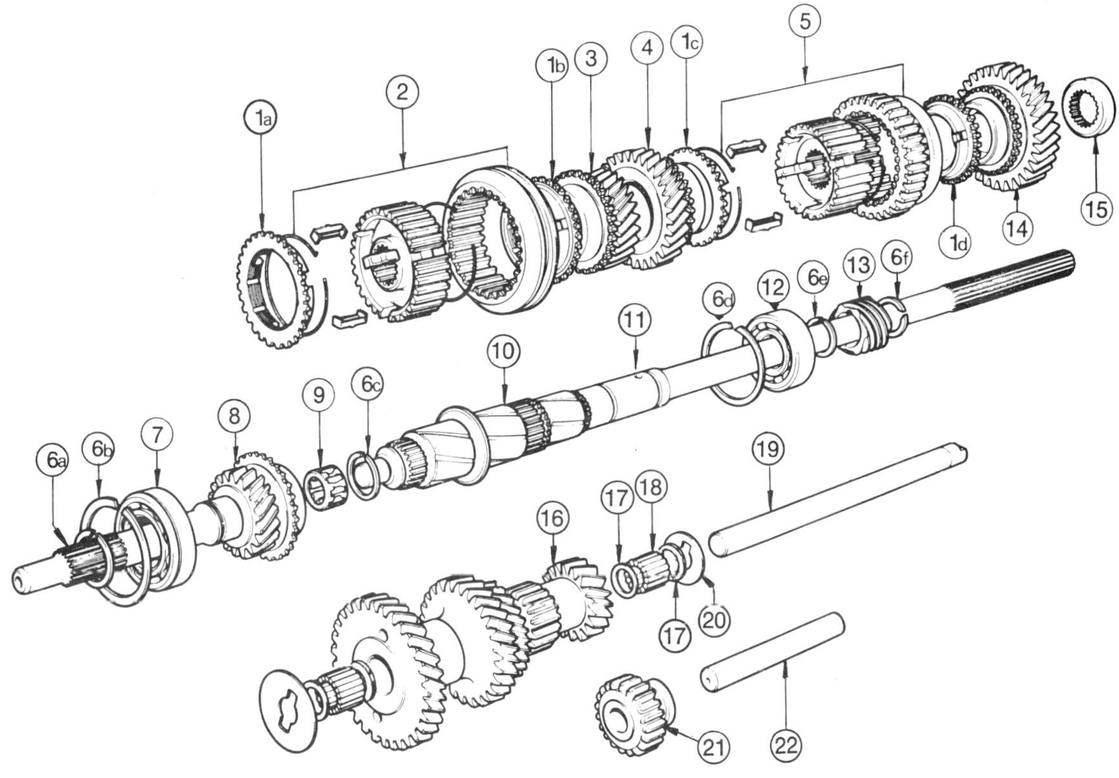

FIG 6:7 Internal components of 'C' type box

Key to Fig 6:7 1 Synchronizers sleeve 2 Synchronizer hub, 3rd/4th gear 3 3rd gear 4 2nd gear 5 Synchronizer hub, 1st/2nd gear 6 Circlips 7 Input shaft bearing 8 Input shaft 9 Needle roller bearing 10 Mainshaft 11 Detent ball 12 Mainshaft bearing 13 Speedometer drive gear 14 1st gear 15 Oil scoop ring 16 Countershaft gear train 17 Spacer shim 18 Needle rollers 19 Countershaft 20 Thrust washer 21 Reverse idler gear 22 Idler shaft

the outer section of the ballrace drive the bearing and input shaft towards the rear and out of the casing.

10 Remove the small circlip 6a in front of the bearing. If the bearing 7 is to be renewed place the assembly on a split slave ring or blocks on the bed of a press and force the shaft through the bearing, support the shaft under the press bed to prevent it falling through and on to the floor.

11 Lift the countershaft gear train, dummy shaft and thrust washers 20 out of the casing, withdraw the dummy shaft and then carefully remove the needle bearings 18 and spacer rings 17.

12 Using tool P7043 extract the reverse idler shaft 22 from the casing and reverse gear 21. If the tool is not available use a $\frac{5}{16}$ inch diameter X 24 t.p.i. bolt of sufficient length and thread to accommodate a spacer tube and washers. The spacer tube should have an ID large enough for the shaft to pass through it and an OD large enough to bear against the face of the casing. Screw the bolt into the shaft and extract it. Retrieve the idler gear and withdraw the relay arm (3 in **FIG 6:6**) from the fulcrum pin.

13 Using a screwdriver prise the retaining plug, 32 in **FIG 6:6**, from the speedometer pinion housing and withdraw the pinion 31.

14 Extract the mainshaft circlip 6d from the rear extension housing and then by ramming the housing onto a wooden base the mainshaft can be forced out of the housing.

15 Refer to **FIG 6:7** and remove the circlip 6c in front of the 3rd:4th synchro hub. Refer to item 10 and separate the synchro hub assembly from the shaft using the same method. Remove the circlip 6f behind the speedometer drive gear 13 and withdraw the drive gear and drive ball 11.

16 Remove the small circlip 6c at the rear of the mainshaft bearing 12, locate the shaft assembly in a press with a split slave ring or blocks underneath the front face of 1st gear 14 and force the shaft through the 1st gear, oil scoop ring 15 and bearing 12. Support the shaft under the bed of the press to prevent it falling.

17 Remove the circlip in front of the 1st:2nd synchro hub assembly, refer to item 16 and adopt the same method to push the shaft through the synchro hub, but locate

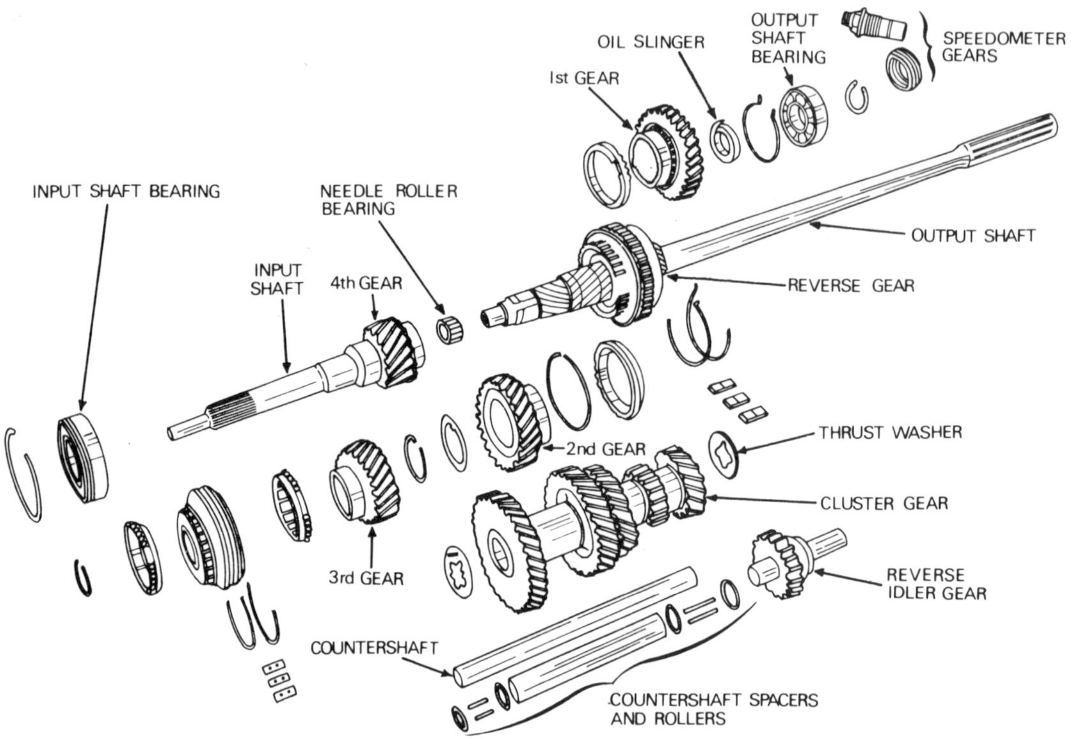

FIG 6:8 Components of transmission

the split slave ring or blocks under the front face of 2nd gear.

18 If necessary, prise the oil seals 19 and 21 (see **FIG 6:6**) out of their housings with a screwdriver.

19 The synchro hubs can be dismantled but if they are worn it is advisable to renew them as an assembly. Note the mating marks relating to the sleeve and hub, take off the circlip wires, noting also their location, and separate the sleeve, hub and blocker bars.

6:4 Assembling the transmission

All components should be carefully cleaned and examined for wear or damage, renewing as necessary. Before assembly dip them all in a specified oil and apply a sealer to those screws which are screwed into the transmission casing. Obtain new circlips throughout.

'H' type:

Refer to **FIG 6:8**. Slide the insert spring, blocking ring, 1st gear and spacer onto the rear of the output shaft with the broad side of the spacer towards the output shaft bearing.

Select a new snap ring for the extension housing output shaft and slide it onto the shaft. The thickness of the new snap ring is selected as follows:

Place the dummy bearing tool T70P-7154 into the extension housing and use feeler gauges to measure the gap between the top face of the tool and the outer edge of the snap ring retaining groove as shown in **FIG 6:9**. The combined thickness of the dummy bearing (.668 inch) and the feeler blades will be the total width between the bearing stop and the outer edge of the retaining groove. From this measurement subtract the width of the bearing to be used and the result is the thickness of the snap ring required. This must be precisely selected as, when installed, the output shaft must have no end float.

Press the bearing onto the output shaft and secure with the new snap ring which must fit **exactly** in the groove. See **FIG 6:10**.

The speedometer gear is pressed into position using the tool T71P-17271-B, shown in **FIG 6:11**. This is most important as this will locate the gear accurately on the output shaft, there being no locking device for the gear. See **FIG 6:12**.

The springs in the 1st/2nd gear synchronizer are positioned offset to one another by placing one end of each spring into the same insert groove as shown in **FIG 6:13** in order to have their tensions in opposition. The inserts are then placed in their grooves and the 1st/2nd gear synchronizer sleeve slid on to the hub with the selector fork collar facing the front end of the output shaft.

Slide the blocking ring, second gear and thrust washer on to the shaft and fit the snap ring in the position shown by **FIG 6:14**.

In order to obtain a tight fit for the output shaft and bearing in the extension housing, the housing should first be heated in an oven or by immersion in hot water. The shaft and bearing may then be slid into place without using any excessive pressure.

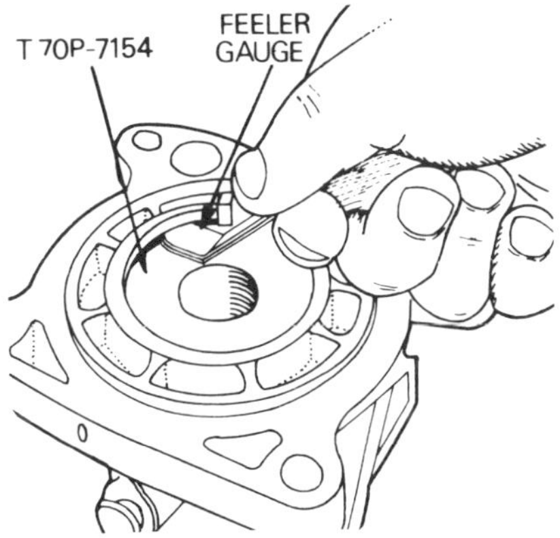

FIG 6:9 Measuring snap ring thickness

Fit the previously selected snap ring to secure the bearing in the housing.

Fit the 3rd/4th synchronizer springs in the same offset manner as for the 1st/2nd gear, position the inserts in their groove and slide the 3rd/4th gear synchronizer sleeve onto the hub with the narrow shoulder towards the rear. Slide the synchronizer assembly on to the output shaft and fit the retaining snap ring.

Press the input shaft bearing onto the input shaft and secure it with a snap ring selected for thickness to give the minimum end play. Fit the shaft and gear into the transmission case and tap it into place with a brass drift applied to the bearing outer race and then fit the snap ring to the periphery of the bearing.

The seal in the input shaft retainer may be renewed if necessary using tool T71P-7050-B before fitting the retainer to the transmission using a new gasket. Make sure that the oil groove in the retainer lines up with the oil passage in the casing and that it is not covered by the gasket. Secure the retainer with the three screws using a suitable sealer on the threads and new lock washers.

The reverse idler gear is fitted with the collar for the selector fork towards the rear and then the idler gear shaft driven into place until it is flush with the wall of the casing.

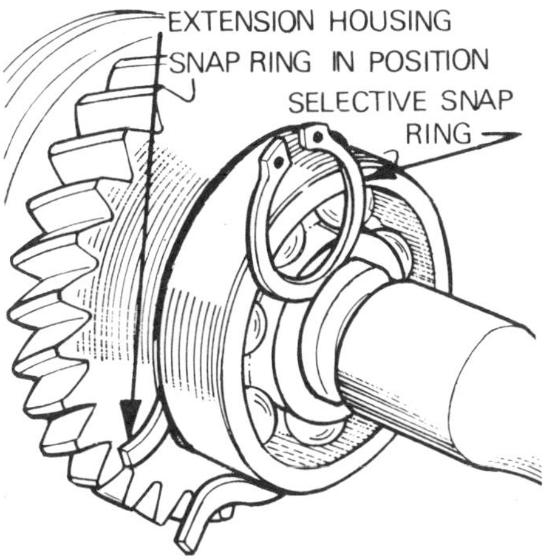

FIG 6:10 Output shaft bearing snap ring

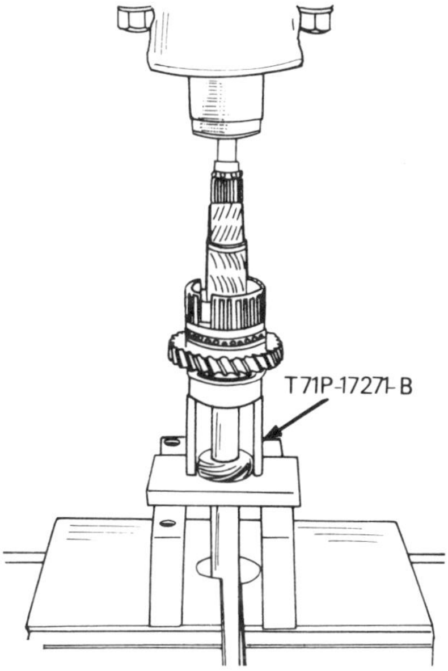

FIG 6:11 Fitting the speedometer gear

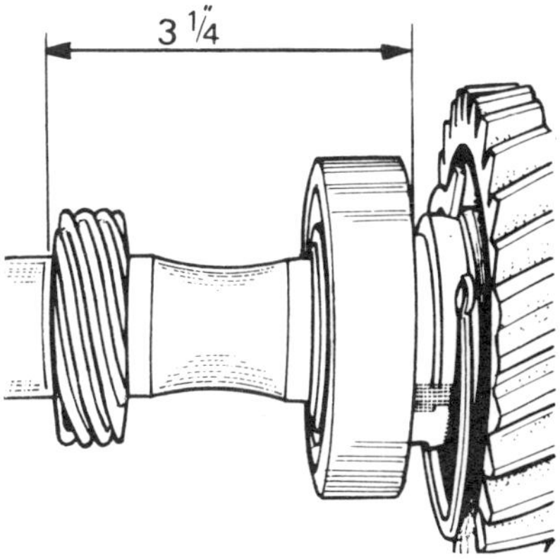

FIG 6:12 Speedometer gear location

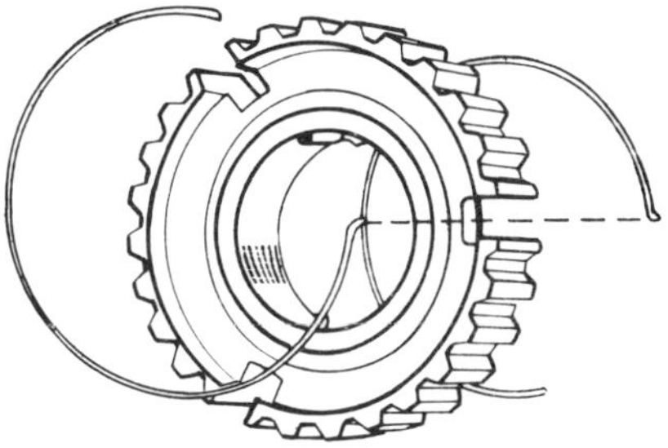

FIG 6:13 Showing typical positions of insert springs

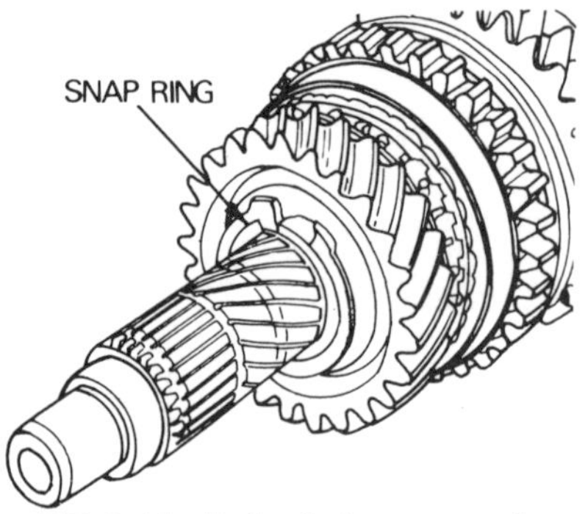

FIG 6:14 Fitting 2nd gear snap ring

The installation of the countershaft assembly is very much a reversal of its removal. Assemble the cluster gear on the dummy shaft and lay it in the bottom of the casing, threading cords underneath it at each end to lift it up into its final position. The rollers and washers may be held in place by smearing liberally with grease or vaseline.

Replace the extension housing gasket with a sealer on both sides, then slide the housing and output shaft into position being very careful not to damage the caged roller bearing. **FIG 6:15**.

Move the extension housing so as to permit access to the countershaft, then pull the cords to raise the cluster gear into mesh with the main gear train and install the countershaft by pushing it into replace the dummy shaft. Be most careful to see that none of the rollers or washers are displaced during this operation, and ensure that the offset lug on the rear end of the countershaft is correctly located to allow the final the final installation of the extension housing.

Secure the extension housing, tightening the screws to a torque of 30-35 lb ft and using sealer on the screw threads.

Fit the speedometer driven gear.

Refer to **FIG 6:16** to assist in identification and install the shift forks. 1st/2nd and 3rd/4th forks are fitted with the number stamped on them facing to the front, while the reverse fork has its stamped number towards the rear. Note that the short leg of the 1st/2nd fork is towards the bottom of the casing.

Fit the gearshift housing on the transmission using a new gasket and sealer and then check that all gears can be selected.

Position the reversing light switch and secure the gearshift housing with its screws. Fit the clutch housing and tighten the screws to 40-47 lb ft. Fit the clutch release lever, hub and bearing.

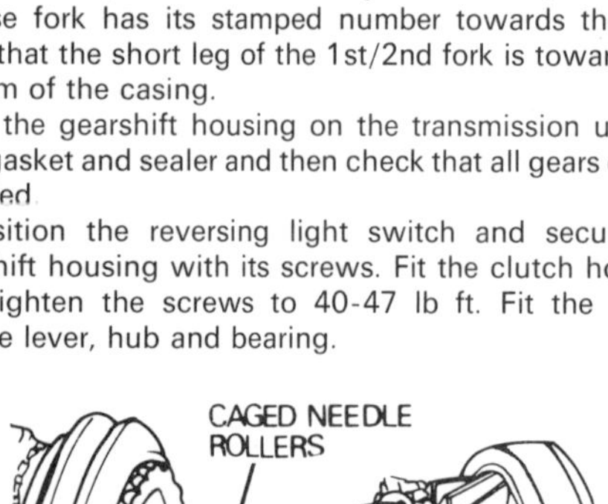

FIG 6:15 Fitting the caged roller bearing

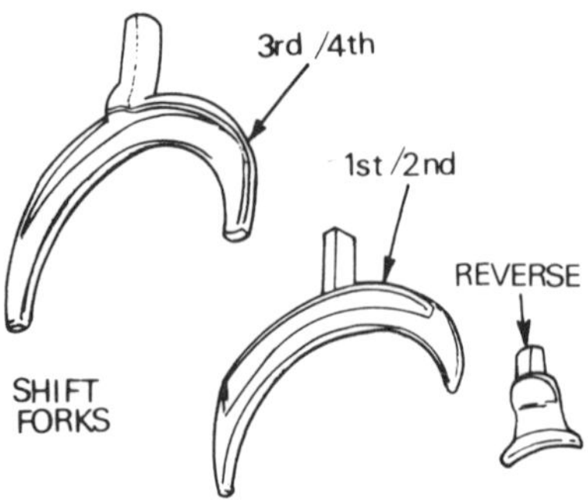

FIG 6:16 Shift fork identification

'C' type:

1 If the synchro hubs have been dismantled, align the mating marks and slide the sleeve over the hub. Fit the blocker bars and when fitting the circlip wires stagger their location by inserting different ends of each spring in the same blocker bar (see **FIG 6:13**). Place the 3rd:4th synchro hub assembly on one side until it is required.

2 Fit the 2nd gear 4 (see **FIG 6:7**) onto the mainshaft so that the reverse dog teeth are orientated to the rear of the shaft. Fit the synchronizer sleeve 1c to the cone of 2nd gear and then slide the 1st:2nd synchro hub assembly 5 onto the mainshaft so that the reverse dog teeth are orientated to the front of the shaft.

3 Place the sub-assembly onto the bed of a press with the split slave ring of the press (or blocks) against the synchro hub. Operate the press and force the shaft downwards and through until the synchro hub is fully home on its seat on the mainshaft. Secure with a new circlip.

4 Fit the synchro sleeve 1d, 1st gear 14 and then fit the oil scoop washer 15 with its broad front face towards 1st gear.

5 If a new ball race 12 or a new rear extension housing is to be fitted, the thickness of a new circlip 6d must be established to obtain a nil end float on the mainshaft. Pick up the extension housing and support it with the bearing housing uppermost. Fit the circlip 6d into its groove in the bearing housing. With a depth gauge measure the depth of the bearing housing from the outer face of the circlip. Now measure the thickness of the new bearing outer track with vernier calipers or a micrometer. Make a note of both readings and deduct the bearing thickness from the measured depth. The result is the thickness of the new circlip to be fitted.

For example:

Measured depth	.70 inch or 17.98 mm
Bearing thickness	**(—) .60 inch** or **(—) 15.92 mm**
Thickness of new circlip	= **.10 inch** or **2.06 mm**

A selection of circlips of varying thickness can be obtained from the service garage stores. See **FIG 6:17** for location.

6 Loosely fit the new circlip 6d (or 3) and the new ball-race onto the mainshaft. Locate the mainshaft sub-assembly on the bed of a press as follows: Fit service

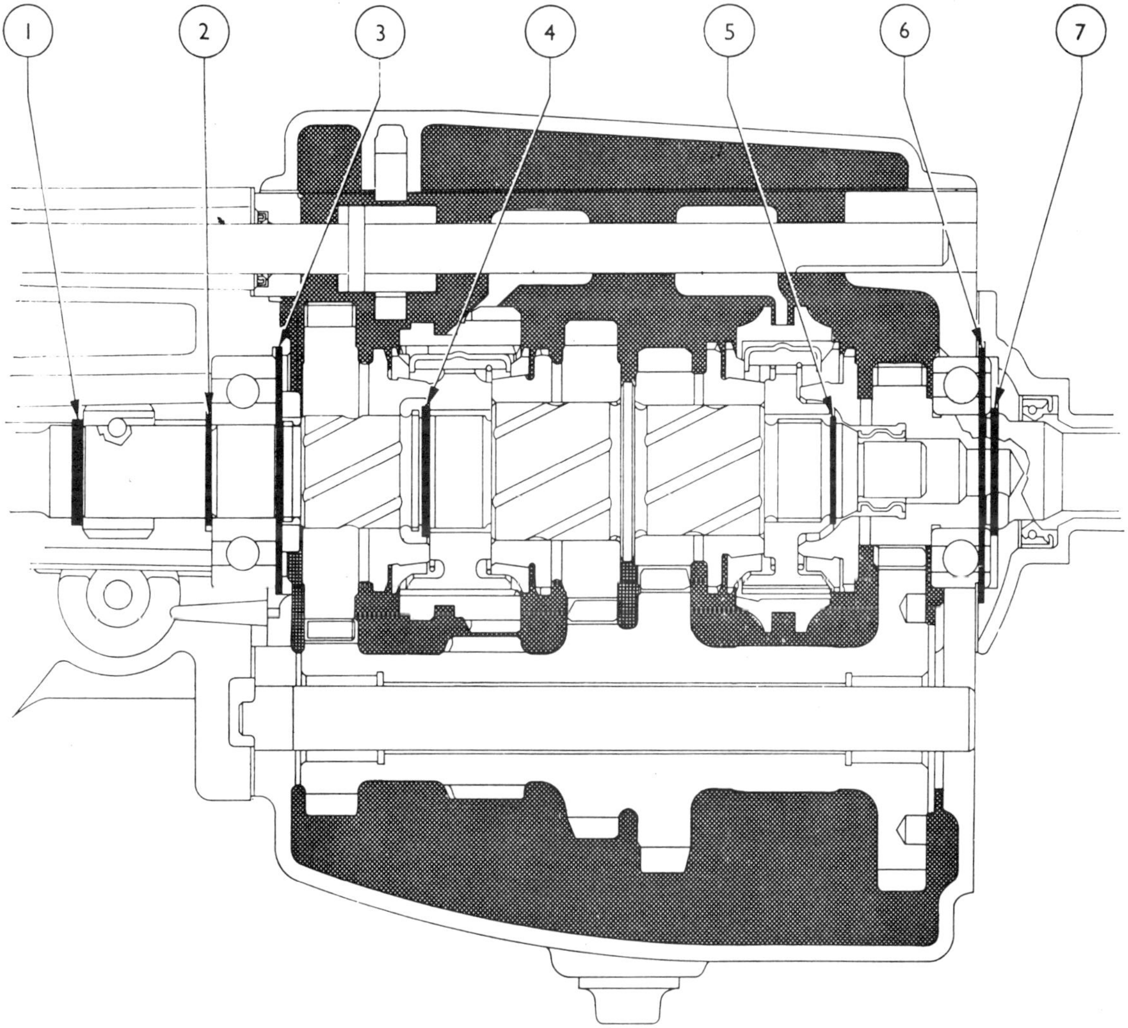

FIG 6:17 Location of circlips in 'C' type box. Circlips 2 and 3 are available in various thicknesses

Key to Fig 6:17 Corresponding Key numbers in Fig 6:7 shown in brackets 1 (6f) 2 (6e) 3 (6d) 4 (not shown) 5 (6c) 6 (6b) 7 (6a)

tool (bearing replacer P4090-7A) with the stepped side adjacent to the inner track of the bearing. Fit the split slave ring or blocks under the service tool. Operate the press and drive the shaft downwards until the bearing is in position.

7 After the bearing has been correctly positioned select a new circlip 6e (or 2) of the correct thickness to fit snugly into its recess and abut on the inner track of the bearing (see **FIG 6:10**). This is to ensure there will be no end float.

8 Fit the detent ball 11 into the mainshaft and slide the speedometer drive gear into position. Fit the circlip 6f (or 1).

9 If the bush 26 and seal 25 (see **FIG 6:6**) have been extracted from the rear extension housing, drift a new bush into the housing with service tool P7150 (German G2-7041B) or a suitably sized universal drift. Bear in mind before and during the fitting of the bush that the small recess should appear at the rear edge of the bush and in line with the oil return groove in the housing. Using the same tool drive a new seal into the housing.

10 Still referring to **FIG 6:6** fit new seals 19 and 21 to the selector rail and speedometer gear orifices.

11 Position the rear extension housing with the forward end uppermost and force the assembled bearing and mainshaft into the bearing housing, secure the large circlip 6d (or 3) into its recess in the bearing housing. To assist in this operation and prevent foreign matter entering the rear of the housing, fit either a discarded propeller shaft yoke or the mainshaft dust cap to the rear of the housing.

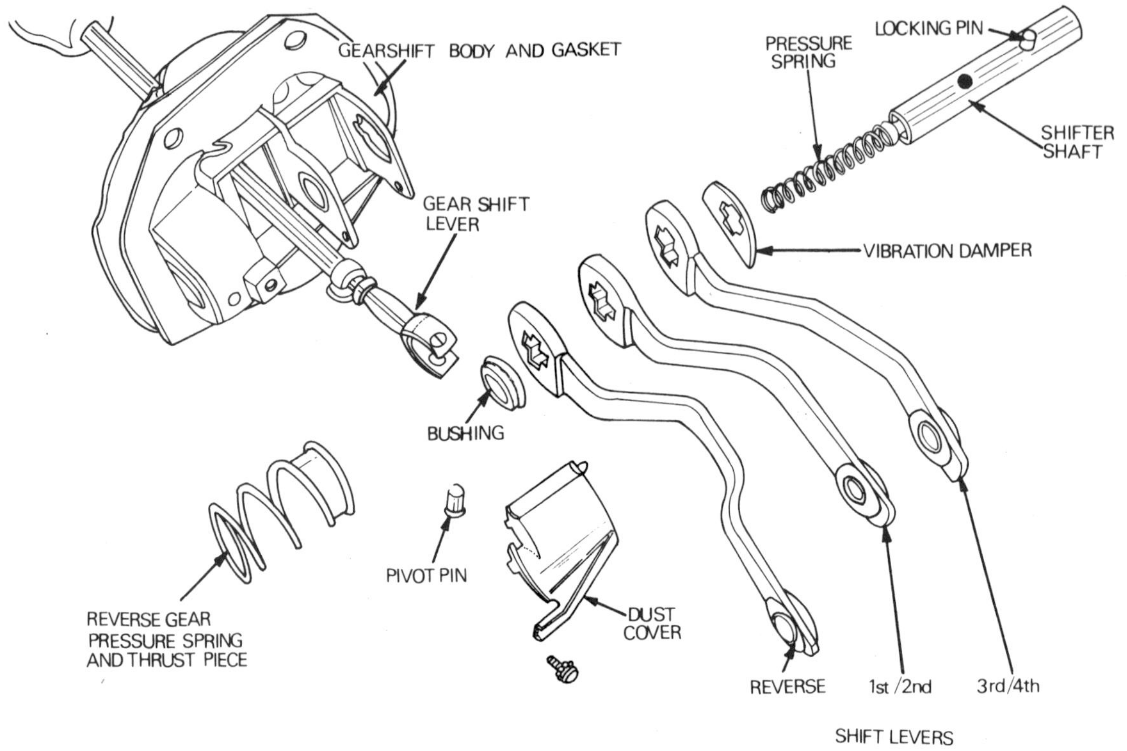

FIG 6:18 Components of gear shift lever assembly

12 Fit and engage the speedometer drive pinion 31, coat the retainer plug 32 with a sealing compound and insert it into the pinion housing.

13 Refer to **FIG 6:7** and fit the 3rd gear 3 onto the mainshaft—with the dog teeth facing forward—and the synchro sleeve 1b. Pick up the assembled synchro hub 2 for 3rd:4th gears and slide it onto the mainshaft with the wide collar of the hub towards the rear of the shaft. Locate the assembly in a press as follows. Fit service tool P4090-9, P4000-31A and the bed taper base 370. Fit the split slave ring and press the synchro hub on to the mainshaft until it bears against its shoulder. Fit a new circlip 6c (or 5).

14 Pick up the reverse relay arm (3 in **FIG 6:6**) and fit it to the fulcrum pin. Locate the reverse idler gear 21 to the relay arm with the groove of the idler gear rearwards and abuting the shaft bore. Use a copper mallet and drive the idler shaft 22 into the casing and through the gear.

15 Pick up the countershaft gear train and the dummy countershaft, insert the dummy shaft into the gear train bore and pack the empty space between shaft and bore with grease. At each end fit a spacer shim 17, needle rollers 18 and another spacer shim 17. Pick up the thrust washers 20, coat the washers with grease and stick them inside the casing, around the countershaft bores, with their lugs bearing against the boss of the gearbox case. Gently lower the gear train into the case.

16 Pick up the input shaft 8 and slide a new ballrace 7 onto the shaft. Place the assembly in a press and force the bearing into position as far as it will go. Fit a new circlip 6a (or 7).

17 From inside the casing, locate the input shaft bearing in its housing and drive it into the casing with a copper drift positioned on the outer track of the bearing. Drive the bearing in only as far as is necessary, to allow for sufficient clearance for the circlip 6b (or 6) to fit snugly into its recess in the bearing. If necessary tap the input shaft in the reverse direction so that the circlip bears on the casing.

18 Refer to **FIG 6:6** and fit a new oil seal 29 into its housing 27, the lips of the seal must face the gearbox case. To avoid damaging the seal when the assembly is slid over the input shaft, wind masking tape around the input shaft splines. Fit a new gasket 28 ensuring that it is correctly positioned on the casing in relation to the lubrication hole. Grease the seal and slide the assembly over the shaft ensuring that the machined recess in the gasket face is positioned over the lubrication hole. Fit the three bolts and tighten to a torque of 12 to 15 lb ft (1.7 to 2.1 kgm). Remove the masking tape.

19 Refer to **FIG 6:7**, pick up and grease the needle bearing 9, fit it inside the input shaft bore, slide the 4th gear synchro sleeve 1a over the cone.

20 Refer to **FIG 6:6** and coat a new gasket 20 with a sealer and stick it to the extension housing face.

21 Engage the rear extension and the mainshaft assembly with the gearbox case. To gain sufficient clearance between the 3rd:4th synchro hub assembly and the countershaft cluster gear, push the synchro hub assembly forward slightly. Make sure the 4th gear synchro sleeve is not displaced.

22 Adjust the position of the extension housing to expose the countershaft bore. Engage the countershaft gear train with the mainshaft and input shaft, holding this position until the true countershaft has been inserted to replace the dummy countershaft. Extreme care must be exercised whilst doing this to avoid dislodging the thrust washers that have been stuck inside the gear case.

23 Pass the true countershaft through the bore, thrust washer, spacer shims, needle rollers and the gear train, without dislodging any of the parts and ensuring that it is in constant contact with the dummy countershaft, until it emerges into the bore at the other end of the case. A plastic or copper mallet should be used to drive the shaft fully home. Note that the lug at the rear of the countershaft must be positioned horizontally to allow for the rear extension alignments.

24 Turn the extension housing into position, coat the securing bolts with sealant and tighten them to a torque of 20 to 25 lb ft (2.8 to 3.8 kgm).

25 Assemble the 1st:2nd and 3rd:4th selector forks and secure them with a new spring pin. Push the synchronizer sleeves 1 rearwards and fit the selector forks, rearrange the sleeves in their idling positions. Apply a little grease to the sliding rail and the seal, refer to **FIG 6:6** and hold the boss 12 and lockplate 14 in line with the bore whilst the selector rail is inserted. Take care not to damage the seal 19. Secure the boss with a new spring pin 13.

26 Coat the cover 24 with sealer and fit it to the extension housing. Fit a new gasket 2, coated with sealer and fit the top cover. Make sure the locating pins 6 are in position and if fitted the detent ball and new spring in the top cover.

27 Refit the clutch housing and associate parts. Reassemble by referring to **Chapter 5** and fill the gearbox with oil.

6:5 The gearshift mechanism ('H type)

The adjustment of the shift linkage was described in **Section 6:2**, but if further work is necessary, proceed as follows:

Removal:

Raise the car and disconnect the three shift rods from the levers by removing the clips as described earlier. Lever out the panel (wood grain) at the rear of the console.

Undo the two screws and slide the plastic cross panel forward and remove it.

Remove the two screws which will be found underneath the rear corners of the handbrake boot. Lever up the rear edge of the front wood grain panel and remove the centre retaining screw.

Remove one screw from each side of the lower front edge of the console, unscrew the knob of the gearlever and move the console to one side.

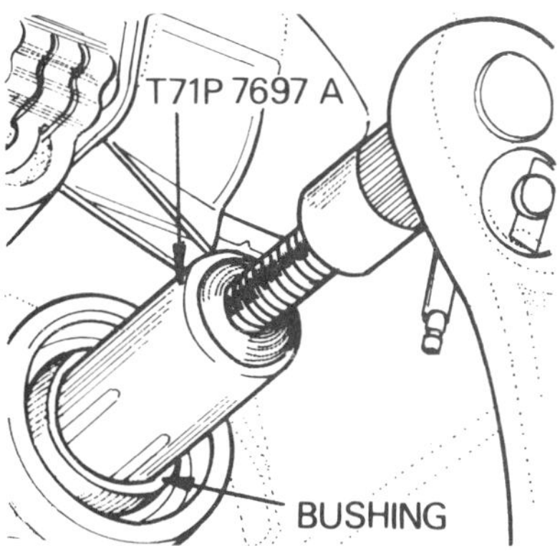

FIG 6:19 Removing the extension housing bushing

Take out the three securing screws and remove the gear shift assembly from the floor pan.

Refitting is a reversal of the above procedure.

Dismantling (see FIG 6:18):

Drive out the pivot pin from the shift lever fork and pull the gearshift lever out of the assembly.

Move all three shift levers rearwards into a horizontal position until it is possible to move the grooved pin through the respective cut-outs in the levers and shaft retainers. Pull out the shifter shaft and drive out the locking pin.

Remove the levers and the vibration damper, also the pressure springs, thrust piece and bushings.

Before commencing to reassemble, give all moving surfaces a smear of a suitable lubricant.

Fit the reverse gear pressure spring on the thrust piece and slide into the gearshift body.

Fit the bushing with the flange towards the levers as shown and then assemble the three levers and vibration damper.

Slide the shifter shaft complete with locking pin and pressure spring into the shaft retainers and levers and then allow the levers to swing into the vertical position.

Fit the gearshift lever and rubber boot and secure it by driving in the front pin.

After assembly, check that the shift operates smoothly and correctly.

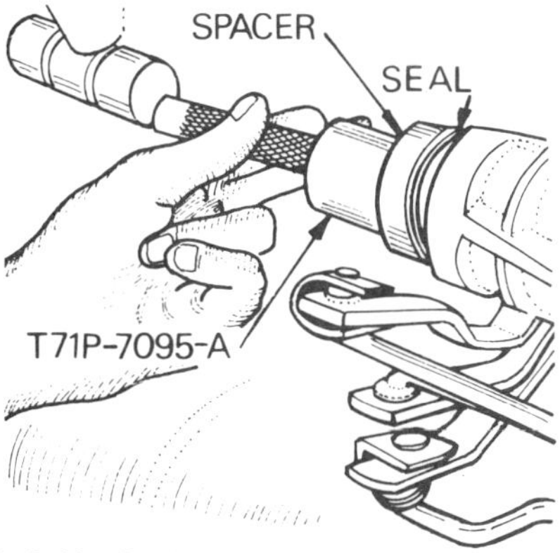

FIG 6:20 Replacing extension housing oil seal

6:6 Installing the gearbox

This operation is described in **Section 5:5**, after which the transmission must be refilled with the specified lubricant and the gearshift linkage adjusted as described in **Section 6:2**.

6:7 Renewing the extension housing oil seal

After long use, wear in the rear end of the extension housing may be indicated by an oil leakage and radial movement of the output shaft.

Remove the four bolts in the flange joint between the drive shaft and the rear axle pinion, being careful to mark the flanges for later assembly.

Remove the bolts securing the centre bearing carrier to its bracket.

Lower the rear end of the drive shaft and slide the front yoke away from the transmission.

To renew the seal and bush on the 'C' type box refer to **Section 6:3** item 5 and **Section 6:4** item 9.

To renew on the 'H' type box screw the tool T71P-7657-A into the seal and extract the seal by screwing in the centre bolt.

The extension housing bush is removed in a similar manner using the service tool (**FIG 6:19**).

Installation:

Fit a new bush on to the replacer service tool (without spacer) and drive it into position, making sure that the split in the bush is uppermost.

The new seal is fitted by driving it, being careful to see that it is kept square, into position with the same tool but this time with the spacer (**FIG 6:20**).

Refit the remaining components in the reverse order to removal and top up the gearbox to make good any loss of oil.

6:8 Fault diagnosis

(a) Jumping out of gear

1 Worn gearshift mechanism
2 Worn selector cams or plunger spring
3 Worn synchromesh coupling dogs, sleeve or hub
4 Worn selector forks or sleeves
5 Excessive end play on shafts

(b) Noisy transmission

1 Insufficient oil
2 Excessive end play on output shaft or countershaft
3 Worn or damaged bearings
4 Worn or damaged gear teeth
5 Excessive running clearances

(c) Difficulty in engaging gear

1 Incorrect clutch adjustment
2 Worn synchromesh cones
3 Worn selector mechanism
4 Selector mechanism out of adjustment

(d) Noisy gearchange

1 Worn or damaged synchromesh cones
2 Blocker bars worn, springs weak
3 Worn or damaged teeth on gears

CHAPTER 7

AUTOMATIC TRANSMISSION

7:1 General description

The automatic transmission fitted to these cars is the Borg-Warner model 35 and comprises a torque converter and a hydraulically controlled epicyclic gearbox with three forward speeds and a reverse. Gear selection is by means of a floor mounted lever mounted in a quadrant giving a choice of six selector positions.

The unit is capable of providing automatic upshifts and downshifts through the three forward ratios and also manual selection of first and second gears.

The selector quadrant is marked with the following lever positions P-R-N-D-2-1 for the following six functions:

P (Park) This position disconnects the engine from the drive and also locks the rear wheels and transmission to prevent the car from moving in either direction. P must never be selected while the car is in motion.

R (Reverse) As its name implies. Never select R while the car is in forward motion.

N (Neutral) In this position the engine may be started and run, as in P, without any drive being transmitted, but no transmission lock is applied.

D (Drive) This is the position for all normal driving. The transmission will give a start in first gear and automatically shift up into second and third (high or top) at speeds dependent upon road speed and throttle position. Downshifts also will be automatically made as road speeds decrease, the actual shifting point being determined according to engine load and throttle position.

2 This position provides a first gear start and automatic shift to second, as in D, but no shift into third. Moving the selector from D to 2 will engage second gear immediately and a shift from second to first will take place as the road speed decreased. To avoid overspeeding the engine, 2 should not be selected at speeds above 65 mile/hour.

1 Provides for moving off in first gear and no further upshift. Upshifts from 1 must be made manually by moving the selector to 2 or D when the driving range provided by those positions will become available. This position, like 2, provides engine braking for the descent of steep hills and if 1 is selected from D when travelling in top gear, the transmission will first shift into second gear and make the move to first gear when the road speed decreases to about 10 mile/hour.

The selector lever has a push button in the handle which must be depressed to release a lock permitting movement of the lever into the P, R, 2 or 1 positions.

Forced downshifts (kick-down) are available at road speeds up to 65 mile/hour in D range whereby an

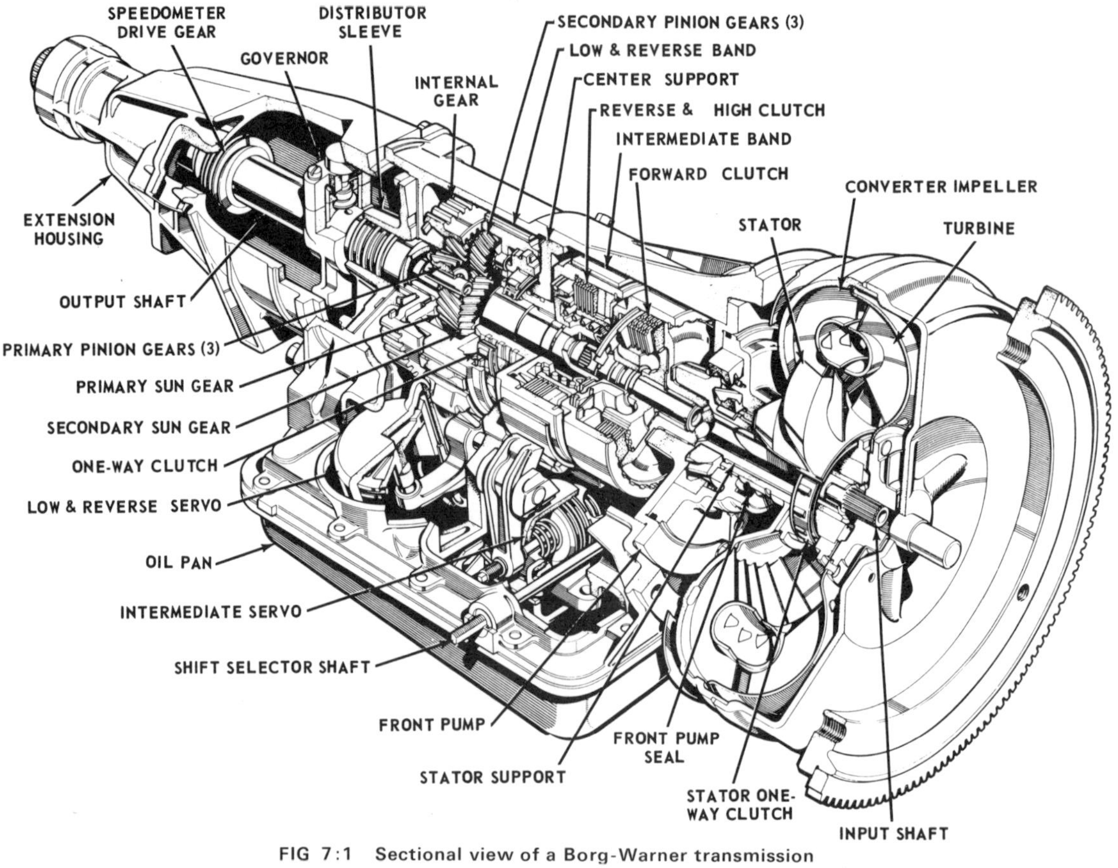

FIG 7:1 Sectional view of a Borg-Warner transmission

immediate downshift from top to second gear is made by completely depressing the accelerator pedal beyond the full throttle position. A kickdown to low is also possible in D range at speeds below 25 mile/hour.

A sectional view of a complete transmission is given in **FIG 7:1**.

The hydraulic torque converter consists of an impeller (pump), turbine and stator, all enclosed and operating in a fluid filled housing. The impeller is directly coupled to the engine crankshaft and the turbine is splined to the input shaft of the gearbox.

As the engine, and therefore the impeller, turns, fluid flows from the impeller vanes into the turbine and causes it to rotate and the fluid returns to the impeller through the blades of the stator which are so shaped as to direct the flow against the impeller blades and assist it in its rotation.

The torque multiplication thus obtained ranges from approximately 2:1, when the turbine is stalled, down to 1:1 when the turbine is being driven at $\frac{9}{10}$ impeller speed and the stator is turning together with the other two elements. At this point the converter operates as a simple fluid coupling.

The initial slip and torque multiplication enable the system to provide very smooth take up of the drive together with maximum flexibility from the three gear ratios.

The planetary gear train consists of a primary sun gear, a secondary sun gear, primary and secondary pinions and an internal ratios are obtained by the operation of hydraulically operated clutches and brake bands controlled by a series of regulator valves according to driving conditions and requirements.

The servicing and overhaul of the automatic transmission are not operations for the home mechanic in view of the many special items of equipment necessary. In the event of a breakdown, the owner is recommended to take his car to a service station for attention and repair or to have a new or replacement transmission fitted.

Towing:

Provided that the transmission is not damaged and the fluid level is correct the car may be towed for distances up to 30 miles at speeds of not more than 30 mile/hour with N selected.

If greater distances are to be covered or higher speeds obtained, or if the transmission is in any way defective, the car should be towed on the front wheels, the rear wheels raised off the road or with the drive (propeller) shaft removed.

It is not possible to start the engine on these cars by towing.

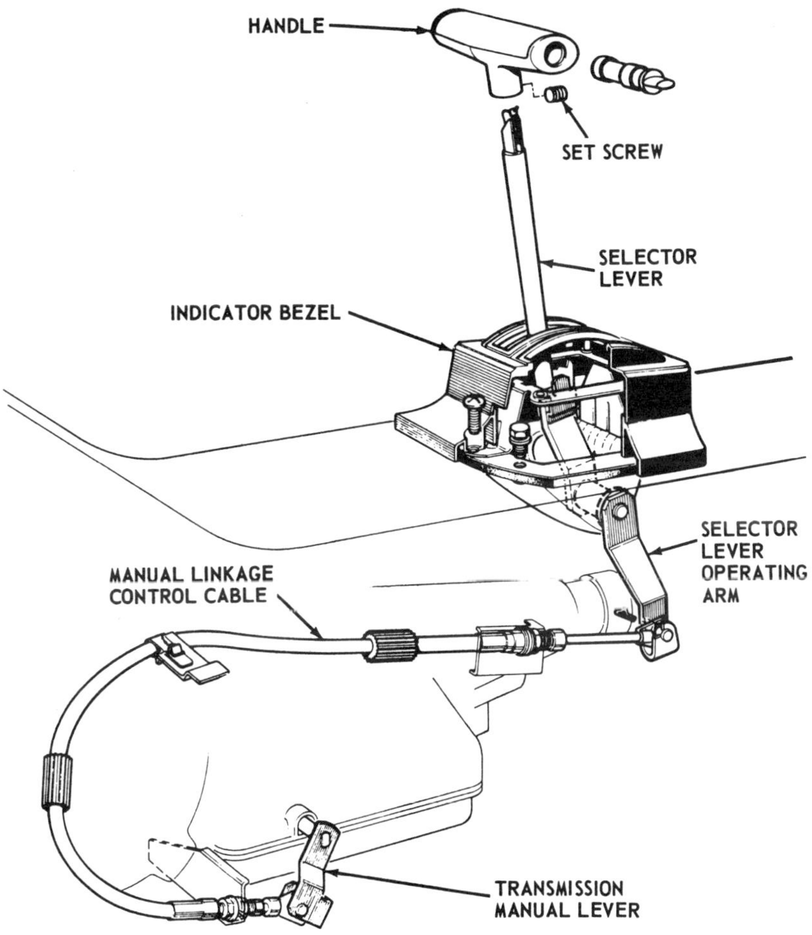

FIG 7:2 The selector mechanism

7:2 Routine maintenance

The only item of routine maintenance is a check on the fluid level at intervals of 6000 miles (10,000 km).

With the engine at full working temperature and the car standing on level ground, allow the engine to run at normal idle speed. Move the selector lever through all positions and place at P.

Clean all dirt from around the dipstick, pull it out, wipe it and check the fluid level being sure to insert the dipstick fully into its tube. The level should be above the MIN mark and enough should be added to bring it up to the MAX mark but do not overfill. Use only the recommended fluid which is ESW-M2C33F.

Replace the dipstick and switch off the engine.

7:3 Adjustments

Manual linkage (see **FIG 7:2**):

Place the selector lever in the D position, then raise the car, remove the clevis pin and disconnect the cable from the transmission selector lever.

Move the transmission selector lever to the D position which is the third detent from the back of the transmission. With both levers at D adjust the cable length until the clevis pin slides easily through the holes in the lever and the cable end.

Secure the clevis pin and check the selector operation in all positions.

Neutral start switch:

This device, sometimes known as the starter inhibitor switch, is fitted to ensure that the starter operates only in the N and P positions. It also includes the back-up or reverse light switch.

Place the selector lever in the D position, then raise the car and disconnect the four leads to the switch.

Loosen the securing locknut ($\frac{11}{16}$ inch) and unscrew the switch by about two turns.

Connect a self-powered test lamp across the two back-up light terminals as shown in **FIG 7:3**. These are the two larger terminals. The test lamp should light up.

Screw the switch in slowly until the lamp goes out and mark the switch position at this point.

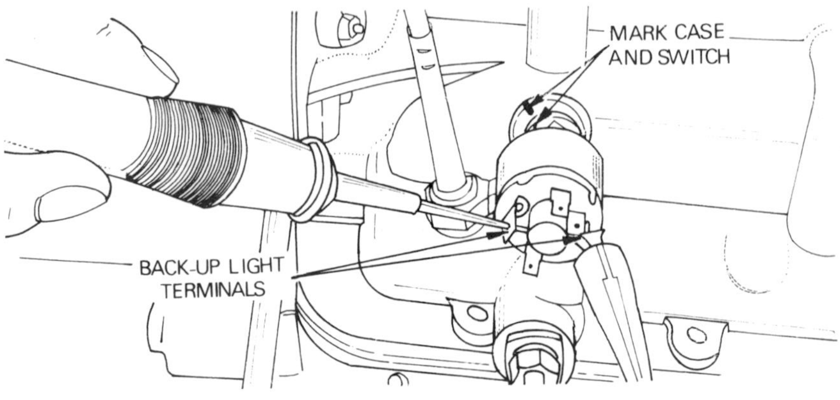

FIG 7:3 Adjusting the inhibitor switch

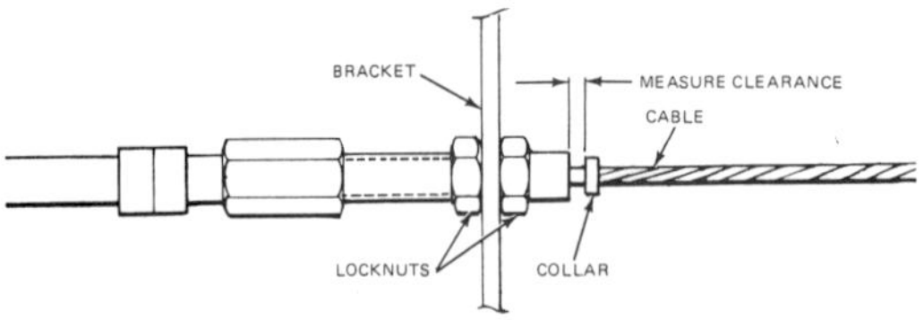

FIG 7:4 Downshift control cable adjustment

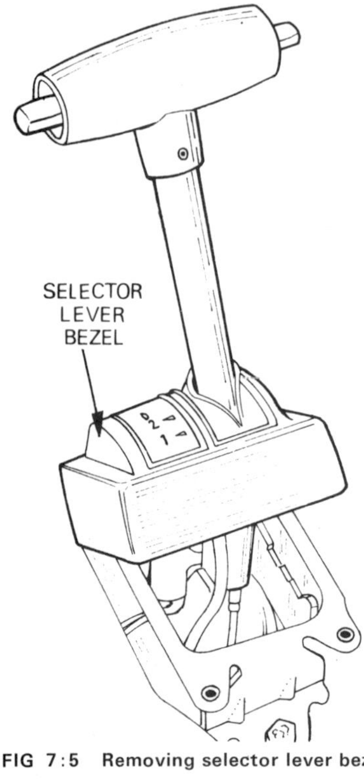

FIG 7:5 Removing selector lever bezel

Connect the test lamp to the two smaller terminals, which are the starter terminals, and continue to screw the switch in until the test lamp lights up again. Mark this new position on the switch.

Unscrew the switch until it is half way between the two positions marked and then tighten the locknut.

Reconnect the four leads and check the operation of the switch in all six lever positions. The starter should operate in the P and N positions only and the reversing light in the R position only. If these services are not obtained as specified the switch must be renewed.

Disconnect the four leads, loosen the locknut and unscrew the switch from the transmission. Note the number of turns required to remove it.

Screw in the new switch by exactly the same number of turns and adjust as described above.

Downshift cable:

The method of adjusting the downshift valve cable to be described can only be used if the accelerator linkage is unworn and the cable is still fitted with its original crimped collar. Otherwise this adjustment requires the use of a pressure gauge and a tachometer.

Refer to **FIG 7:4**. With the engine hot, idle correctly adjusted and the accelerator linkage correctly set, slacken the locknuts and adjust the position of the collar to give a clearance of .030 inch between the collar and the cable outer casing.

7:4 The selector mechanism

Adjustment of the selector mechanism is described in **Section 7:3**, but if for any reason it is required to remove it from the car, the procedure is as follows:

Raise the car and support it on stands. Remove the clevis pin and disconnect the selector lever cable and bushing from the selector lever operating arm. **FIG 7:2**.

Lever out the woodgrain panel at the rear of the console. Remove two retaining screws and slide the plastic cross panel forward and remove it.

Remove the two screws under the rear corners of the hand brake lever boot.

Lift up the rear edge of the front woodgrain panel and remove the centre retaining screw. Remove the screw from each side of the forward lower edge of the console and move the console to one side.

Lift upward on the selector lever indicator bezel shown in **FIG 7:5** and remove the three bolts holding the selector lever housing to the floor pan.

Disconnect the indicator light and remove the selector lever and housing assembly.

Loosen the setscrew retaining the handle on the selector lever, press in the push button and lift off the handle.

Remove the plug from the side of the selector housing and remove the retaining nut on the bottom of the selector lever shown in **FIG 7:6**.

The selector lever and bushings may now be removed by tapping out the operating arm shaft using a soft drift. Similarly tap out the cable retaining pin at the upper end of the selector lever.

Refer to **FIG 7:7** and remove the cable adjusting nut and remove the detent plunger spring and bushing. The cable may now be withdrawn from the selector lever.

Reassembly:

Insert the cable into the selector lever and fit the retaining pin.

Fit the bushing, spring and detent plunger over the cable and into the lower end of the lever. Press in the plunger and fit on the cable adjusting nut.

Fit the selector lever and bushings on to the operating arm and tighten the retaining nut.

Fit the handle and push button to the selector lever and tighten the setscrew.

Refer to **FIG 7:6** and with the selector lever in the centre detent, turn the cable adjusting nut until the clearance between the bottom of the pawl and the detent is between .005 and .010 inch. Check that the release mechanism operates correctly and replace the plug in the side of the selector housing.

Hold the selector lever and housing in place on the floor pan and fit the securing bolts.

Connect the indicator light and fit the indicator bezel.

Refit the console and install the remaining parts in the reverse order of removal.

Lower the car, check the operations of the selector lever in each position and adjust if necessary as described in **Section 7:3**.

7:5 Removing the transmission

Although the dismantling of an automatic transmission is not considered a task suitable for the home operator, if a replacement becomes necessary or professional attention to the unit required, he may wish to take it out of the car himself either for convenience or in the interests of economy.

Lift the car up on to suitable stands and disconnect the battery.

Remove the transmission dipstick, disconnect the throttle linkage downshift valve control cable, remove the drain plug and drain the fluid from the unit, bearing in mind that if this is done just after using the car the fluid will be **very hot**.

Remove the four bolts securing the drive shaft to the rear axle pinion flange after marking it for later reassembly.

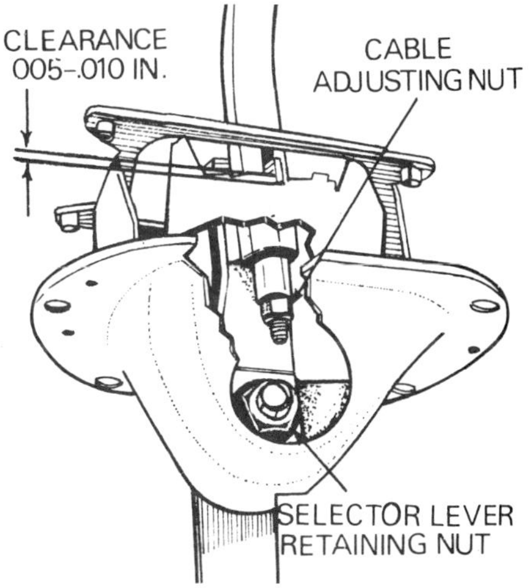

FIG 7:6 Manual selector lever adjustment

Remove the two bolts securing the drive shaft centre bearing to the frame.

Lower the drive shaft assembly and withdraw from the transmission.

Disconnect the exhaust pipe bracket from the transmission mounting, loosen it on the exhaust pipe and swing it to one side.

Remove the snap ring retaining the speedometer cable to the transmission and pull out the cable.

Disconnect the cables to the starter relay, unbolt and remove the starter. Unbolt and remove the front cover of the converter housing.

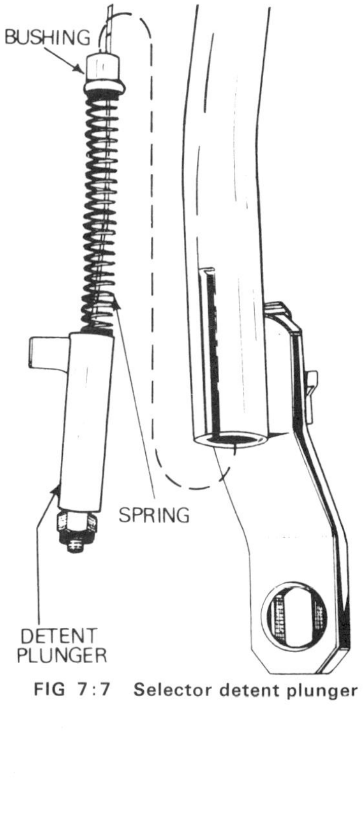

FIG 7:7 Selector detent plunger

Remove the four capscrews securing the flexplate to the converter.

Remove the selector control cable from the lever on the transmission. Disconnect the leads to the starter inhibitor switch, noting their positions for later re-installation.

If a proper transmission jack is not available, very carefully protect the pan and support the transmission on a trolley jack.

Remove the four engine support to body bolts. Remove the six bolts securing the converter housing to the engine. Remove the transmission filler tube.

The complete transmission assembly may now be disengaged towards the rear, at the same time exerting pressure with a suitable lever between the flexplate and the converter in order to prevent the converter from from the transmission during the operation.

Lower the transmission/converter assembly on the jack and remove from underneath the car.

It may be noted here that no servicing is possible on the converter. If it is faulty it must be renewed.

7:6 Installing the transmission

Make sure that the converter is properly installed and then place the assembly on the jack. To avoid any possibility of falling off it may be desirable to secure it with a chain.

Raise the assembly into position and fit all but the centre bolt on the right of the six bolts securing the converter housing to the engine. The sixth bolt is used when the fluid filler tube and O-ring are fitted to the casing.

Move the rear engine support into position and fit the four securing bolts. Remove the jack from under the transmission.

Fit the four capscrews between the flexplate and converter and tighten to 40-45 lb ft. Fit the front cover to the converter housing.

Install the starter assembly and connect up the cables to the terminals on the starter relay.

Fit the exhaust pipe bracket to the transmission bracket. Fit the speedometer cable and secure it with its snap ring.

Refit the selector control cable and bushing to the selector lever and reconnect the leads to the neutral start switch, taking care to fit them in their original positions.

Fit the drive shaft into rear of the transmission, line up the coupling flanges and fit the bolts to the rear axle pinion, position the centre bearing carrier and bolt it to its body bracket.

Lower the car and refit the cable for the throttle linkage downshift valve and adjust as described earlier.

Fill the transmission with the specified oil ($6\frac{3}{4}$ US qts), check the controls and inspect for leaks.

7:7 Testing

Road testing will reveal faults and enable a check to be made on adjustments, but the tests should be carried out in an ordered sequence and even when a fault has been found it may well be beyond the scope of the home operator to rectify. It is clearly essentail that all other services are functioning correctly.

Stall test:

If the turbine in the converter is held stationary and the impeller is driven by the engine, the consequent heavy braking effect on the engine results in much lower engine speeds at full throttle. The condition of the converter, and the engine, can be judged by observing engine speeds under these conditions.

These tests must be made with the engine and transmission at normal working temperature and, to avoid overheating, must not be prolonged beyond ten seconds. After each stall test the selector should be moved to neutral with the engine running at about 1000 rev/min for 15 seconds to cool the transmission. Normal stall speed is 2050 to 2250 rev/min (2000), 1950 to 2150 rev/min (1600 GT), and 1750 to 1950 rev/min (1600).

Set the handbrake and fully apply the footbrake. Select 1 and fully depress the accelerator pedal for not more than 10 seconds. Note the indicated engine speed.

A stall speed lower than specified indicates either a slipping one way clutch in the converter which must be renewed or an engine in need of an overhaul or tune-up.

A high stall speed indicates either slipping in the transmission or faulty clutches or brake bands. If slipping is indicated, release the throttle immediately.

Road testing:

If the stall speed test is satisfactory, proceed on the road as follows:

Select D, release the brakes and accelerate away with minimum throttle. Check the 1-2 and 2-3 upshifts against the table below.

Stop the car and repeat the test with full throttle and again note the shift speeds.

At 25 mile/hour in high gear give full throttle without kick-down and the car should accelerate without shifting down to second gear.

At 30 mile/hour in high gear press the throttle through the detent into kick-down. There should be an immediate downshift to second. If repeated at 15-20 mile/hour there should be a downshift to first.

At 40-45 mile/hour in high gear release the accelerator pedal and select 2. Check for the downshift to second gear and engine braking followed by the shift down to first.

Stop and accelerate with full throttle up to 20 mile/hour. There should be no upshifts and listen for clutch slip or squawk.

Brake to a stop on a hill and select P. Release the brakes and confirm that the parking pawl holds the car stationary. Repeat the test with the car facing in the opposite direction.

Table of gearshift speeds in mile/hour

Shift	*Light throttle*	*Full throttle*
1-2	6-8	35-43
2-3	9-12	62-68
	Closed throttle	*Full throttle kickdown*
3-2	12-16	54-65
2-1	7-10	25-37

CHAPTER 8

FINAL DRIVE, REAR AXLE AND SUSPENSION

8:1 The drive shaft

The two piece tubular drive shaft is of conventional design, having a universal joint at each end and one in the middle. This is shown in **FIG 8:1** which also shows the centre bearing, mounted on the body, located just in front of the middle universal joint.

The forward end of the shaft is splined to the output shaft of the transmission and bolted through a flange to the differential pinion.

Removal:

Mark the shaft and the pinion flanges to ensure correct reassembly and then remove the four securing bolts and lockwashers.

Remove the two bolts and washers securing the centre mounting to the body.

Lower the rear end of the shaft and slide the shaft assembly out of its engagement in the transmission. Steps should be taken to catch oil escaping from the transmission when the shaft is removed.

Refitting:

Slide the splined front yoke into the transmission being careful not to damage the oil seal or bearing in the extension housing.

Line up the marks made earlier and fit the four bolts to the rear flange and the differential pinion flange. Tighten to a torque of 43-47 lb ft.

The centre bearing carrier is bolted to its bracket when the car is standing, loaded normally, on its wheels. The bolts should be tightened to 13-17 lb ft.

Check the oil level in the transmission and top up if necessary.

Centre bearing:

Mark the relative positions of the front and centre universal joints for correct reassembly. Bend back the locking tab for the bolt at the rear end of the front shaft, slacken the bolt, remove the U shaped plate and separate the two halves of the drive shaft.

Remove the front shaft and bearing assembly from the rubber insulator and remove the insulator from its carrier by bending back the locating tabs.

Use a suitable puller to remove the bearing and protective caps from the shaft.

Check the bearing for wear and the rubber insulator for deterioration.

Refitting:

Using a length of suitable tubing, drive the ball bearing and the protective caps on to the shaft.

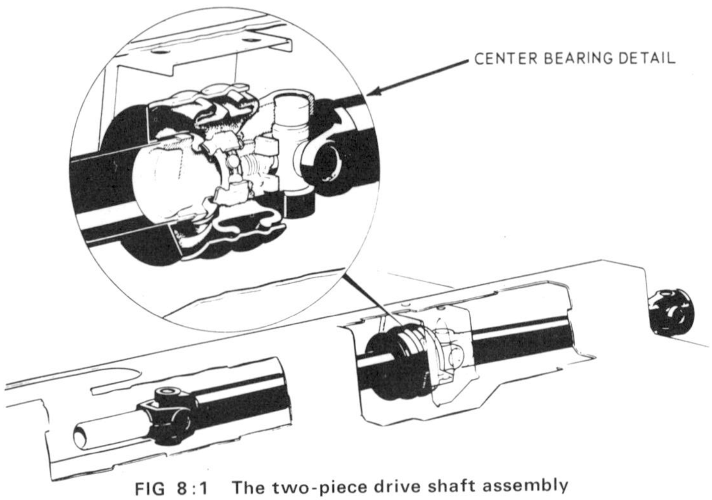

FIG 8:1 The two-piece drive shaft assembly

Insert the rubber insulator into its carrier with the boss upwards and bend the six tabs back over the beaded edge of the insulator.

Slide the carrier and insulator over the bearing assembly.

Fit the securing bolt with a new locking tab on to the shaft, leaving enough space for the insertion of the U plate.

Line up the mating marks on the two universal joints and assemble the shafts. Insert the U plate with its smooth face towards the fork under the retaining bolt head and tighten the bolt to 25-30 lb ft. Bend up the locking tab.

Install the drive shaft as described earlier.

Universal joints:

The components of a universal joint are shown in **FIG 8:2** and they may be dismantled as follows:

After removing the drive shaft, extract the snap ring from each spider bearing and remove the bearing cups and rollers by gently tapping on the yoke.

Remove the spider and prise off the oil seal and retainer from each spider journal. Kits of spare parts are available to rebuild the joints.

Fit new oil seals to the retainers and fit them on the shoulders of the spider journals with the oil seals outwards.

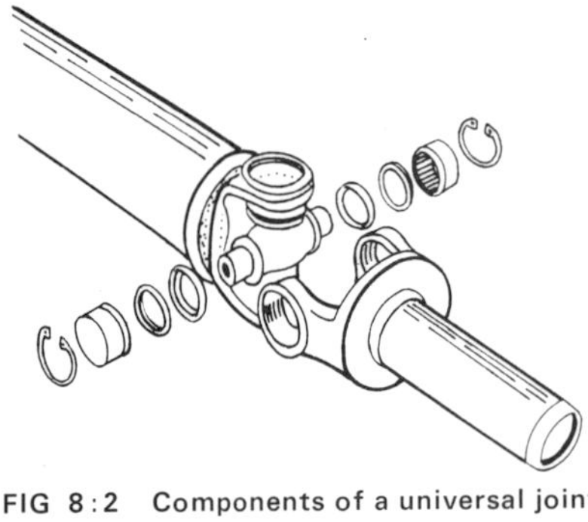

FIG 8:2 Components of a universal joint

Fit the spider in the drive shaft yoke and assemble the needle rollers in each bearing cup. Pack the bearings with a multi-purpose lithium grease, leaving a certain amount of room for expansion when hot.

Tap the bearings squarely into place, taking care not to displace the rollers. Refit the snap rings and install the drive shaft.

8:2 The rear axle

This is of conventional design with the pinion, differential unit and crown wheel assembled into the axle casing from the rear.

The driving pinion runs in two taper-roller bearings which are pre-loaded by a selective tubular spacer placed between them, the depth of meshing with the crown wheel being controlled by a selective shim between the pinion head and the rear bearing. The crown wheel is bolted to the differential case which is carried in two taper-roller bearings, the sideways location being determined by selective shims on either side which also give a degree of pre-loading on the bearing.

The differential is of the conventional two pinion type with the two axle half shafts being splined to the side gears and supported at the outer ends by ball races with built-in oil seals secured in the outer ends of the axle casing.

It should be noted that all the bolts used in this axle assembly use metric threads. This, of course, makes no difference to the servicing procedure, but does mean that many home operators will need to obtain some extra tools for the procedures outlined in this section.

8:3 Removing and refitting the axle

Jack up the rear end of the car support it on stands and remove the road wheels.

Release the handbrake and disconnect the cable from the lever on the rear of the axle housing. Disconnect the brake hydraulic pipe at the junction on the axle and plug the aperture to prevent fluid loss.

Mark the drive shaft and pinion flanges and remove the four bolts and washers.

Jack up the centre of the axle and remove the bolts securing the lower ends of the shock absorbers. Lower the jack.

On the pre 1973 models remove the bolts to release the rear end of the radius arms from the axle, noting that as these bolts are under load it may be necessary to assist with a screwdriver and C clamp.

Since 1973 the radial arms have been superceded by an anti-roll bar. Remove both anti-roll bar brackets from the rear axle. During the operation pull the anti-roll ball towards the rear axle using a suitable clamp to eliminate the preload from the bolts.

Remove the nuts from the U bolts and detach the bolts and plates. Lift the axle and remove it sideways through a wheel arch.

Refitting:

Slide the axle sideways into position on the springs, making sure that the spring insulators and retainers are correctly located on the spring spigots and the retainers in the holes in the axle pads.

Fit the U bolts over the axle, slide on the lower plates and tighten the locknuts to an initial torque of 5 lb ft.

To refit the anti-roll bar use a suitable clamp to press the bar onto its seating, fit the brackets and bolts and tighten fully.

Jack up the axle and install the lower shock absorber mounting bolts. Lower the jack.

Pull the radius arms into position, using a screwdriver and C clamp as when dismantling, and fit the bolts but do not tighten them at this stage.

Line up and reconnect the drive shaft to the pinion flange, tightening the bolts to 43-47 lb ft.

Remove the plugs and reconnect the brake pipes through the bracket on the axle casing. Reconnect the parking brake cable to the lever on the axle and adjust the cable as necessary.

Adjust the brakes if required by moving the parking brake levers on the brake carrier plates in and out. Bleed the braking system.

Fit the road wheels and lower the car to the ground. Now that the weight of the car is being carried on its wheels, the rear bolts for the radius arms and the U bolts nuts can be tightened. The specified torques are 22-27 and 18-26 lb ft respectively.

8:4 The axle shafts

1 Jack up the rear of the car, support on stands and remove the road wheels. Release the handbrake.
2 Remove the screw securing the brake drum and lift off.
3 Remove the screws securing the bearing retainer plate to the axle casing. These are accessible through the holes in the axle shaft flange.
4 Pull the axle shaft and bearing assembly out of the axle case using the service tool and sliding hammer.
5 Loosen the inner retaining ring by nicking it deeply with a cold chisel in several places (see **FIG 8:3**) and slide it off.
6 Press the bearing and seal off the axle shaft.

Installation:

Before replacing the axle shaft it should be inspected for any signs of roughness on the machined surfaces and if these are present they should be carefully removed or, if too severe, the worn or damaged part renewed.

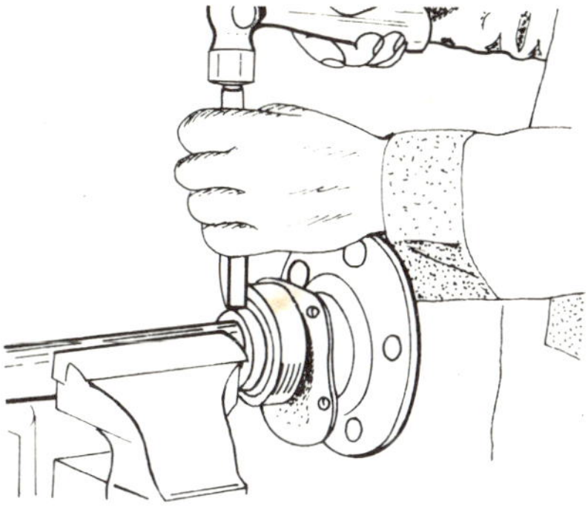

FIG 8:3 Removing a rear wheel retainer ring

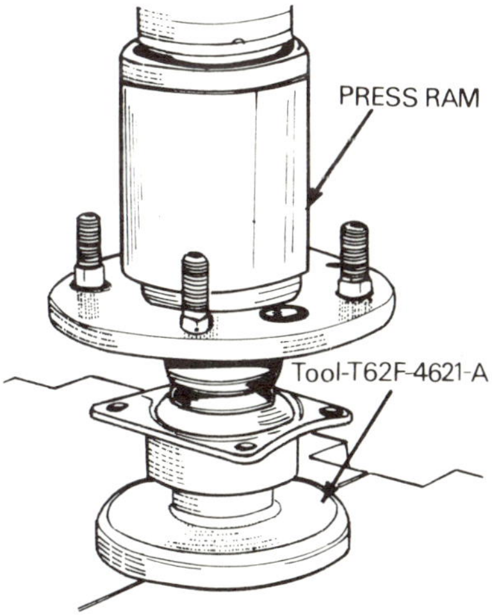

FIG 8:4 Fitting a rear wheel bearing retainer ring

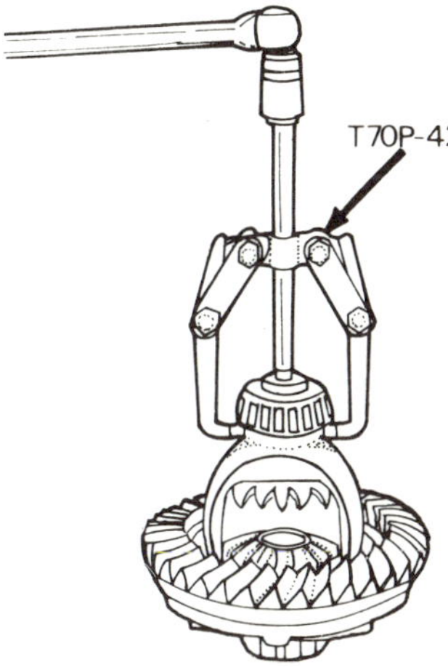

FIG 8:5 Removing differential side bearings

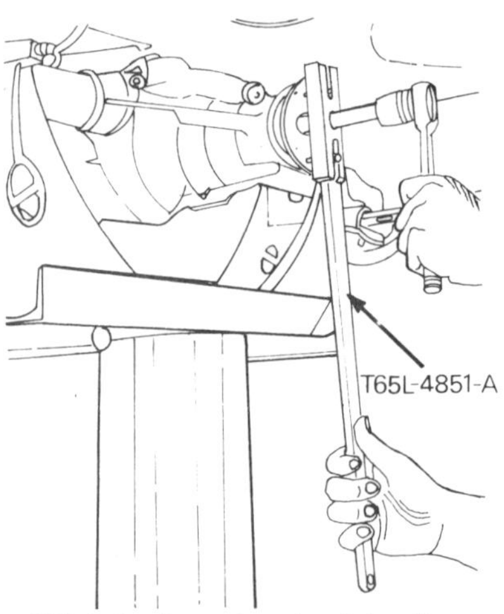

FIG 8:6 Removing the pinion flange

Coat the bearing bores with axle lubricant then place the bearing retainer plate on the axle shaft and press on a new bearing, noting that the shaft journal and the inside of the retainer must be clean and dry.

Press the bearing inner retaining ring on the shaft using the tool shown in **FIG 8:4** until the retainer seats firmly against the bearing.

Insert the shaft into the axle casing, engage the splines in the differential side gear and tap it fully home.

Secure the bearing retainer plate with the four bolts and spring washers, tightening to 15-18 lb ft.

Replace the remaining parts in the reverse order of removal.

8:5 Servicing the differential

Before describing the procedure for this operation, the operator is advised that it is not simple and it requires the use of tools and instruments which may not be available. Under these circumstances he may find it preferable to take the assembly to his local service station for attention.

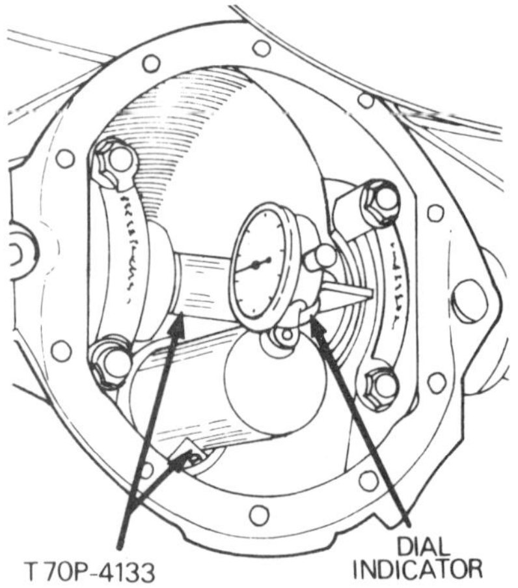

FIG 8:7 Checking pinion depth

Carry out Items 1 through 4 of **Section 8:4** then:

Remove the drive shaft from the pinion flange. Remove the ten retaining bolts and lift off the rear axle cover and gasket, placing a suitable container to catch the oil as it flows out. The gasket should be discarded and the cover cleaned. On the German and U.S.A. manufacture the retaining bolts are at the rear of the casing.

Mark the differential bearing caps for later assembly then undo the cap retaining screws and remove the caps.

Use two tapered lengths of wood to lever the differential assembly out of the casing.

Remove the taper roller bearing from each side of the assembly using the tool shown in **FIG 8:5** and take the adjusting shims out of the housing.

Unscrew the bolts securing the crown wheel and remove it.

Tap out the locking pin securing the differential pinion shaft in the housing, then remove the differential pinion shaft, the pinion, side gears and adjusting shims.

Hold the drive pinion flange and remove the pinion nut. This self-locking nut may be retained for assembly and checking, but must be renewed on final assembly. Pull off the pinion flange using the tools shown in **FIG 8:6**.

Remove the pinion from the axle casing and pull off the spacer.

Pull the large roller bearing off the pinion shaft with the service tool or other suitable puller and remove the spacing shim from the pinion shaft.

Remove the small taper roller bearing and oil seal from the casing using a suitable drift. Similarly drive out the bearing outer races.

Clean all parts thoroughly and inspect. Renew any worn or damaged parts and any bearings which are rough in action when dry. Renew the oil seal.

Assembling the differential:

Fit first the small then the larger bearing races into the casing using the Ford service tool, being most careful to see that they are squarely and fully positioned.

The next step is to determine the thickness of shimming required for the correct depth of pinion mesh. First position the crossbar of the tool Ford service in the casing together with the side bearings as shown in **FIG 8:7**. Fit the bearing caps (number to number) and tighten the retaining bolts.

Slacken back the bolts and re-tighten with the fingers only.

Hold the bar and rotate the nut by hand. This pre-loads the side bearings by expanding the crossbar. Rotate the crossbar several times to seat the bearings and check that they are still pre-loaded. Do not over expand the bar. Tighten the retaining bolts to a torque of 43 lb ft.

Install the dummy pinion part of the service tool with the bearings but without the shims into the axle case. Lightly lubricate the bearings. Tighten until the correct pinion bearing pre-load of 13 to 19 lb inch is obtained.

Rotate the dummy pinion several times to ensure seating of the bearings. **It is essential that the torque reading be recorded and adhered to for the further adjustment of the drive pinion.** This torque must also be checked after the installation of the actual pinion (with the selected spacer).

Mount a dial indicator on the mounting bracket and position it at zero on the dummy pinion. Slowly rotate the dial indicator over the crossbar and read the total deflection of its pointer. This reading gives the exact thickness of shims to be used. When the pinion gear is marked minus one (1) or minus two (2) this amount must be added to the indicator reading to obtain the correct shim thickness. When the pinion gear is marked plus one (1) or two (2) this amount must be subtracted.

Select a spacer shim of the exact thickness as calculated.

Slide the shim(s) on to the pinion to be installed and press on the large taper roller bearing, wide end towards the gear. Position the side gears with one shim each in the differential case, the grooved side of the shim being towards the gear.

Place both differential pinions and thrustwashers simultaneously between the side gears. Push the pinion shaft into position in the differential case taking care to align the locking pin bores.

Measure the play of each side gear with a feeler gauge and if necessary new shims must be fitted to obtain a clearance between .0004 and .006 inch.

Secure the differential pinion shaft with a locking pin.

Place the crown wheel on the differential case and pull it evenly into position with the four old bolts. Remove the bolts and fit **new bolts** and tighten to 50-54 lb ft. Note that the crown wheel and pinion are supplied only in matched pairs bearing the same number.

To determine end play of differential assembly:

Press the taper roller bearings without shims onto the differential case using the tool shown in **FIG 8:8**.

Fit pressure blocks into the axle tubes on either side of the differential (see **FIG 8:9**) and fit the differential case and bearings into the axle housing.

Fit the bearing caps and tighten the screws. Slacken off the screws and then retighten them finger tight.

Tighten a pressure spindle as shown in **FIG 8:10** in either tube to a torque of 43 lb inch, rotate the differential several times and re-check the torque at the pressure spindle.

Mount a dial indicator on the axle housing so that the stylus contacts the inner side of the crown wheel flange and the pointer is at zero.

Place the pressure spindle into the other housing tube and tighten to 43 lb inch. Read the dial gauge for the total sideways deflection of the differential assembly. Keep a record of this figure. Say, for example, that it is .053 inch (1.35 mm).

To determine thickness of pinion bearing spacer:

Slide the master spacer service tool on to the pinion shaft. Form a ring with soft solder wire of approximately .08 inch (2 mm) diameter to fit closely round the drive pinion shaft and slide it into place on the gauging tool.

Fit the pinion into the axle casing and slide on the small taper roller bearing and the pinion flange.

Screw on the old self-locking nut which had been retained during dismantling. Hold the drive pinion flange with the special wrench and slowly tighten the nut until the same torque is obtained as that recorded earlier when adjusting the master pinion. If this torque is exceeded the procedure must be repeated with a new piece of solder wire.

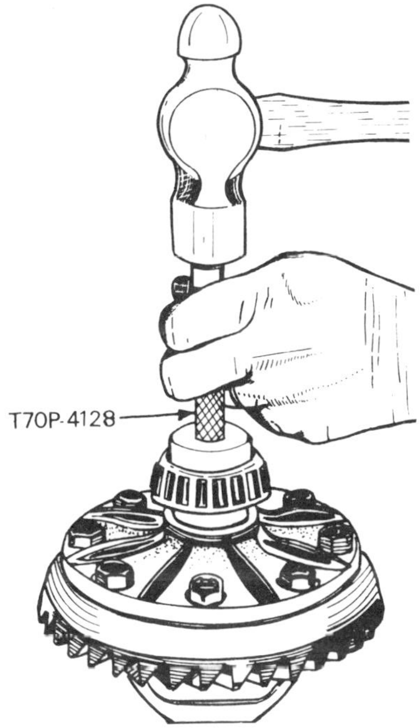

FIG 8:8 Fitting differential side bearings

Remove the compressed solder ring and measure its thickness at two opposite points and take the mean reading.

Add this value, for example .05 inch (1.21 mm), to the gauge spacer ring, which is .374 inch (9.50 mm), giving the spacer thickness required, i.e. .05 + .374 = .424 inch (1.21 + 9.50 = 10.71 mm). Select a spacer of this thickness from the range of 60 available.

Fit the pinion with the selected spacer, small taper roller bearing, drive pinion flange and the old self-locking nut. Tighten the nut to 72-87 lb ft. Rotate the pinion several times and then carefully check the torque in lbs inch. This must be the same as that recorded on initial

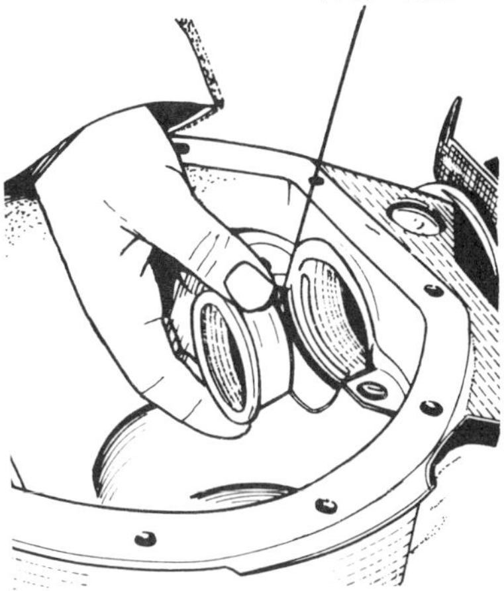

FIG 8:9 Fitting pressure blocks

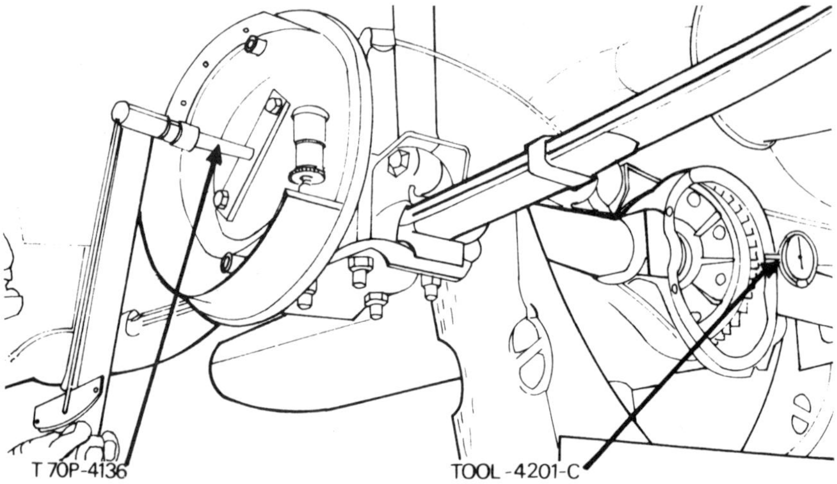

FIG 8:10 Differential set-up spindle and blocks installation

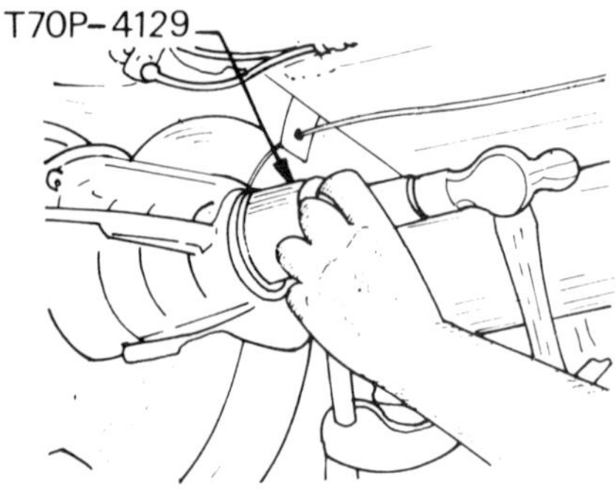

FIG 8:11 Fitting the drive pinion oil seal

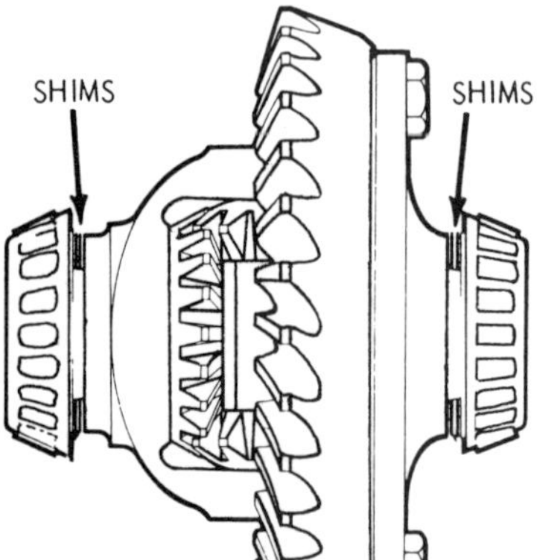

FIG 8:12 Showing location of differential side shims

assembly with the dummy pinion. Fit a thicker spacer if the torque is exceeded or a thinner one if the specified torque is not reached. Remove the old nut.

Apply some grease between the two sealing lips of a new seal and some sealing compound on the other side and fit the seal as in **FIG 8:11**. Fit a **new** self locking nut and tighten to 72 to 87 lb ft.

To determine shim thickness for differential bearings:

Replace the pressure blocks back into the axle tubes and place the differential case with the bearing races into the axle casing. Fit the bearing caps and tighten the screws. Loosen the screws and then do them up again finger tight. Using the pressure spindle press the differential case **away** from the drive pinion with a torque of 43 lb inch. Rotate the drive pinion several times.

Set up a dial gauge with the stylus at right angles to a tooth on the crown wheel and measure the backlash. Measure the tooth backlash at three more points at 90 deg. intervals. Deviations of backlash must not exceed .002 inch (.05 mm). Insert the pressure spindle into the other axle tube and screw in slowly until the backlash is .0004 inch (.01 mm).

Set up the dial gauge with the stylus on the flange of the crownwheel. Zero the gauge, insert the spindle into the other axle tube and torque to 43 lb inch. Make a record of the dial reading. For this example let us say .025 inch (.64 mm).

Remove the pressure spindle, differential case and pressure blocks from the axle case.

As an example. If total play is .053 inch (1.35 mm) and .002 inch (.05 mm) is added for pre-load the result would be .055 inch (1.40 mm). The correct pre-load is between .0012 and .0031 inch and a value between these two must be added to the play to give an even figure for the total.

If the shim thickness as measured in the example is .025 inch (.64 mm) subtract from this the desired tooth backlash of .005 inch (.12 mm) and the result is .020 inch (.52 mm). (Note that the backlash value of .005 inch is a constant established as a result of many tests.) This is the thickness of shim required behind the crownwheel.

The remaining shims must be placed on the tooth side of the crownwheel. With total play of .055 inch (1.40 mm), subtract the backside shim thickness of .020 inch (.52 mm) and this thickness is .035 inch (.88 mm).

Remove the differential case bearings as shown in **FIG 8:5** and then position the correct shims on the the differential case as shown in **FIG 8:12**.

Check the contact surfaces and press the taper roller bearings on to the differential case. Insert the case into the axle housing and position the bearing caps as previously marked. Insert the screws with sealing compound and tighten to 43-39 lb ft.

Check the backlash with a dial gauge on one of the crownwheel teeth as before and if it is outside the limits of .005 to .009 inch (.12 to .22 mm) the setting operation must be repeated. If the backlash is too great, remove shims from the crownwheel face (tooth) side and transfer to the rearside. If backlash is too small reverse the procedure. Do not increase or decrease the number of shims, but simply transfer between one side and the other.

Checking tooth contact pattern:

New crownwheels will show the desired contact pattern from the test run at the factory and should appear as in **FIG 8:13**. If new components have been fitted it will be necessary to check the tooth contact pattern after setting the gears as instructed in the proceding operations.

Coat the teeth of the crownwheel with a marking compound, then, using a wooden wedge as a brake on the crownwheel, turn the drive pinion by a number of turns in both directions corresponding with the number of teeth on the crownwheel.

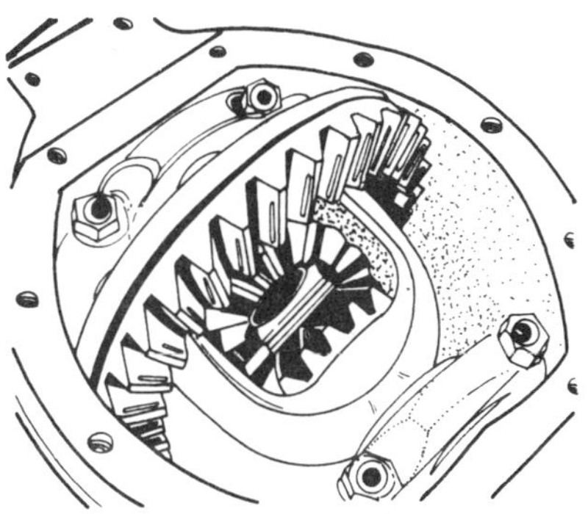

FIG 8:13 Correct gear tooth contact pattern

Backlash has a great effect on the contact pattern, so try altering the backlash between the prescribed limits if the pattern is not satisfactory. The number of shims may not be changed, only moved from one side to another.

When satisfactory, fit a new gasket and the cover and tighten the bolts to 22-29 lb ft.

Fit the parking brake operating lever to the axle casing and connect the return spring to its bracket. Fit the rear brake assemblies on the axle ends.

Connect the parking brake cable to the operating levers on both backplates.

8:6 Servicing the rear springs

The components of the semi-elliptic leaf suspension system are shown in **FIG 8:14**, and a leaf assembly is removed as follows:

Chock up the front wheels, jack up the rear end of the car and fit stands under the body jacking points. Take the weight of the rear axle on a trolley jack.

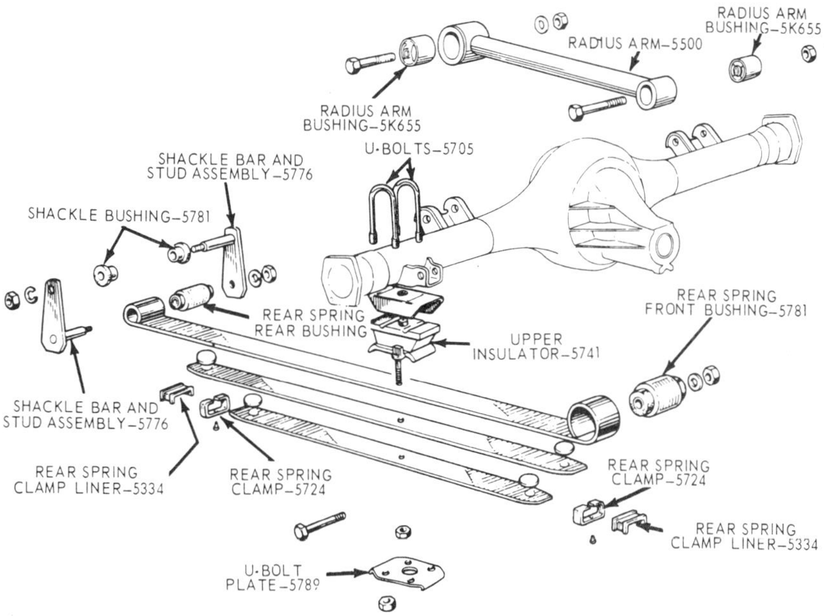

FIG 8:14 Components of the rear suspension

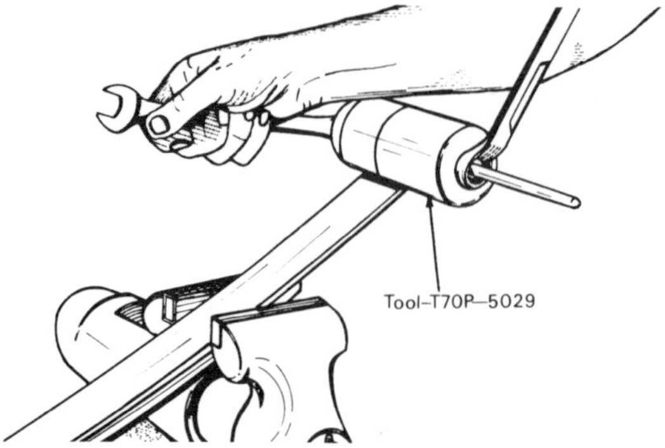

FIG 8:15 Removing the spring bushes

Remove the nuts and washers and detach the combined plate and bolt assemblies. Remove the two rubber bushes.

Unscrew the nut from the front mounting bracket and withdraw the bolt. Remove the U bolt nuts and the attachment plates and lower the spring assembly.

Remove the insulator and retaining plate from the spring.

Using the service tool as shown in **FIG 8:15**, pull the bushes out of the front eye of the springs. The same tool is used for removing the bushes from the spring rear eyes.

Clean all the parts and check for wear or damage, particularly on the rubber bushes and insulators.

Dismantling:

Remove the spring centre bolt and nut. Drill out the rivets securing the spring clips and slide the clips along to the end of the springs thus freeing the two shorter leaves.

Check the condition of the leaves and renew the pads if necessary.

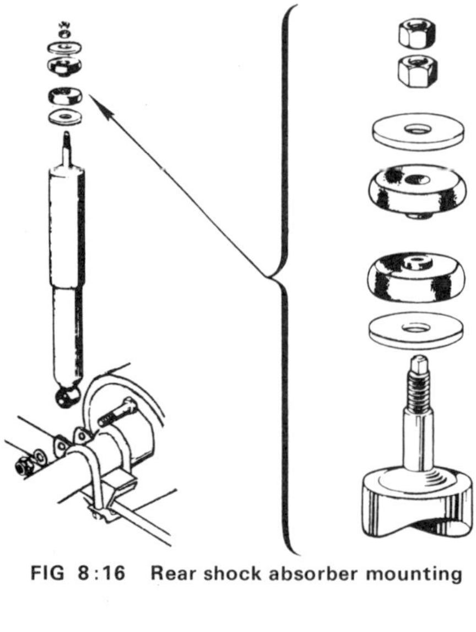

FIG 8:16 Rear shock absorber mounting

Make sure that the rubber pads are correctly located between the end of the leaves, then assemble and fit the centre bolt and nut. It will be noted that this bolt has a special head.

Replace the clips and rubbers and rivet the clips to the spring.

Installation:

Press new bushes into the spring eyes, being careful to see that they are fitted squarely in the apertures. Assemble the front eye to the mounting bracket, insert the bolt but do not yet tighten up the nut.

Fit the rubber insulating sleeve round the spring and position its retainer plate. Lift the spring up into position and refit the U bolts and retainer plate. Tighten these nuts initially to a torque of 5 lb ft.

Fit new rubber bushes in the body holes for the rear shackle, hold the spring in place, assemble the bolt and plate assemblies, fit the nuts and washers but do not tighten.

Remove the jack under the axle and lower the car to the ground.

With the weight of the car on its wheels tighten the front and rear attachment bolts and the U bolt nuts to torques of 27-32, 8-10 and 18-26 lb ft respectively.

8:7 The shock absorbers

These are hydraulic, double-acting, telescopic units and are fitted between the rear axle casing and a reinforced mounting point on the floor pan. They are sealed and no periodic attention is required and none is possible. In the event of failure a new unit must be fitted. It is in fact desirable when replacing one shock absorber to replace also the other so as to maintain symmetry in the suspension.

The method of mounting is shown in **FIG 8:16** and removal is as follows:

Chock up the front wheels, jack up the rear of the car and support it on stands under the body jacking points.

From inside the luggage compartment remove the two nuts from the top of the shock absorber, using a second wrench on the flats of the piston rod to prevent it turning. Lift off the top metal washer and the rubber bush.

Remove the nut and bolt from the lower end of the shock absorber and detach it from the bracket on the axle casing. Pull the damper downwards and clear of the body.

Refitting:

Fit the large steel washer and the rubber bush on the top of the unit insert through the hole in the body and then fit the upper bush with the spigot, the washer and the nut, which is not tightened at this stage.

Fit the lower end of the shock absorber into the axle bracket and then insert the bolt. Tighten the nut to a torque of 40-45 lb ft.

Lower the car to the ground and tighten the top mounting nut to 15-20 lb ft. Replace the locknut.

8:8 Anti-roll bar

Removing:

1 Disconnect the handbrake primary cable from the transfer lever at the rear of the axle.

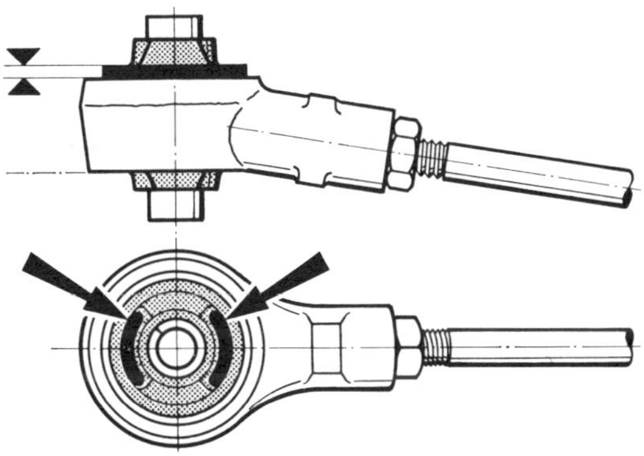

FIG 8:17 Press in the new bush, chamfered side first, but note the correct location of the two semi-circular rubber bush recesses in the final position

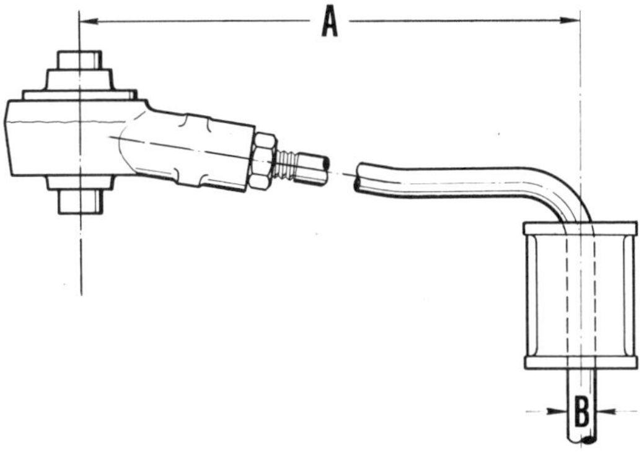

FIG 8:18 Screw on the end pieces to obtain a dimension (A) of 10.24 + .1 inch (262 + 2.5 mm). (B)=.39 inch (10 mm)

2 Unscrew and remove the securing bolts securing the antiroll bar to the axle. Use a clamp to secure the anti-roll bar to its lower bracket to eliminate the pre-load on the securing bolts.

3 Disconnect the anti-roll bar from the floor assembly. Withdraw the bar.

Refitting:

4 Locate the anti-roll bar ends into the floor brackets and secure them with the eyebolts. The bolt heads should be on the inside position. Fit the washers and nuts but do not tighten at this stage.

5 Using a suitable clamp, force the anti-roll bar on to the rear axle lower brackets. Fit the saddle and the bolts and tighten fully.

6 Tighten the floor bracket bolts fully.

Renewing bushes:

1 Remove the anti-roll bar, slacken the locking nuts and unscrew the end pieces. Pull off the rubber trunnion bushes.

2 Lubricate the new trunnion bushes with glycerine and slide them on to the bar.

3 To remove the rubber bushes from the eye-pieces, mount the eye-piece on a piece of tube, with sufficient length and ID to accept the old bush. Place them on a press bed. Obtain a piece of tube with a slightly less OD than the bush, place it squarely on the top of the bush and operate the press to force the old bush out of the eye-piece.

4 Refer to **FIG 8:17** and press in the new bush, chamfered side first, noting the final position of the bush recesses.

Adjusting end pieces:

1 Refer to **FIG 8:18** and screw the end pieces on to the bar to obtain dimension 'A' 10.24 inch $\pm$ .10 inch, (262 mm $\pm$ 2.5 mm). B = .39 inch (10 mm). Tighten the locknuts.

2 Refit the anti-roll bar to the car.

8:9 Fault diagnosis

(a) Noisy axle gears

1 Insufficient or incorrect lubricant
2 Worn bearings or gears
3 Incorrect backlash
4 Incorrect meshing of gears
5 Insufficient preload on bearings

(b) Excessive backlash

1 Worn gears, bearings or housings
2 Worn axle shaft splines or side gears
3 Worn universal joints or gearbox splines
4 Loose or broken wheel studs

(c) Oil leakage

1 Defective pinion shaft or axle shaft seals
2 Defective seals on universal joint spiders
3 Faulty gasket or damaged faces of rear cover

(d) Vibration

1 Drive shafts out of balance
2 Worn universal joints
3 Rear universal joint flange not mated correctly
4 Yokes on universal joints 90° out of phase
5 Centre bearing carrier defective

(e) Rattles

1 Worn damper mountings
2 Worn radius arm bushes
3 U bplts or spring clips loose
4 Faulty rubber bushes
5 Broken spring leaf

(f) 'Settling' of suspension

1 Weak or broken spring leaf
2 Badly worn spring eye bush or shackle pin

NOTES

CHAPTER 9

FRONT SUSPENSION AND HUBS

9:1 General description

The arrangement of the front suspension can be seen in **FIG 9:1**. The vertical damper (shock absorber) and spring unit 1 is attached to the body at the top end. The bottom end of the unit is controlled by a track control arm 2 and a stabilizer or anti-roll bar 3. The spring unit carries the front wheel and brake assembly and incorporates a steering arm 5 which is connected to the rack and pinion steering mechanism by track rods 6.

To allow the spring unit to turn for steering purposes, it is connected to the outer end of the track control arm by a ball joint 4. This joint also accommodates the up and down movements due to road shocks and suspension loading. The arrangement is clearly shown in inset 'Y'.

Inset 'X' is a view of the rubber bush 7 which forms the inner pivot of the track control arm.

9:2 Routine maintenance

The suspension and damper units are sealed and do not require topping up. After the first 600 miles (1000 km), at 3000 miles (5000 km) or three months and then at subsequent 6000 mile (10,000 km) or six monthly intervals, do the following:

1 Check the torque of the front suspension crossmember retaining bolts. Correct torque is 25 to 30 lb ft.

2 Check boots or gaiters on steering and suspension joints. Renew if deteriorated or faulty.

At 6000 miles (10,000 km), check and adjust front wheel bearings. Check tracking. At 27,000 and 51,000 miles (45,000 and 85,000 km), repack front wheel bearings with grease and adjust (see **Section 9:8**). Repeat at 24,000 mile (40,000 km) intervals.

9:3 Servicing the track control arm

The bush at the inner end of the arm can be renewed as follows:

1 Jack up the front of the car and fit stands. Refer to **FIG 9:1**.

2 Remove pivot bolt 8 at the inner end. Pull arm 2 downwards and remove bush using a $\frac{3}{4}$ inch bolt.

3 Fit a new bush, using the same tool. Position the arm and fit the pivot bolt, head to the front, flat washer and self-locking nut to the rear. Do not fully tighten nut.

4 Lower the car and tighten nut to a torque of 22 to 27 lb ft.

Removing arm:

With front of car lifted and stands fitted, release stabilizer bar 3 from arm (see inset 'Y'). Remove pivot

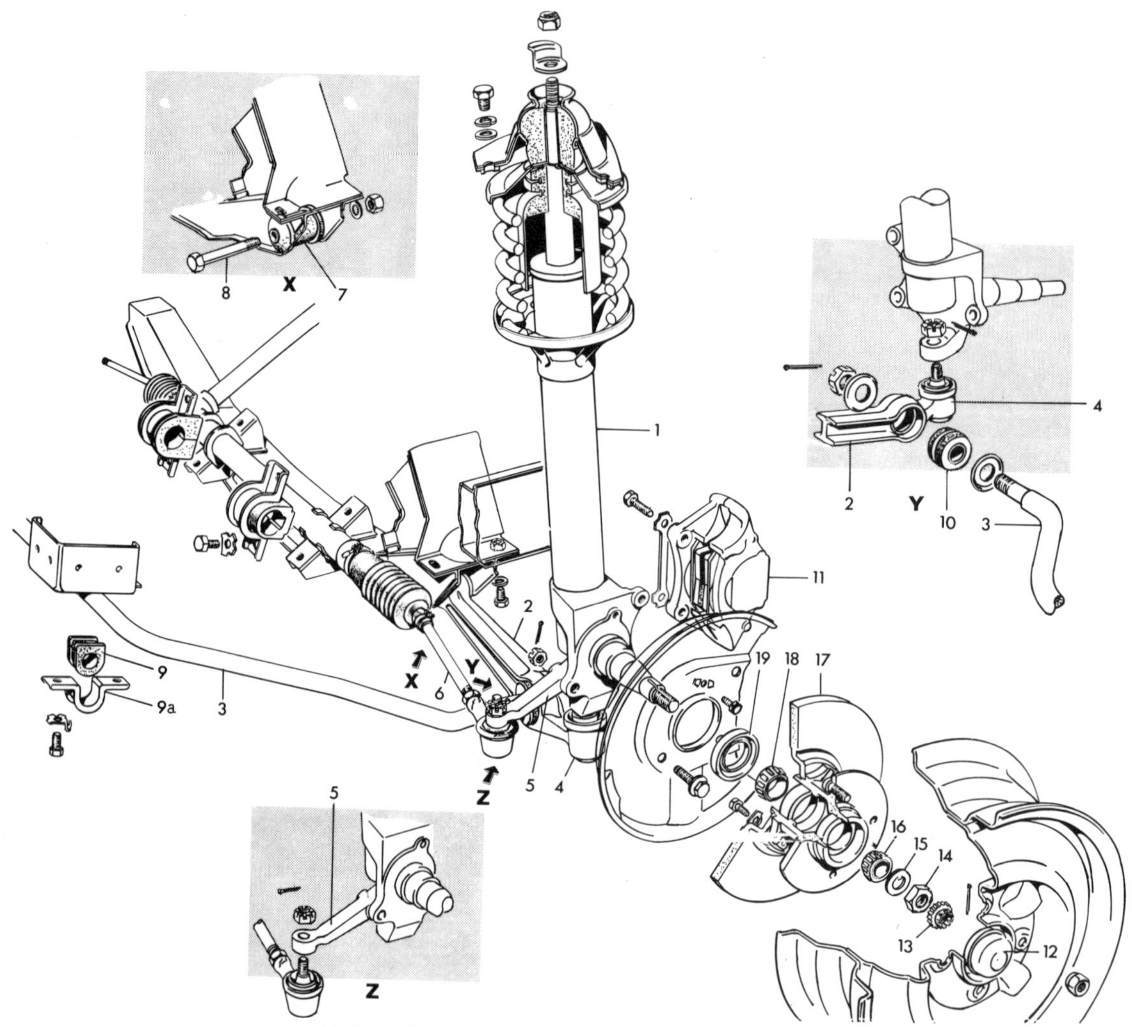

FIG 9:1 Components of the front suspension system

Key to Fig 9:1 1 Suspension unit 2 Track control arm 3 Stabilizer bar 4 Ball joint 5 Steering arm 6 Steering track rod 7 Pivot bush 8 Pivot bolt 9 Mounting bush 9a Clamp 10 Bush 11 Caliper 12 Dust cap 13 Locknut 14 Adjusting nut 15 Washer 16 Outer bearing cone 17 Hub and disc 18 Lower bearing cone 19 Seal

bolt 8. Release ball joint 4 from suspension unit (see inset 'Y').

If track control arm has been damaged in a crash, scrap it. Make no attempt to straighten it. Check condition of ball joint and seal 4 and renew assembly if defective.

Installing arm:

Refit the ball joint stud to the suspension unit, tightening the castellated nut to a torque of 30 to 35 lb ft. Fit a new splitpin. Refit stabilizer bar end to arm and tighten castellated nut to a torque of 15 to 45 lb ft when car is on the ground. Fit the pivot bolt (preceding operations 3 and 4).

9:4 Servicing stabilizer bar

Renewing the bushes (car lifted at front, stands fitted, handbrake applied):

Mounting bushes 9 and control arm bush 10 can be renewed by releasing the stabilizer bar 3 from the arm (see inset 'Y'), after removing clamps 9a (2 bolts each, with locking tabs). Pull stabilizer bar forward and out of arm, removing sleeve and large washer.

Slide mounting bushes off the ends of the bar. Fit the new bushes.

Reassemble bar in reverse order, tightening stabilizer bar clamp bolts to a torque of 15 to 18 lb ft when the car is on the ground. Turn up the lock tabs. Also when the car is on the ground, tighten the bar-to-control-arm nut to a torque of 15 to 45 lb ft then fit a new splitpin.

The bar itself can be renewed while the bushes receive attention. Check for wear due to faulty bushes and look for cracks and bends due to accident damage. Lying the bar on a flat surface will quickly show whether the ends are out of alignment. Do not try to straighten a bent bar.

9:5 Removing and installing suspension unit

Removing:

1 Jack up front of car and fit stands. Remove road wheel(s).
2 Release flexible brake pipe from bracket on unit. Fit plugs to open ends of both unions. Put a jack under the track control arm (2 in **FIG 9:1**) and jack up the suspension unit.
3 Detach track rod end from steering arm 5 (see inset 'Z'). Use tool 3290-C to release the taper pin. Remove the jack. Release ball joint 4 from the bottom end of the unit (see inset 'Y').
4 Release the top end of the unit from the side apron panel (3 bolts) and lift unit away, complete with brake assembly.

Installing:

Fit top end of unit to side apron panel (3 bolts to a torque of 15 to 18 lb ft. At bottom end, fit ball joint stud (castellated nut to a torque of 30 to 35 lb ft). Fit new splitpin.

Fit track rod end to steering arm (castellated nut to a torque of 18 to 22 lb ft). Fit new splitpin.

Remove brake line plugs and connect flexible pipe to bracket on unit. Bleed the brakes (see **Chapter 11**). Fit wheel(s) and lower car to ground.

9:6 Servicing a suspension unit

Removing:

With the unit removed from the car, fit the adjustable spring restrainers, tool P-5045 (see **FIG 9:2**). Refer to **FIG 9:3** and remove top nut and cranked retainer 1. Lift off top mount 6, the dished washer 6a, upper spring seat 10, spring 11 and the bump rubber 3 or 3a.

Remove the brake pads (see **Chapter 11**). Detach the caliper (2 bolts and lockplate). Remove the hub and disc assembly (see **Section 9:7**). Remove the disc shield. Detach the steering arm.

The suspension unit can now be renewed, or overhauled as instructed later.

Refitting:

Refit the steering arm, tightening the nuts to a torque of 30 to 24 lb ft. Fit shield, followed by hub and disc assembly. Adjust hub bearings as instructed in **Section 9:8**. Fit caliper, using new lockplate (bolt torque 45 to 50 lb ft) turn up lock tabs. Refit brake pads (see **Chapter 11**).

Reassemble the spring and other parts in the reverse order to dismantling. The dished washer 6a on top of spring seat 10 has its convex side upwards. The piston rod nut is initially tightened to 5 to 10 lb ft after applying Loctite to threads. Remove spring restrainers. Assemble unit to car and lower to ground.

Now slacken the piston rod nut. Turn the front wheels to the straight-ahead position and set cranked retainer 1 so that it points inwards towards the engine. Retighten the nut to 28 to 32 lb ft.

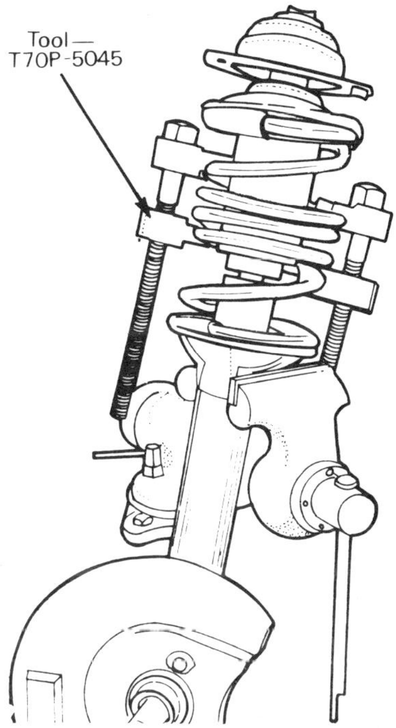

FIG 9:2 Compressing a spring

Overhauling:

Fit restrainers to spring (tool P-5045). Remove top nut, cranked retainer (1 in **FIG 9:3**), top mount 6, dished washer 6a, seat 10, spring 11 and bump rubber 3 or 3a. Check spring.

Refer to **FIG 9:4** and unscrew the bump stop platform 1, using a suitable wrench. Lift platform off unit. Remove O-ring 2. Do not remove the guide bush and gland assembly 3 until the top machined edge of the piston rod 4 has been examined for burrs. Stone off any which may be present. Pull the rod upwards until the bush and gland assembly is clear of the casing and lift off the assembly. Empty the fluid from the casing.

Pull out the piston rod complete with cylinder 5 and compression valve 6. Press on the rod to push out the valve, then withdraw the rod. If necessary, remove the piston ring from the piston.

Clean all the parts and examine for wear or damage. The piston and piston rod are serviced as an assembly. Do not try to dismantle them.

Reassembling:

If the ring was removed, fit a new one to the piston. Insert piston rod into cylinder and fit compression valve into base of cylinder. Carefully fit the assembly into the outer casing. Fill the unit with 326 cc of the correct fluid.

Fit the service tool guide on the end of the piston rod. Slide the gland and bush assembly over the guide and push it down until it enters the cylinder and the complete internal assembly is below the top of the outer casing. Fit the O-ring and locate it correctly round the bore of the outer casing. Screw the bump stop platform into the outer casing using a suitable wrench tightening securely to a torque of 55 to 60 lb ft.

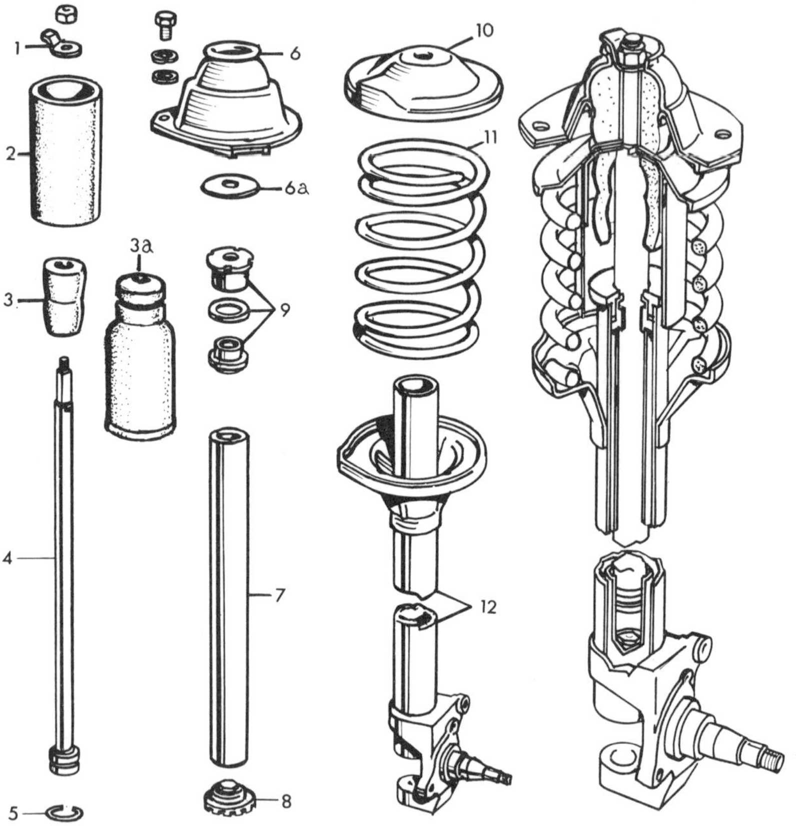

FIG 9:3 Components of front suspension unit

Key to Fig 9:3 1 Cranked retainer 2 Gaiter 3 Bump rubber (early) 3a Bump rubber (later) 4 Piston rod 5 Piston ring 6 Top mount 6a Dished washer 7 Cylinder 8 Compression valve 9 Bump stop platform 10 Upper spring seat 11 Spring 12 Outer casing

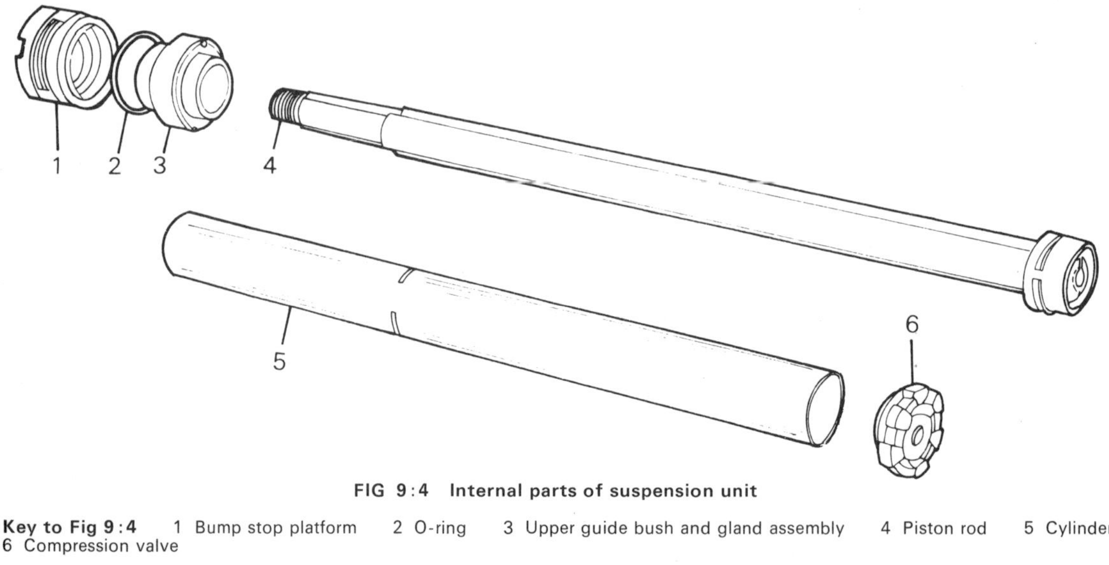

FIG 9:4 Internal parts of suspension unit

Key to Fig 9:4 1 Bump stop platform 2 O-ring 3 Upper guide bush and gland assembly 4 Piston rod 5 Cylinder 6 Compression valve

Reassemble the remaining parts and refit according to the instructions in 'Refitting'.

Renew top mount, bump rubber and piston rod gaiter.

These will be readily accessible by following the first paragraphs of instructions in this Section. Renew all rubber parts which show signs of deterioration, softening, or break-up. Reassemble and refit according to the second part of 'Refitting' in this Section.

It is most important to verify that both springs are of the same colour. Never mix springs, as the suspension systems will then be of unequal height, which will upset the handling of the car.

Renewing springs (units out of car):

After the restrainers are fitted to the spring, the top mount is removed, followed by the dished washer and the upper spring set. The spring can then be lifted off.

To fit a new spring, hold the lower end in soft jaws in a vice and fit the spring restrainers. Reassemble in the reverse order.

9:7 Removing and installing front hub

Removing:

With car jacked up and front wheel removed, do the following:

1 Detach brake pipe from bracket on suspension unit and plug both unions.
2 Remove brake caliper 11 (see **FIG 9:1**) from suspension unit (bolts with locking tabs). Remove dust cap 12 from hub. Remove splitpin and items 13, 14, 15 and 16.
3 Pull off the hub and disc assembly 17 to 19.
4 Separate disc from hub (4 bolts with locking tabs).

A new hub will be supplied complete with bearing cups and cones. Check that the cups and cones are of the same make. The name is on the cone and the initial letter of the name is stamped on the hub. For example, T = Timken and S = Skefko.

Installing:

1 Clean mating faces of hub and disc. Align mating marks, fit bolts and new locking plates and tighten to 30 to 34 lb ft. Turn up locking tabs.
2 Pack hub with lithium base grease but do not completely fill, to allow for expansion. Leave space for the spindle. Fit inner bearing cone 18. Fit seal 19 with lip towards bearing using the Ford service tool.
3 Fit assembly to wheel spindle, followed by outer bearing 16, thrust washer 15, and adjusting nut 14. Turn hub while tightening nut to 27 lb ft. Slacken nut by 90 deg. and fit retainer 13 with slot in retainer aligned with spindle hole. Fit new splitpin but do not bend up.
4 Check disc runout with dial gauge. Measured near the periphery of the face, the total runout should not exceed .0035 inch (.089 mm). If excessive, check mating faces of hub and disc. Check bearings and cups for damage.

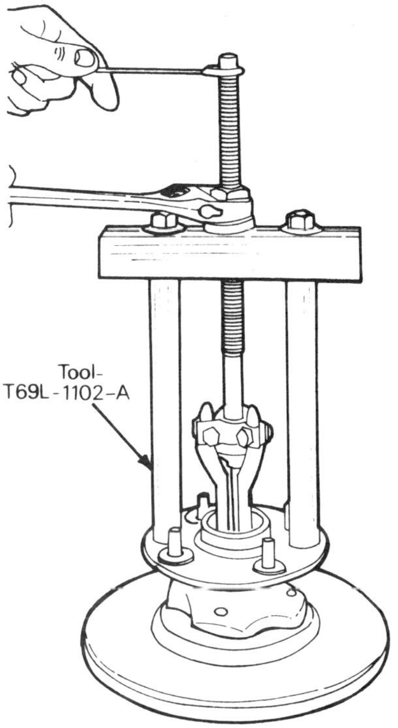

FIG 9:5 Removing front wheel bearing cups

5 When satisfied, bend up splitpin and fit dust cap. Fit caliper, using new locktabs and tightening bolts to 45 to 50 lb ft. Remove plugs and reconnect brake pipes. Refit road wheel. Torque for wheel nuts is 50 to 55 lb ft. Bleed the brakes (see **Chapter 11**).

9:8 Overhauling front hubs

Renewing wheel stud:

With road wheel removed, drive out defective stud. Locate new stud in splined hole and draw into place using a spacer, such as a short piece of suitable tubing, and the wheel nut reversed.

Lubricating:

At 27,000 and 51,000 miles (45,000 and 85,000 km), pack the front hubs with fresh grease. Remove the hub as described in **Section 9:7** but do not part the hub and disc and do not remove the oil seal unless renewal is required.

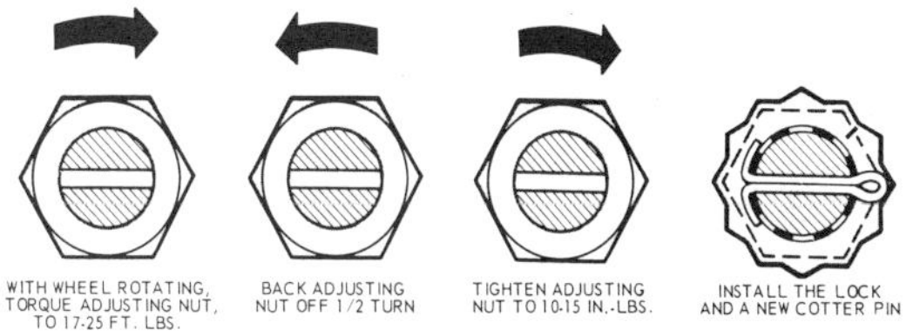

FIG 9:6 Adjusting a front wheel bearing

Wash the parts free from old grease with a solvent and allow to dry. Pack the hub with fresh lithium base grease but do not fill completely. This will allow for expansion. Leave enough space for the spindle.

Refit the hub and adjust the bearings as instructed in 'Installing' in the same Section. At all times keep grease off the brake discs.

Renewing bearings:

Remove the hub as described in **Section 9:7**. Remove the inner and outer bearing cups, using the Ford service tool as shown in **FIG 9:5**. The same tool is used to fit new cups.

When renewing cones, always fit new cups as well and make sure that cups and cones are of the same make.

If required new hubs may be obtained complete with bearing cones and cups. The cups are already fitted but check that the cones and cups are of the same manufacture. When the cups are fitted the initial letter of the manufacturers name is stamped on the hub. Example T = Timken and S = Skefco.

Refit the hub, after fitting a new seal and packing with grease, as described in the same Section. Adjust the bearings and bleed the brakes.

Front wheel bearing adjustment:

This operation will be necessary if the wheel is loose on the spindle or does not rotate freely.

Raise the car until the appropriate wheel is clear of the ground then lever off the wheel cover and remove the grease cap from the hub.

Wipe any excess grease away and remove the adjusting nut, cotter pin and nut lock.

Loosen the bearing adjusting nut three turns, then rock wheel, hub and brake disc assembly in and out several times to push the brake pads away from the disc (rotor).

Refer to **FIG 9:6**, rotate the wheel and at the same time torque the adjusting nut to 17-25 lb ft to seat the bearings.

Back off the adjusting nut one half turn and then retighten it to 10-15 lb inch or finger tight.

Locate the locknut on the adjusting nut so that the slots in the locknut are in line with the cotter pin hole in the spindle. Fit a new cotter pin and bend over as shown.

Check the front wheel rotation. If it is in order, refit the grease cap and hub cap. If movement is still rough, clean or renew the bearings as necessary.

Before driving the car, pump the brake pedal several times to restore normal brake operation.

9:9 Suspension geometry

The camber, castor, and kingpin angles are given in Technical Data at the end of this manual. All these angles are set during manufacture and they are not adjustable.

Defects in the suspension and steering which affect the handling of the car, particularly if they seem to follow accident damage, may be due to incorrect angles. These must be checked on an alignment gauge. Faults and possible checks are as follows:

Incorrect castor angle:

Check that stabilizer bar is not bent, and that its attachment bolts are tight.

Incorrect camber or kingpin inclination:

If kingpin inclination is correct but camber angle is wrong, check the wheel spindle for distortion. If both angles are wrong, check track control arm for distortion and control arm ball joint for slackness and excessive wear. Also check the inner mounting of the track control arm for wear and distortion.

9:10 Fault diagnosis

(a) Wheel wobble

1 Worn or slack hub bearings
2 Broken or weak front springs
3 Uneven tyre wear
4 Bent stabilizer bar or track control arm
5 Loose suspension mountings, worn bushes
6 Loose wheel nuts

(b) 'Bottoming' of suspension

1 Check 2 in (a)
2 Rebound rubbers defective
3 Dampers not working
4 Broken stabilizer bar

(c) Heavy steering

1 Front tyres under-inflated
2 Wrong suspension geometry

(d) Excessive tyre wear

1 Check 4 and 5 in (a); 3 in (b) and 2 in (c)

(e) Rattles

1 Check 2 and 5 in (a) and 4 in (b)
2 Stabilizer bar clamps loose

(f) Excessive rolling

1 Check 2 in (a); 3 and 4 in (b) and 1 in (c)

CHAPTER 10

THE STEERING SYSTEM

10:1 Description

The layout of the steering system is shown in **FIG 10:1**, from which it will be seen that it is of the rack and pinion type with the steering gear mounted in rubber insulators on brackets attached to the front crossmember.

The components of the steering column and the steering gear assemblies are shown in **FIGS 10:2** and **10:3**. The steering wheel has a bellows type hub which will collapse on impact with the drivers body in the event of a severe frontal impact and so minimize possible injury.

Steering wheel movements are transmitted to the pinion shaft through the steering gear shaft and the flexible coupling and universal joint assembly. At the lower end of the pinion shaft is a helical pinion which meshes with the rack and rotation of the pinion in either direction results in a transverse movement of the rack inside its housing.

The outer ends of the rack carry ball jointed track rods which in turn, are ball jointed to the steering arms on the suspension units. Adjusting the length of the tie rods enables the tracking of the front wheels to be set to the specified values.

Shims are used to set the preload on the pinion bearings. Shims also adjust the degree of damping on the rack exercised by the rack adjusting bearing or slipper. Preload on the track rod inner ball joint is regulated by movement of the ball housing screwed on the end of the rack.

10:2 Routine maintenance

When working on the car with the front wheels clear of the ground, do not move the wheels quickly from lock to lock. Such movement builds up hydraulic pressure that may burst or blow off the bellows, and possibly also damage the gear teeth.

1 At the first 600 miles (1000 km) check the front wheel toe-in.

2 At every 6000 miles (10,000 km) or six-monthly intervals, examine the rack bellows for leaks or damage, and check the gaiters on the track rod outer ball joints for splits or deterioration. Also check the condition of the steering shaft universal joint and the flexible coupling.

Section 10:4 gives details of the method of introducing oil into the rack housing after renewing a bellows in situ. Note the warning which is given to ensure that the housing is not overfilled, otherwise the bellows may be split or blown off due to a build-up in hydraulic pressure.

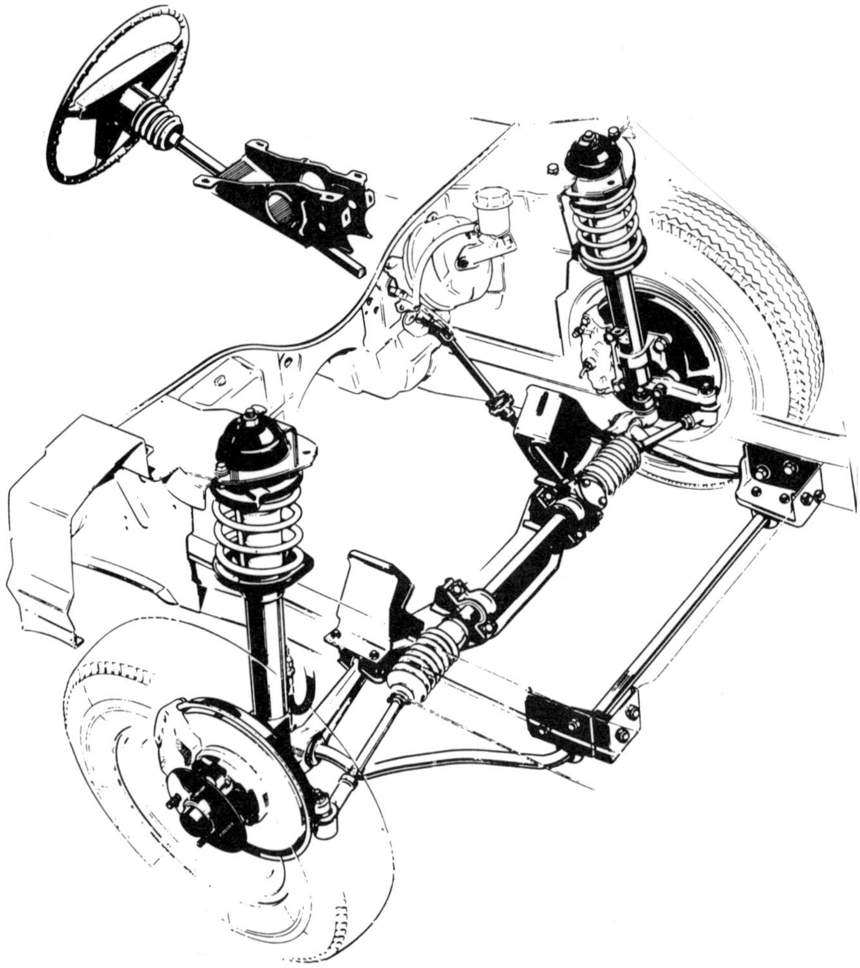

FIG 10:1 Layout of the steering system

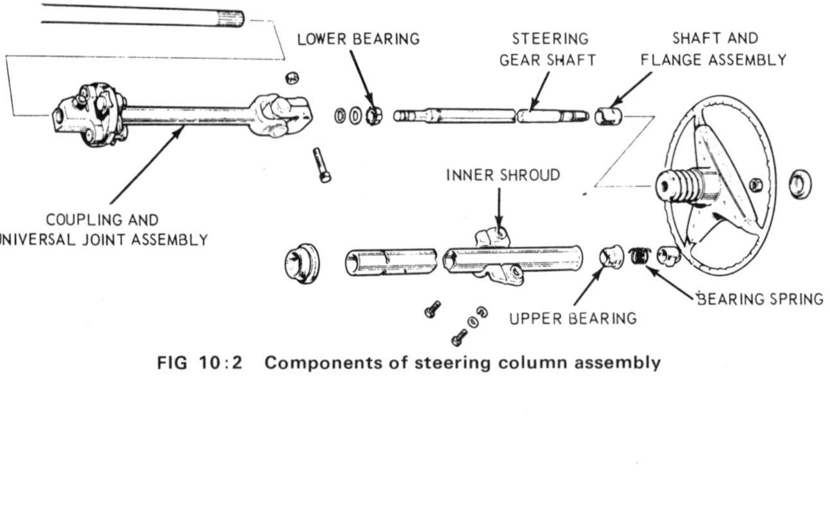

FIG 10:2 Components of steering column assembly

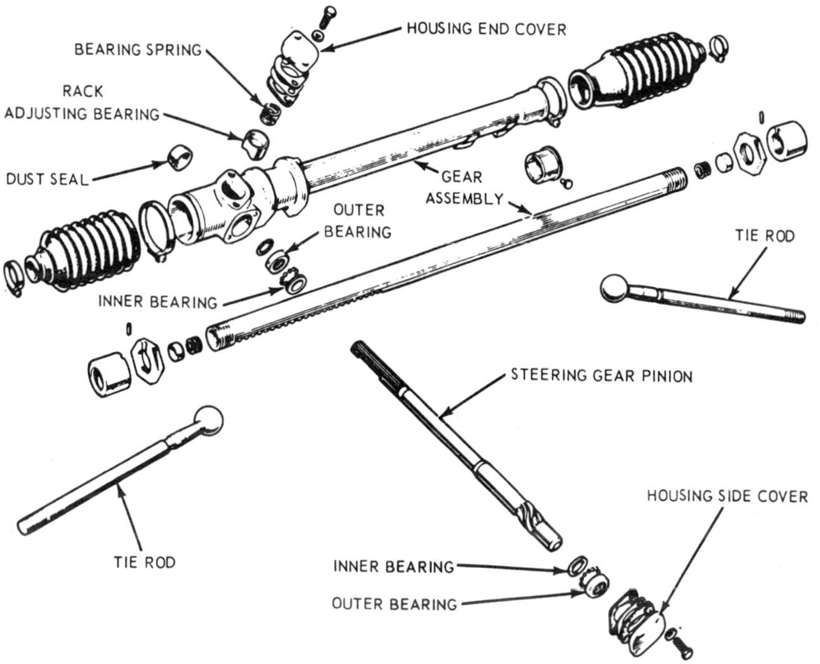

FIG 10:3 Components of the steering gear

10:3 Toe-in and steering angles

The correct figures for toe-in, and wheel lock angles are given in Technical Data. **If either the wheel lock angles or toe-in is adjusted, then both must be re-checked after the adjustment.** As the normal owner is not equipped to check the wheel lock angles, it is recommended that these, and alignment checks are made by a garage which has accurate gauges for the job.

Before making checks, the tyres must be correctly inflated, the wheels must be running true and the hub bearings correctly adjusted. The stabilizer bar clamps must be tightly secured and there must be no excessive play in the ball joints. Check springs for correct seating. The toe-in can be roughly checked as follows:

1 Bring the car to rest after running forward. Set the front wheels straight-ahead.

2 Measure the distance between the rims at wheel centre height at the front. Mark the points with chalk and roll the car forward for half a turn of the wheels. With the marks now at the rear, measure the distance between them. This dimension should exceed that at the front by .06 to .25 inch (1.5 to 6.4 mm) or by the nominal fraction of $\frac{5}{32}$ inch. The wheels will then toe-in.

3 If adjustment is needed, slacken the locknuts securing the ball joints at the outer ends of the track rods (see **FIG 10:4**). Slacken the small clips at the outer ends of bellows.

4 Turn the track rods until the toe-in is correct, making sure that the rods are approximately equal in length (within $\frac{1}{4}$ inch or 6.35 mm). The number of threads exposed will be a good guide. If necessary, screw one rod into its outer ball joint and unscrew the other rod by an equal amount, remembering that one is a right-hand thread and the other a lefthand. This will rectify any inequality without affecting the toe-in. Screwing both rods into (or out of) the ball joints by equal amounts will then adjust the toe-in correctly.

Wheel lock angles:

These must be checked on suitable equipment. When a lock angle of 35 deg. is set on one wheel, the front lock angle of the other must be 32 deg. 15 min. to 33 deg. 45 min. If the steering is turned onto left lock, the back lock angle is taken on the left wheel and the front lock angle on the right, and conversely for a turn on right lock.

Repeat on the other lock. If readings are incorrect or unequal, alter the track rod lengths. To keep toe-in correct, turn the rods equal amounts. If one rod is screwed into its outer ball joint and the other unscrewed by the same amount (or vice versa), the toe-in will not be affected.

Recheck the wheel lock angles and then recheck the toe-in. When satisfied, tighten the outer ball joint locknuts and the clips on the bellows.

Incorrect wheel lock angles:

If the angles are incorrect, comparing one lock with the other, first check the toe-in. If this is correct, check that the track rods are approximately equal in length. Minor differences in length up to a maximum of $\frac{1}{4}$ inch (6.35 mm) are acceptable, to compensate for manufacturing tolerances.

If both toe-in and track rod lengths are satisfactory, examine the steering arms and track rods for distortion. Also check the steering linkage ball joints for wear or slackness.

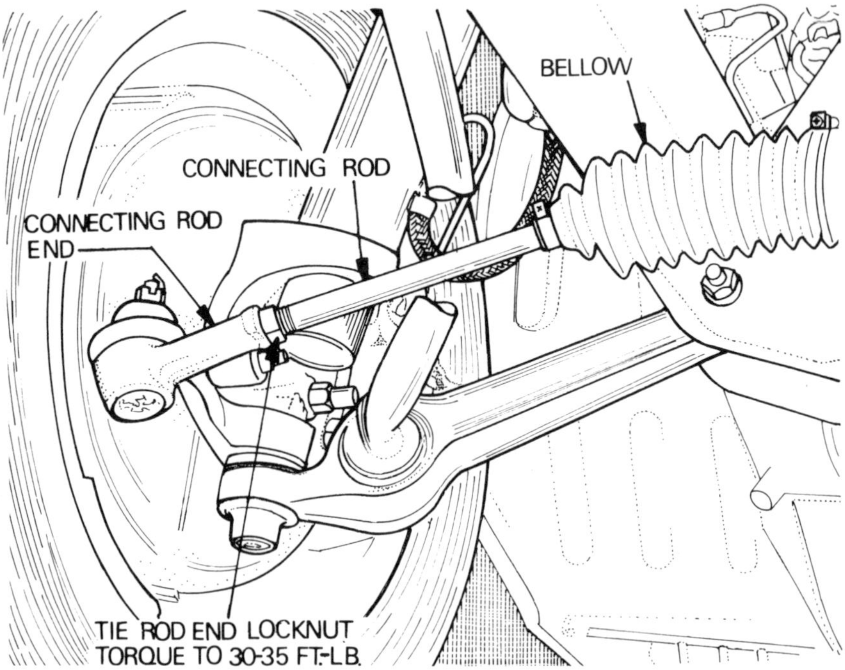

FIG 10:4 Showing the steering connecting (track) rod and ball end

Checking steering angles:

These must be checked on a suitable wheel alignment gauge. Before starting operations, refer to the figures given in Technical Data for castor angle, camber angle, and kingpin inclination.

Refer to **Section 9:9** of the preceding Chapter for possible faults which may lead to incorrect angles, remembering that there are no adjustments.

10:4 Renewing bellows in situ

These are shown in **FIG 10:3** and they must always be renewed as soon as they are seen to have split or deteriorated. **The entry of road grit and the loss of lubricant will otherwise have a disastrous effect on the rack mechanism.** Renewal is possible without removing the rack from the car, as follows:

1 Apply the handbrake, jack up the front of the car and support it on stands. Remove the splitpin and nut from the ball joint pin on the connecting rod end (see **FIG 10:4**). Extract the pin from the end of the rod.

2 Remove the ball joint end from the connecting (track) rod. Count turns required to remove joint so that it can be replaced in the same location, to keep the toe-in correct.

3 Slacken clips at each end of bellows. There may be soft iron wire instead of a clip at the inner end. Cut this away and use a screw clip as a replacement. Set a container to catch draining oil and pull off the bellows. Move the steering from lock to lock several times to ensure that all lubricant is drained from the steering gear. **If any remains, and the specified quantity of fresh oil is introduced, there will be a chance that overfilling will lead to a bellows being blown off due to hydraulic pressure.**

4 Fit the new bellows and tighten the large inner clip, leaving the small one loose. Refit the ball joint to the outer end of the track rod, screwing it on as far as its original position.

5 Fit ball joint pin to steering arm, tighten nut to 18 to 22 lb ft and fit a new splitpin. Lower car to ground.

6 Check toe-in and wheel lock angles (see **Section 10:3**). Tighten the ball joint locknut and the small clip on the bellows.

7 Refer to **FIG 10:3** and remove housing end coverplate. Withdraw the spring and slipper, taking great care of the joint and shims. Pour in .25 pint (.03 US pint or .15 litre) of SAE.90.EP oil through the damper hole.

8 Refit the slipper, spring, shim pack, joints and coverplate, tightening the bolts to 6 to 8 lb ft.

If both bellows need renewal, the operations remain the same, but make sure the clips on both sides are tightened before introducing the oil.

10:5 Renewing track rod ends

Track rod ball joints at the outer ends are sealed and are not adjustable. Damaged or deteriorated rubber boots will permit the entry of road grit and loss of lubricant. If this has happened, the joint assembly must be renewed. Do this by following the instructions for removal in operations 1 and 2 in the preceding Section. Fit wheel stands (not chassis stands) or raise car on hoist so that wheels are loaded. Fit the new parts according to operations 4, 5 and 6. If adjustment to toe-in is necessary, refer to **Section 10:3**.

10:6 Renewing steering arms

A steering arm can be seen in **FIG 9:1** in the preceding Chapter. If it has been bent in an accident, or if this is suspected because alignment checks prove that something is wrong, the arm must be renewed. **No attempt should be made to straighten it.** Remove as follows:

1 Jack up front of car, fit stands and remove wheel. Detach brake supply pipe from bracket on suspension unit and plug both open pipe ends.
2 Unlock and remove bolts securing brake caliper and lift caliper away.
3 Remove hub and disc assembly (see **Section 9:7** in preceding Chapter).
4 Remove track rod end from steering arm (see operation 1 in **Section 10:4**).
5 Remove splitpins and nuts to detach steering arm from suspension unit.

Installing:

1 Secure the arm to the suspension unit, using a torque of 30 to 34 lb ft on the nuts. Fit new splitpins.
2 Refit track rod end to arm, tightening nut to 18 to 22 lb ft. Fit new splitpin.
3 Refit hub assembly (see **Section 9:7** in preceding Chapter), adjusting the bearings as instructed.
4 Fit the brake caliper. Use new locktabs and tighten bolts to 45 to 50 lb ft. Reconnect brake pipes and tighten securely. Fit road wheel.
5 Bleed the brakes as instructed in **Chapter 11**. Lower car to ground.

10:7 Overhauling steering gear

Removing:

In this operation the wheels must remain loaded, so that it is not practicable to fit chassis stands. Either raise the car on a hoist, fit wheel stands, or block up the wheels when the car is jacked up, lowering the car onto the blocks after making sure the rear wheels are chocked and the handbrake applied. The steering wheel must be straight-ahead. Then proceed as follows:

1 Referring to **FIG 10:2**, look under the bonnet and identify the flexible coupling. Remove the nut and bolt clamping the coupling to pinion shaft.
2 Release the steering gear from the body crossmember. The clamps can be seen just below inset X in **FIG 9:1** in the preceding Chapter. The clamp bolts have lock-plates.
3 Detach the track rod outer ball joints from the steering arms as instructed in operation 1 of **Section 10:4**. Unscrew the joints as in operation 2.
4 Put one wheel on lock to remove steering gear, so that opposite end will clear stabilizer bar.

Overhauling:

Those operations which can be carried out without complete stripping of the steering gear will be covered first.

Renewing bellows:

When pulling off bellows, be ready to catch the oil which will drain out of the gear. Remove the bellows as instructed in operation 3 in **Section 10:4**. Expel all oil by holding rack vertically, then traverse from lock to lock.

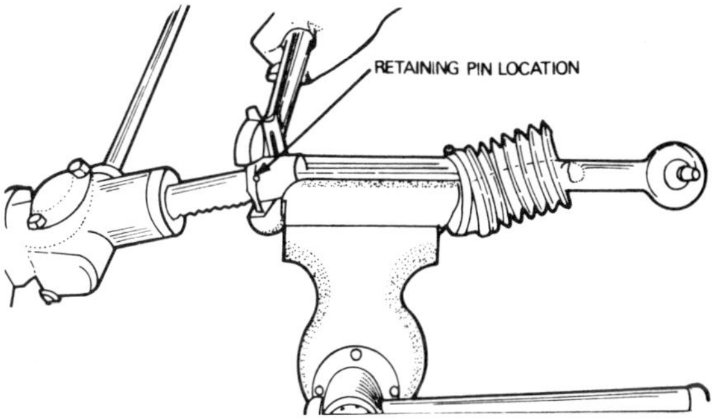

FIG 10:5 Adjusting connecting rod inner ball joint

To fit new bellows, mount gear vertically in soft jaws in a vice. This assumes that one bellows is already in position and is at the bottom end.

Into the space between the casing and the track rod inner ball joint, pour .25 pint (.03 US pint or .15 litre) of SAE.90.EP oil. Traverse the rack to help the flow of oil. Fit the new bellows, securing both ends with clips and not wire. Refit the outer ball joints.

Renewing track rod inner ball joint:

Each end of the steering rack (see **FIG 10:3**) carries a ball joint assembly for the tie rod and adjustment of this joint is possible by screwing the ball housing along the rack.

To dismantle the joint, drill out the pin shown but be careful not to drill too deeply. Hold the locknut and screw the ball housing off the end of the rack shaft using a suitable wrench. Remove the spring and ball seat from the recess in the rack and discard.

Examine the bearing surfaces of the track rod ball and the ballhousing for wear and damage. Renew the parts if defective, as accurate adjustment will otherwise be impossible.

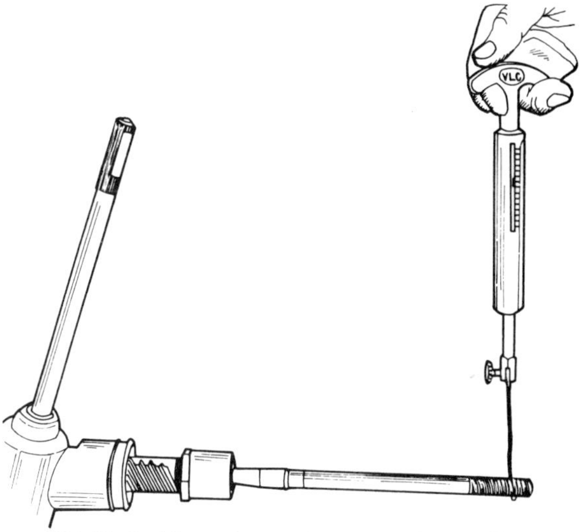

FIG 10:6 Measuring track rod articulation effort

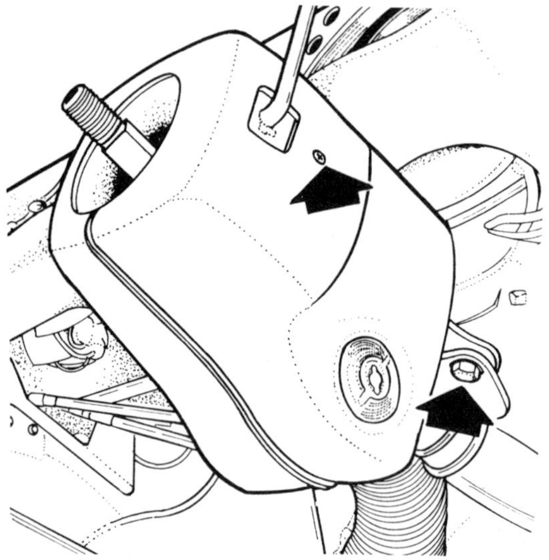

FIG 10:7 Showing location of steering column and shroud mounting screws

Reassemble by fitting a new spring and seat into the rack. Smear SAE.90.EP oil on the ball, seat and housing. Fit the parts to the rack and tighten the housing until articulation of the track rod shows signs of stiffness. Effort to articulate joint is measured as in **FIG 10:6**. Before doing this, turn the track rod through at least seven revolutions, so that the reading will be true. A spring pull scale reading up to 10 lb (5.6 kg) will be suitable.

Fit a piece of wire to the scale and hook it round the rod about $\frac{1}{4}$ inch (6.3 mm) from the end. With the rod parallel to the rack as shown, screw the ballhousing either in or out as required until the scale records a pull of 5 lb before the rod begins to move. Tighten the locknut on the housing and check that the effort required to articulate the rod is still 5 lb.

Do not fit a locking pin in the existing hole if it happens to line up. Always drill a fresh hole, half in the locknut and half in the housing. Use a $\frac{1}{8}$ inch (3.18 mm) drill to a depth of $\frac{3}{8}$ inch (9.525 mm). Tap the pin into position and secure it by peening the hole.

Dismantling gear:

Refer to **FIG 10:3** for details of the internal parts. The steering pinion shaft runs in ball bearings in which the balls are fitted loose. There are fourteen balls in each bearing and great care must be taken to see that none fall into the rack during these operations. Dismantle as follows:

1 Remove the pinion dust seal, remove the housing side cover and the bearings and then pull out the pinion shaft.

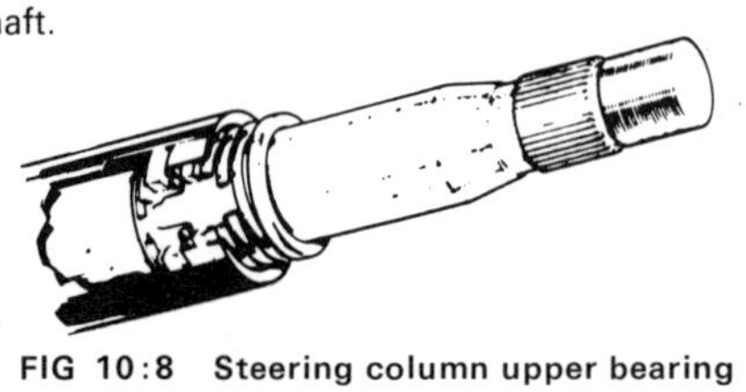

FIG 10:8 Steering column upper bearing

2 Pull out the rack from the pinion end of the casing in order to avoid damage to the support bush on the rack teeth. Remove the outer and inner bearings.

Clean the parts and inspect for wear or damage. If the teeth of rack or pinion are damaged a complete new gear assembly must be fitted. Renew the rack support bush if worn, as slackness here may lead to rattles. Renew the ballbearings if the races are worn or pitted.

Reassembling:

Fit a new pinion oil seal into the casing, followed by the upper bearing. Stick the balls into place with grease. Fit the rack with its teeth correctly positioned for engagement with the pinion. Set it centrally by checking the length protruding at each end of the casing.

Fit the lower ballbearing to the pinion shaft and slide the shaft into place in the casing with the alignment mark on the pinion vertical (as if seen with the gear assembled in the car). Now do the following:

Pinion bearing preload:

Fit the coverplate without shims or gaskets and tighten the bolts evenly until the plate is just touching the pinion bearing. Use feeler gauges to check the gap between the coverplate and the casing. If the gap varies when measured adjacent to the bolts it shows that they have not been tightened evenly.

The shim pack must include two gaskets, one on each outer face. Make up this assembly so that the total thickness is .002 to .004 inch (.05 to .10 mm) less than the gap measured by the feeler gauges. Steel shims are available in thicknesses of .002, .005 and .010 inch (.051, .127 and .254 mm) and paper gaskets are .005 inch (.127 mm) thick. Fit the shims, gaskets and coverplate and tighten the bolts to 6 to 8 lb ft (.85 to 1.1 kg m). Use sealer on the bolt threads. The pinion bearings should now be correctly preloaded.

Rack damper adjustment:

Correct adjustment is essential to avoid 'knocking' from the steering gear or steering stiffness. Do the following:

Locate slipper in the rack housing so that it fits snugly on the back of the rack, pushing it right home. Place a straightedge across the face of the casing which takes the damper coverplate. Use feeler gauges to measure the distance between the top of the slipper and the underside of the straightedge. Make up a shim pack, sandwiched between paper gaskets so that the total thickness exceeds the feeler gauge dimension by .0005 to .0035 inch (.013 to .089 mm). The shims and gaskets are available in the same thicknesses as those for the pinion bearing preload as specified in the preceding instructions.

Fit the spring in the recess in the slipper, position the shim pack, gaskets and coverplate and tighten the bolts to 6 to 8 lb ft (.85 to 1.1 kg m). Put sealer on the bolt threads.

Next measure the torque required to turn the pinion. This should be between 10 and 18 lb inch and if it is not within these limits, the adjustment is incorrect or there is is undue friction somewhere. Check the shimming of the damper cover, and if this is not the cause, look for tight bearings, damaged gear teeth, or lack of lubricant. Continue reassembling by fitting bellows and track rods as described earlier.

Installing steering gear:

Screw the locknuts on the track rods by the number of turns required to remove them. Set the steering wheel in the straight-ahead position. With the steering gear also in the straight-ahead position (the rack should be protruding equally from each end of the rack housing), offer it up to the mounting brackets on the crossmember. Before securing it, check the condition of the mounting rubbers, and align the splines on the pinion shaft and in the flexible coupling. Press the pinion shaft into the coupling and fit the mounting clamps, tightening the bolts to 15 to 18 lb ft. Use new lockplates.

Attach the track rod ends to the steering arms, tightening the slotted nuts to a torque of 18 to 22 lb ft. Fit new splitpins. Tighten the locknuts.

Tighten the flexible coupling clamp bolt to a torque of 12 to 15 lb ft and lower the car to the ground. Check the toe-in and wheel lock angles. Check steering wheel position.

10:8 Removing and installing steering wheel

Set the front wheels straight-ahead. Refer to **FIG 10:2** and prise out the central emblem. Remove retaining nut and pull wheel off splines.

When refitting, make sure that the road wheels are still straight-ahead and then press the steering wheel into place with the spokes correctly set. Tighten the retaining nut to 20 to 25 lb ft. Press the emblem into place with the lug at the bottom.

10:9 Removing and installing column couplings

Disconnect the battery, and the choke cable from the carburetter. Refer to **FIG 10:2** and remove the clamp bolt securing flexible joint to pinion shaft. Remove the clamp bolt from universal joint.

Refer to **FIG 10:7**. Remove the shroud from the column (two cross-head screws, one each side). Remove the two bolts from the column bracket, one of which is indicated by the lower arrow. Disconnect the electrical wiring plugs from their connectors.

Pull the column to the rear enough to permit removal of the joint and coupling assembly.

When reassembling in the reverse order, first check that the steering gear and the steering wheel are both in the straight-ahead position before engaging the coupling splines. Also make sure that the rubber grommet 8 is properly fitted, where the column passes through the floor.

Tighten the coupling clamp bolts to 12 to 15 lb ft, tightening the one for the universal joint first. Reconnect the wiring plugs.

When fitting the two screws for the column shroud, note that one is self-tapping and the other threaded. Secure the column bracket and shroud to the underside of the facia panel. Reconnect choke cable and battery.

10:10 Overhauling steering column

To remove the steering column, repeat the instructions in **Section 10:9** but do not remove the clamp bolt from the lower flexible coupling. An extra item is to lift off the indicator cancelling cam and spring and remove the two screws securing the indicator switch to the top of the column. Remove the wiring loom strap and switch assembly. Withdraw the column.

Dismantling:

Refer to **FIG 10:2**. Pull shaft out of column. Remove lower bearing assembly by prising off the circlip. The upper bearing is shown in **FIG 10:8** and it can be driven out from below with the steering shaft.

Check the shaft splines and the bearings. A new upper bearing can be tapped into place, and a new lower bearing can be fitted to the shaft, using a new washer and circlip.

Before introducing the shaft into the column from the lower end, check that the pin of the steering lock (if fitted) does not protrude into the column. Ensure this by turning the key to 'Ignition' and back to 'Off'. Do not remove the key. Reassemble in the reverse order to dismantling.

Installing:

Follow the instructions in **Section 10:9** to refit the column into the car. When the direction indicator switch has been refitted to the top of the column, fit the spring and indicator cancelling cam to the shaft. With road wheels straight-ahead, the 'ear' on the cam must be midway between the cancelling levers of the indicator switch.

10:11 Fault diagnosis

(a) Wheel wobble

1 Unbalanced wheels and tyres
2 Worn or loose steering connections
3 Incorrect wheel alignment angles
4 Excessive play in steering gear
5 Worn or slack hub bearings
6 Rack damper ineffective, spring broken

(b) Wander

1 Check (a)
2 Uneven tyre pressures or tyre wear
3 Misalignment of suspension unit

(c) Heavy steering

1 Check 2 in (a) and 3 in (b)
2 Very low tyre pressures
3 Lack of oil in rack housing
4 Wrong wheel tracking
5 Pinion preload or rack damping excessive
6 Steering shaft or column bent, faulty bearings
7 Defective flexible or universal couplings
8 Defective steering ball joints

(d) Lost motion

1 Slack pinion bearings
2 Rack damper not working
3 Loose steering wheel
4 Loose couplings, worn splines
5 Worn or badly adjusted ball joints
6 Rack housing loose in mountings
7 General wear in steering gear

NOTES

CHAPTER 11

THE BRAKING SYSTEM

11 :1 Description

Hydraulically operated brakes are used on all four wheels with disc units on the front and drums at the rear. A dual system is employed in which a tandem type master cylinder supplies pressure through one circuit to the front brakes and another, quite separate, to the rear wheels. These are operated by a pendant type pedal which is coupled directly to a power brake booster (vacuum servo) fitted to the rear bulkhead of the engine compartment. The master cylinder is bolted to the front face of the booster and these two items are replaced as a unit.

The floor mounted handbrake between the front seats operates the rear wheel brakes through a two cable linkage and at the same time causes the self-adjusting mechanism on these brakes to set itself and compensate for any wear on the friction linings.

The layout of the braking system is shown in **FIG 11 :1**.

11 :2 Maintenance and bleeding the system

Very little maintenance is required as both front and rear brakes are self-adjusting, but a regular check should be made on the level of the fluid in the master cylinder reservoir.

Clean the area around it and remove the reservoir filler cap. Fill up with the specified brake fluid, USA reference CZAZ-19542-A (ESA-M6C25-A), UK reference ME-3833-F, making sure that both halves of the container are filled.

At about 6000 mile intervals the following checks should be made:

Check the friction linings and pads for wear and renew as described later in this chapter if necessary.

Lubricate the handbrake linkage.

Check all the pipelines and fittings for possible damage or deterioration. This includes the possibility of chafing on the flexible hoses.

Bleeding the system:

This is not an item of routine maintenance and should be necessary only if air has been admitted into the system after a servicing operation or if the fluid level has been allowed to drop too low in the reservoir. The need for this operation is usually indicated by a spongy feeling or excessive travel on the brake pedal.

It is important to ensure that the piston assembly in the pressure differential valve is held in the central position. This may be done by using a screwdriver with the

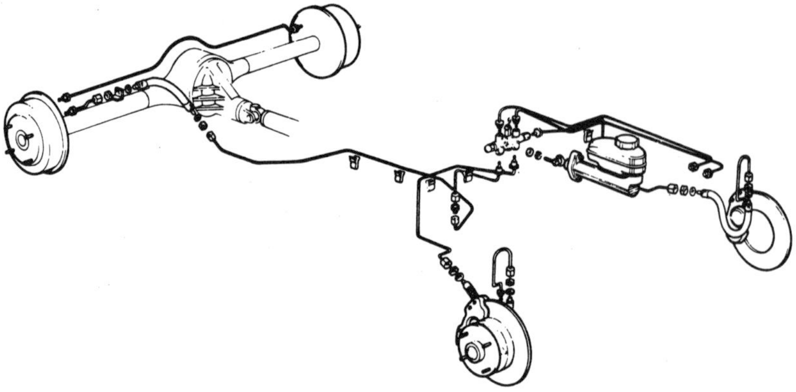

FIG 11:1 Layout of the hydraulic system

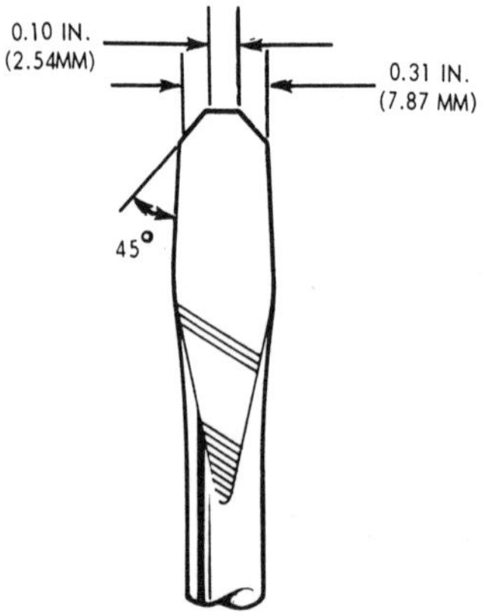

FIG 11:2 Dimensions of tool for centralising the pressure differential valve

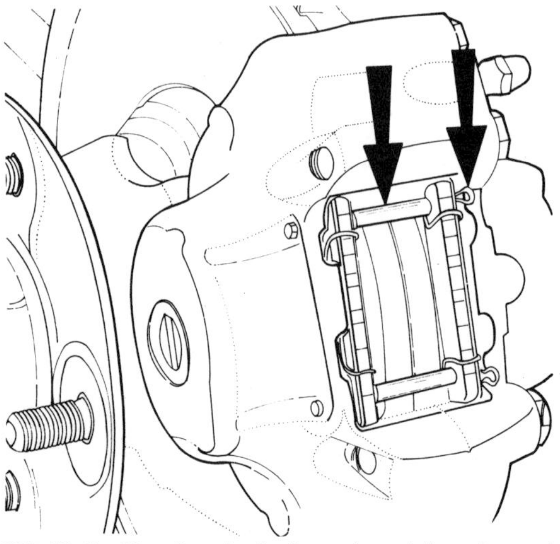

FIG 11:3 Showing the brake pad retaining pins and clips

blade modified as shown in **FIG 11:2**. It should be inserted through the aperture in the base of the assembly after the rubber has been removed.

Fill up the reservoir and be prepared to top up as the operation proceeds in order to replace the fluid as it is used. Do not re-use the fluid expelled in the course of the bleeding.

Remove the dust cap from the righthand front bleed nipple and fit a length of suitable tubing with the free end immersed in a quantity of brake fluid in a clean glass jar.

Unscrew the bleed valve about half a turn and have an assistant to depress the brake pedal fully and allow it to return. Pause for two or three seconds and repeat.

At first the fluid being pumped into the jar will contain bubbles of air and the process should be continued until no air bubbles are present. The bleed valve may then be tightened and the operation repeated on the other front brake and then the rear brakes.

Do not forget to watch the fluid level in the reservoir and top up as necessary.

Replace the bleed nipple covers and the reservoir cap, after seeing that the vent hole is free. Remove the centralizing tool from the differential valve.

Switch on the ignition and depress the brake pedal several times. The warning light should not illuminate.

With the ignition still on, operate the test switch and ensure that the warning light does illuminate.

11:3 Renewing the front brake pads

These should be renewed as soon as they have worn down to a thickness of $\frac{1}{8}$ inch and the procedure is as follows:

Apply the parking brake, jack up the front of the car and support it on stands. Remove the front wheels.

Refer to **FIGS 11:3** and **11:4**. Pull out the retaining clips, withdraw the retaining pins and remove the brake pads, tension springs and shims using, if necessary, a pair of thin nosed pliers.

Before fitting the new pads, check that they are the correct type and colour code and ensure that the disc is undamaged and free from dirt and oil. It will also be necessary to push the pistons back into their bores. This will cause the fluid level in the reservoir to rise and perhaps overflow if some fluid is not siphoned out.

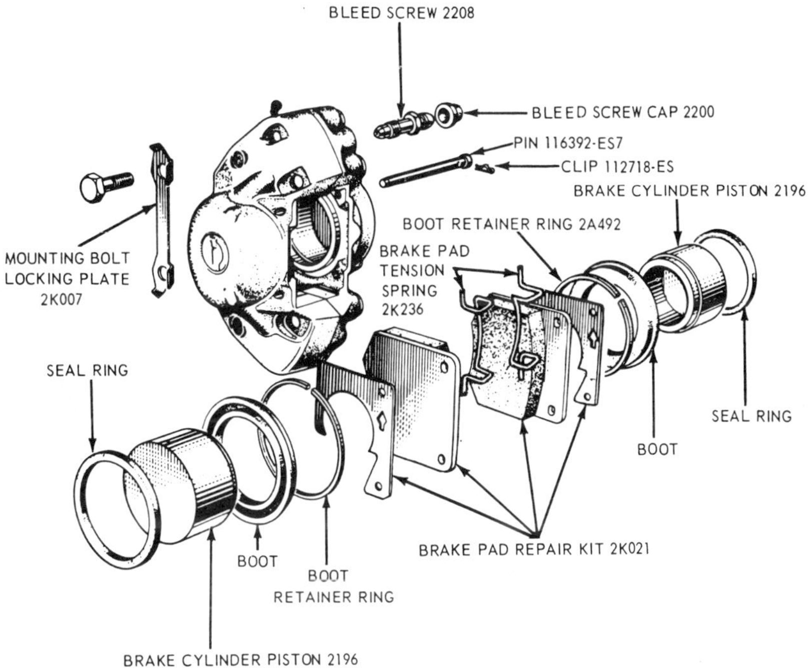

FIG 11:4 Components of a front brake caliper assembly

Place the brake pad tension springs on the pads and shims and fit them into the caliper. The pads can go in only one way, but the shims may be fitted either way up. Refit the retaining pins and secure them with the clips, noting that the clips are on the side of the pins away from the piston seal. See also that the tangs of the pad tension springs are underneath the retaining pins.

Operate the brake pedal several times to bring the pads fully into position against the disc, then check that the pads have a little free movement to indicate that the retaining pins are not fouling the pads.

Refit the road wheels and lower the car to the ground.

11:4 Servicing the calipers

Removal:

Raise the front of the car and remove the appropriate road wheel.

Remove the brake pads as described in **Section 11:3**. Piston removal will be facilitated if the brake pedal is now depressed to push them out of their bores.

Disconnect the fluid supply pipe from the union on the the rear of the caliper and plug each open end to prevent the entry of any foreign matter.

Bend back the locking tabs, remove the two securing bolts and lift away the caliper assembly.

Dismantling:

Under no circumstances should the two halves of the caliper body be separated.

Partially extract one piston and remove the circlip and the sealing bellows from the groove in the piston. The piston may now be withdrawn with the fingers assisted, if necessary, by a little air pressure.

Ease the bellows from the groove in the bore and withdraw the piston sealing ring.

Repeat for the other piston and then clean all the parts in methylated spirit or brake fluid, but do NOT use a mineral base cleaner such as petrol, kerosene or carbon tetrachloride. Check that all the items are fit for further use or renew where necessary. Rubber parts should always be renewed.

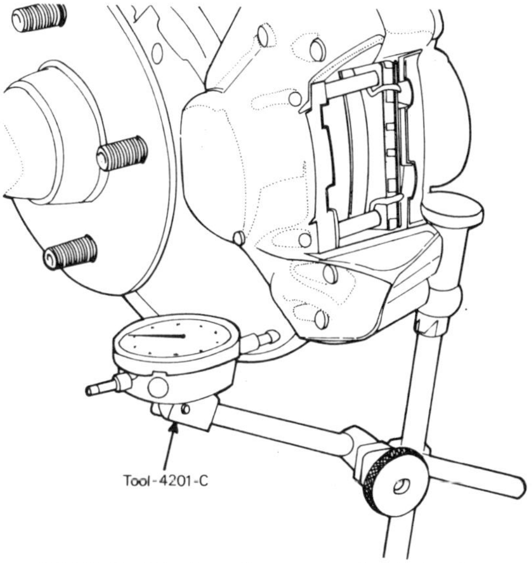

FIG 11:5 Checking the runout of a brake disc

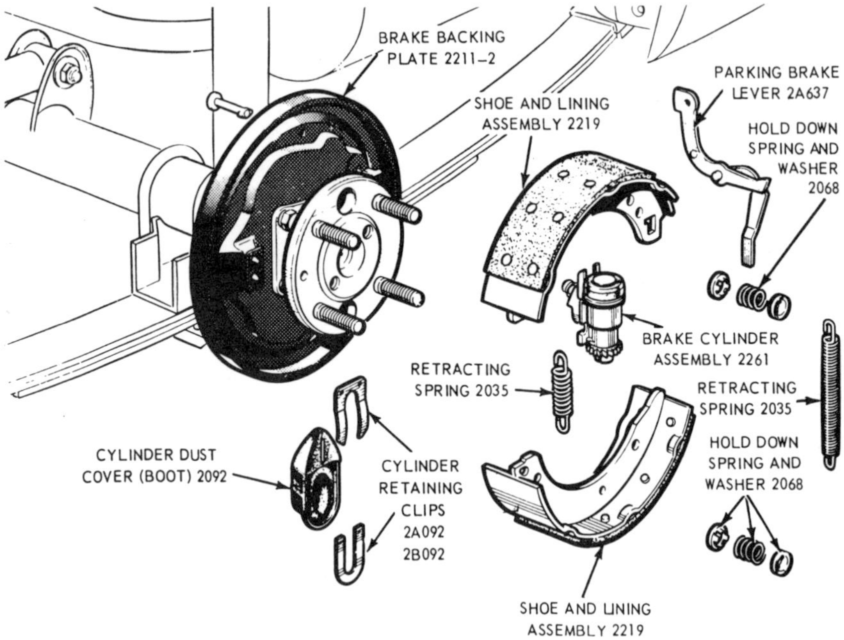

FIG 11:6 Components of a rear drum brake assembly

Reassembly:

Fit a new piston sealing ring in each cylinder bore and fit the rubber bellows to the cylinder with the out-turned lip firmly in the cylinder groove.

Dip the pistons in clean brake fluid and insert them carefully, crown first, through the bellows into the cylinder Fit the inner edge of the bellows in the annular groove in the piston skirt.

Push the piston as far as possible into the bore and then secure the bellows to the caliper with the circlip.

Reinstallation:

The caliper assembly is refitted using a new locking plate and tightening the bolts to a torque of 45 to 50 lb ft (6.22 to 6.91 Mkg). Bend up the locking tabs.

Reconnect the hydraulic pipe to its union.

Refit the brake pads as described in **Section 11:3**, pushing the pistons back as necessary and ensuring that the piston seals are correctly fitted.

The remainder of the parts are fitted in the reverse order of removal, after which the brakes must be bled as described earlier in **Section 11:2**.

11:5 The hub and disc assembly

Removal:

Remove the grease cap from the end of the hub. Remove the cotterpin and the adjusting nut retainer, then unscrew the adjusting nut and remove the thrust washer and the outer bearing race.

Pull off the hub and disc assembly from the stub axle, make alignment marks on both parts and separate the disc from the hub after bending back the locking tabs and removing the bolts. Both locking plates and bolts should be discarded and new ones obtained.

Refitting:

Clean thoroughly both mating faces, align the mating marks and fit the disc to the hub, tightening the bolts to 30-34 lb ft (4.15 to 4.70 mkg). Secure with the locking tabs.

Replace the assembly on to the stub axle and fit the outer bearing race, thrust washer and adjusting nut, which should be tightened to 27 lb ft (3.73 mkg) while rotating the disc to ensure the correct seating of the bearings.

Slacken the nut back by one quarter of a turn and fit the nut retainer so that one of the castellations lines up with the cotterpin hole in the axle. Fit a new cotterpin.

The disc run-out is now checked as follows:

Disconnect the connecting rod from the steering arm at its outer end, after removing the cotterpin and castellated nut and separating the ball joint.

Mount a dial gauge on the steering arm as shown in **FIG 11:5**, rotate the disc and check the total indicator reading. It must not be more than .0035 inch (.089 mm).

If, after eliminating the possibility of dirt between the mating surfaces or misalignment of the hub bearings and trying a new location of the disc assembly on the axle, the run-out is still in excess of the specified dimension, a worn or distorted disc is indicated and must be renewed.

Remove the gauge, refit the connecting rod end and tighten to 18-22 lb ft (2.48-3.04 mkg) using a new cotterpin. Replace the grease cap.

Caliper splash shield:

After removing the disc assembly as just described the splash shield is detached by bending back the integral locking tabs and removing the securing screws.

Refitting is a reversal of the removal procedure.

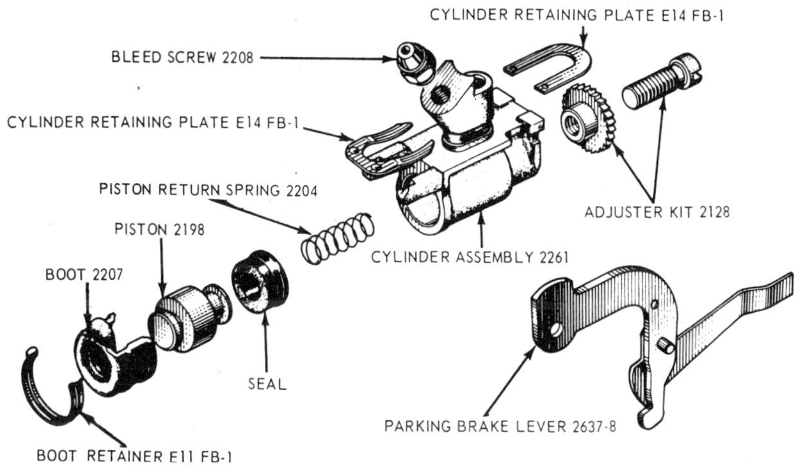

FIG 11 :7 Components of a rear wheel cylinder

11 :6 Servicing the drum brakes

Dismantling. (See **FIG 11 :6**):

The shoes should be examined at intervals of about 6000 miles (10,000 km) to see that there is at least $\frac{1}{32}$ inch (.93 mm) of lining material above the rivet heads and that the linings are not contaminated by oil or grease. In either case new shoes should be fitted as it is not possible to satisfactorily remove all traces of the contamination, nor is the home operator likely to be able to reline the old shoes himself.

Chock up the front wheels, raise the rear end of the car and support it on stands. Remove the road wheels, release the handbrake then remove the brake drums by taking out the securing screw.

Remove the hold down springs by giving the top washer a quarter of a turn and pulling outwards.

Pull each shoe out of its slot in the fixed pivot and wheel cylinder. Lift the shoes away and detach the two return springs.

A warning should now be given not to allow the brake pedal to be operated while the drums are off otherwise the wheel cylinder pistons may be ejected together with a quantity of brake fluid. To prevent this, the piston should be retained with a rubber band or a wire clip.

Withdraw the ratchet wheel assembly from the wheel cylinder and, in order to facilitate the fitting of the drum over the new shoes, rotate the wheel until it contacts the shoulder of the slot headed bolt. This moves the brakes into the fully off position.

Reassembly:

Before commencing, apply a smear of grease to the various rubbing surfaces such as the brake shoe support pads on the backplate, the shoe-pivots, the threads of the ratchet wheel and the recess in the wheel cylinder.

Fit the return springs onto the shoes, noting that they are fitted on the drum side of the shoe, and then fit the shoes onto the backplate assembly with the rear shoe in its location on the fixed pivot and engaging the parking brake link.

Fit the hold down pins and secure them with a washer, spring and then the second washer, which is turned through 90° to secure it. Check to make sure that the shoes are properly seated and that the springs are not binding on the backplate or wheel cylinder.

Refit the brake drum and secure it with the countersunk screw.

Now bring the shoes into adjustment by operating the parking brake lever behind the backplate for as long as is necessary to cause the clicking to stop.

With the ratchet wheel in the fully off position it is possible for the indexing lever on the parking brake link to over-ride the ratchet and remain in that position. It is necessary, therefore, to ensure that it returns to the fully off position every time.

Refit the road wheel and lower the car to the ground. Operate the handbrake several times to bring the brakes into correct adjustment and check by carrying out a road test.

Rear wheel cylinder:

Having removed the brake shoes, disconnect the hydraulic supply lines, note that there are two on the right handbrake plate, and plug the open ends.

Disconnect the handbrake link on the inside of the plate by removing the spring clip and clevis pin.

Lever off the rubber boot from the rear of the plate and then pull off the two U shaped retainers securing the cylinder to the backplate.

Remove the wheel cylinder and the handbrake link.

Refer to **FIG 11 :7** and remove the boot retainer. Prise off the boot and withdraw the piston complete with seal and spring from the cylinder bore. Detach the seal from the piston.

Remove the ratchet wheel and slot headed bolt from the other end of the cylinder.

Clean all parts as previously detailed, inspect for wear or damage and renew as necessary.

Dip the piston and a new seal in brake fluid and fit the seal on the piston with its flat face next to the rear shoulder of the piston. Insert the spring into the cylinder bore.

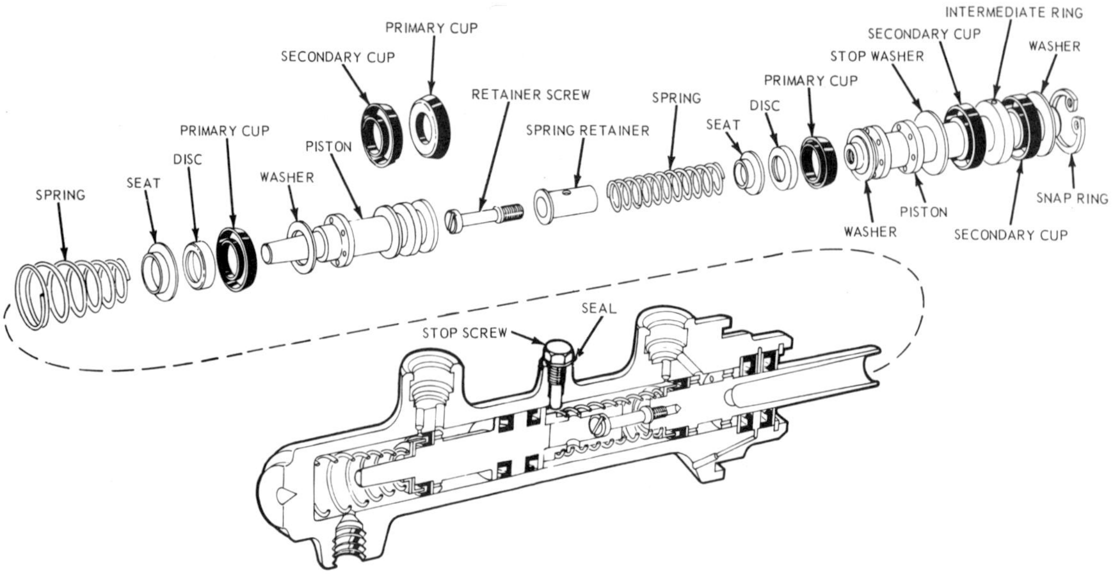

FIG 11 : 8 **Components of the master cylinder**

Dip in brake fluid and insert the piston assembly into the bore with the seal end innermost and being careful not to damage the seal in the process.

Fit the rubber boot and its retainer.

Rotate the ratchet wheel to the fully off position, abutting on the shoulder of the bolt head, smear with grease and insert into the wheel cylinder.

Apply also a smear of grease to the sliding surfaces of the backplate and the wheel cylinder, then pass the handbrake link and the neck of the wheel cylinder through the aperture in the backplate and secure with the U shaped retainers. Note that the spring retainer is fitted from the handbrake link end and the flat retainer on top of it from the other end.

Fit the rubber boot over the cylinder and the handbrake link, ensuring that the cylinder is still free to slide in the plate.

Operate the handbrake link to check the self-adjusting action of the ratchet wheel. There is a right handed screw on the righthand wheel cylinder and a left handed screw the lefthand cylinder.

Refit the shoes as described earlier, reconnect the hydraulic supply pipes, fit the drums and the road wheels and bleed the system as described in **Section 11 : 2**.

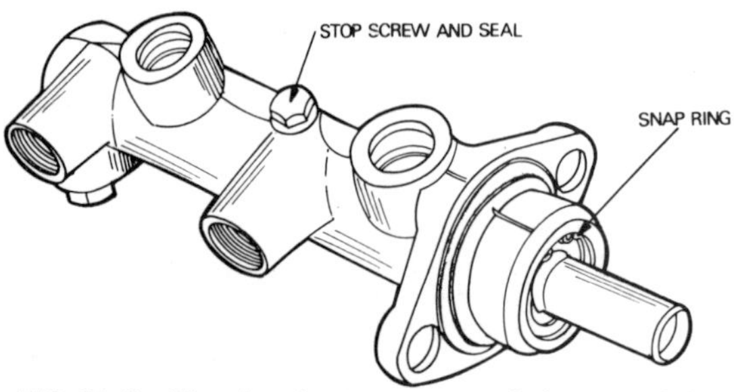

FIG 11 : 9 Showing the stop screw and piston retaining snap ring

11 : 7 Servicing the master cylinder

Dismantling:

Refer to **FIG 11 : 8**. Disconnect the hydraulic supply pipes from the cylinder body, taking steps to catch any fluid spillage, and plug the ends of the pipes.

Undo the two securing nuts and lift the master cylinder away from the servo unit.

Lift off the fluid reservoir and remove the rubber plugs. Loosen the stop screw at the centre of the cylinder body (see **FIG 11 : 9**), push the piston inwards and remove the snap ring using a pair of thin nosed pliers.

Withdraw the stop washer and the primary piston assembly, then, using compressed air, carefully press out the secondary piston assembly.

Wash all parts clean in methylated spirit or commercial alcohol and allow to dry. Do not use a cloth from which any fluff might adhere. Renew all parts showing any sign of rust, scoring or other damage or wear. All rubber seals, which will be found in the repair kit, should be renewed.

Reassembly:

Before starting to assemble the master cylinder, immerse all parts in clean brake fluid and study **FIGS 11 : 8** and **11 : 10** as it is essential to fit the new cups in the correct directions.

Assemble the secondary piston with filler washer, cups, pressure disc, spring and spring seat and carefully insert it into the cylinder as shown. Push it down to the end of its bore and fit the stop screw and seal. Release the piston and allow it to slowly contact the stop screw. Do not alter the length of the stop screw or the thickness of the seal.

Next assemble the primary piston with filler washer, primary cup, pressure disc and spring, spring seat, retainers and retainer screw. Do not over-tighten this screw.

Assemble the rear end of the piston in the order shown, press it carefully into the cylinder bore and fit the stop washer and snap ring.

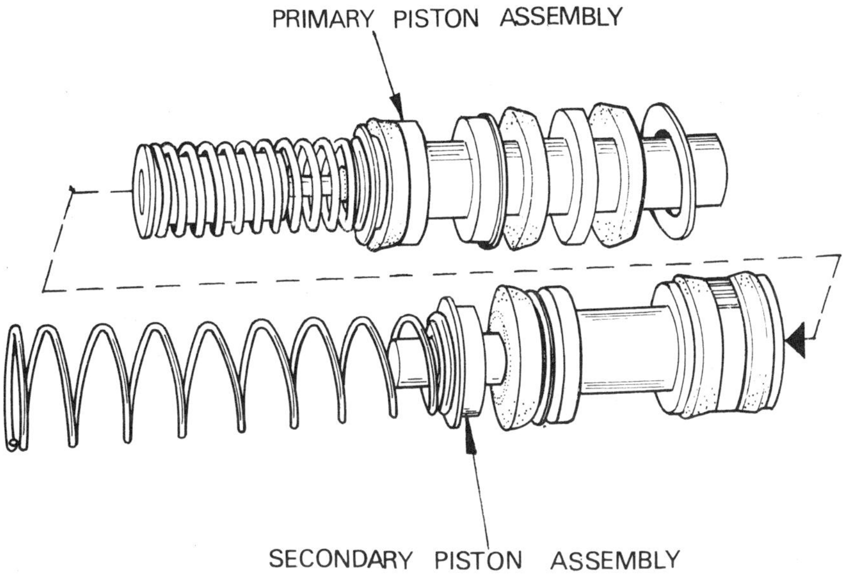

FIG 11 :10 Primary and secondary piston assemblies

Note that the booster unit push rod which operates the master cylinder is of a specific length and is not adjustable.

Place the master cylinder and fluid seal correctly onto the pushrod and hold it in position while screwing in the hydraulic pipe unions by a few turns.

Bolt the master cylinder to the booster unit and tighten the fluid pipe unions.

Refit the rubber plugs and the reservoir. Fill the reservoir with the specified fluid (see **Section 11 :2**). Bleed the entire brake system and test on the road.

11 :8 The pressure differential valve

This component, which is shown in the exploded view of **FIG 11 :11**, is bolted to the rear of the engine compartment. It is connected in series with the fluid supply lines to the front and rear brakes and with normal and equal pressure in each circuit the split piston assembly is maintained in its central position. In the event of a failure in either circuit the pressure will fall and the piston move towards that side and in so doing operate the plunger of the warning switch. This illuminates the light on the instrument panel to warn the driver of the fault and advise him that only one half of his braking potential is available.

Removal:

Disconnect the five hydraulic pipes from the ports on the valve body and plug the ends of the two pipes from the master cylinder.

Disconnect the wiring from the switch terminal.

Unscrew the securing bolt and remove the valve assembly.

Dismantling:

Unscrew the end plug and the adaptor and discard the copper washers. Unscrew the switch.

Very carefully push the two pistons out of the bore, remove and discard the two seals. Pull off the dust cover and discard it.

Clean and inspect all the pieces and renew any that show signs of wear or corrosion.

Assembly:

Fit new seals on the pistons with the larger diameter of each seal towards the slotted end of the piston and dip in clean brake fluid.

Insert the longer piston into the bore with the slotted end towards the outside, as shown in the illustration, until the groove is in line with the hole for the switch plunger and then screw the switch into position and tighten to 2 to $2\frac{1}{2}$ lb ft (.28-.34 mkg).

Insert the shorter piston also with the slotted end outermost.

Using new copper washers, screw in the adaptor and the end plug noting that the adaptor is fitted into the end adjacent to the hole for the mounting bolt. Tighten both to 16-20 lb ft (2.2-2.8 mkg).

Fit a new dust cover.

Testing:

After any of the operations described above or after repairing or disturbing any part of the braking system, it is essential to check the functioning of the system.

Switch on the ignition and momentarily depress the test switch. The warning lamp should light up. If it does not look for an electrical fault in the wiring or connections, or a blown bulb.

Depress the brake pedal several times. The warning light should not illuminate, but if it does there is a fault in the hydraulic system.

Switch off the ignition after making the test.

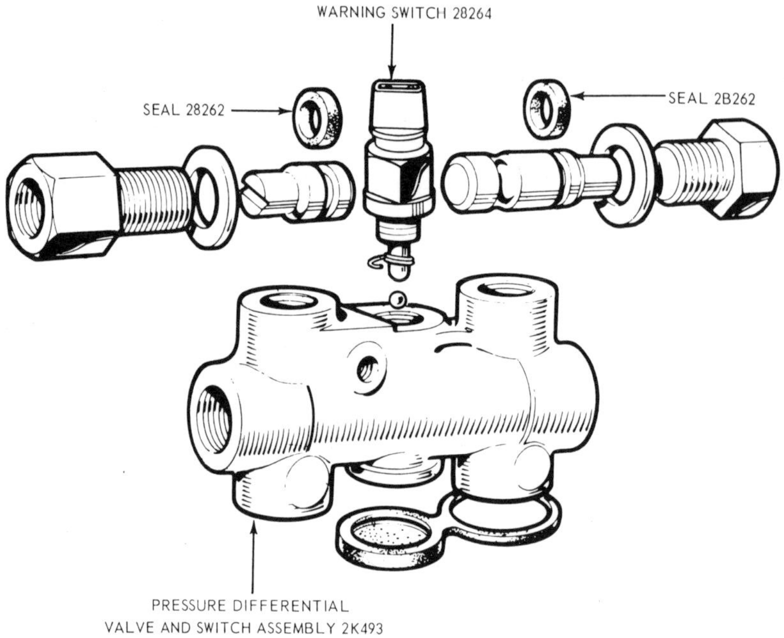

FIG 11:11 Components of the pressure differential valve

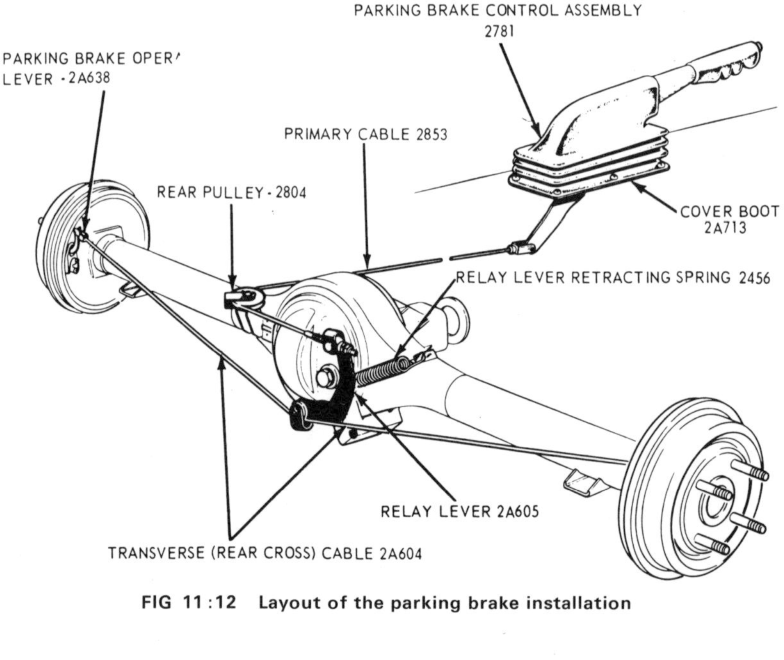

FIG 11:12 Layout of the parking brake installation

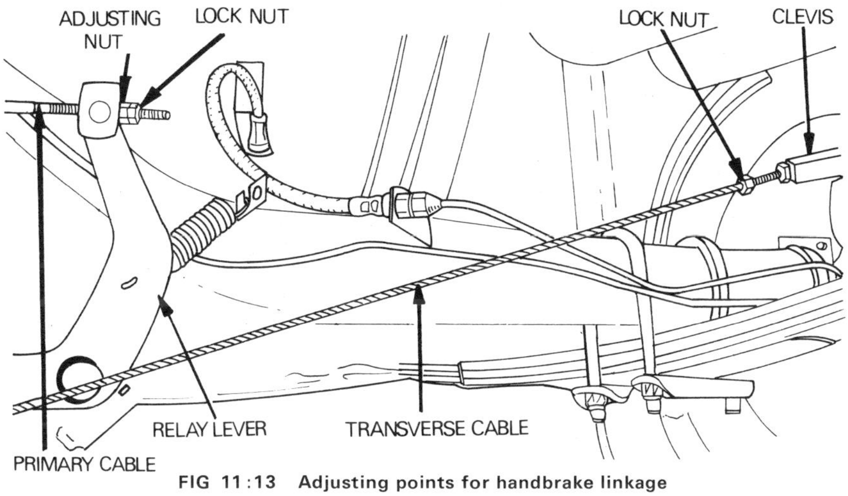

FIG 11:13 Adjusting points for handbrake linkage

11:9 The power brake booster

This item, also known as the vacuum servo unit, is mounted on the engine compartment bulkhead and is operated directly by the brake pedal at one end and drives the master cylinder at the other. As mentioned earlier, the booster and the master cylinder are replaced as a unit and the home operator is not advised to attempt any servicing on the booster, but to remove it in the event of failure and take it to his service station for attention or renewal.

Removal:

First detach the vacuum supply pipe from the unit and then the fluid pipes from the master cylinder, taking care to avoid fluid spillage or the entry of dirt into the open ends.

Remove the two retaining nuts and lift off the master cylinder, taking care not to damage the fluid seal.

Disconnect the clevis pin from the brake pedal and booster push rod and remove the two bolts securing the booster to the panel bracket. If desired, the bracket can be taken off with the booster and separated after removal from the car.

Fitting:

Fit the booster to its bracket with a new gasket and secure it to the panel. Connect the push rod to the brake pedal with the clevis pin and secure the pin.

Attach the master cylinder to the booster, using a new seal if the old one is in any way damaged, and tighten the two nuts.

Refit the hydraulic pipes to the master cylinder and the vacuum hose to the booster unit. Top up the reservoir and bleed the brake system as described in **Section 11:2**.

11:10 The parking brake

This is hand operated through a cable linkage by a lever mounted on the floor between the two front seats. It also incorporates a mechanism to actuate the self-adjusting devices in the rear brakes as and when necessary. The layout of the whole system is shown in **FIG 11:12**.

As mentioned, the wheel brake units are self-adjusting and this automatically maintains the setting for the parking brake also. If, after a long period of use, it is found that excessive travel on the hand lever is required to obtain satisfactory results and it is known that the brakes do not need new linings, the cause may be stretched brake cables.

Adjustment:

The mechanism for adjusting the linkage to compensate for cable wear is shown in **FIG 11:13** and is set as follows:

Jack up the rear of the car, chock up the front wheels and release the handbrake. Check that the primary cable follows its correct run and that all cables and guides are well lubricated.

First adjust the effective length of the primary cable by slackening the locknut on the end of the cable at the relay lever on the rear axle and turning the adjusting nut until the primary cable has no slack in it and the relay lever is just clear of the stop on the axle casing.

Next, the effective length of the transverse cable must be adjusted. Slacken the locknut on the end of the cable adjacent to the righthand wheel unit, check that the parking brake operating levers are fully back on the stops in the off position and then adjust so that there is no slack in the cable. Confirm that the operating levers are still against their stops and tighten the locknut.

Lower the car to the ground and remove the jacks.

Handbrake lever:

If it is necessary to remove this, proceed as follows after jacking up the front of the car and chocking the rear wheels.

Release the handbrake and remove the carpet around the brake lever.

Disconnect the primary cable from the end of the handbrake lever under the car by removing the spring clip and clevis pin.

Unscrew the six self-tapping screws and remove the rubber boot, then remove the two securing screws and lift out the handbrake lever assembly.

Replacement is a reversal of the above, after which the cable adjustment should be checked as described earlier. Ensure that all moving parts are well greased.

11:11 Pipe lines and flexible hoses

Metal pipe lines should be checked at regular intervals for corrosion or accidental damage and renewed if any fault is found. Stocks of pre-fabricated pipe lines are not carried by agents, but replacements are made up from lengths of tubing using the old pipe as a pattern. They are made from Bundy tubing with a wall thickness of .028 inch (.7 mm). Fuel type tubing must not be used as it is not capable of withstanding the much higher pressures used in the braking system.

Flexible hoses should also be inspected and renewed if there is any doubt about their condition. It is recommended that they are renewed after three years use, or 36,000 miles (60,000 km).

Never attempt to remove a flexible hose by turning either end with a spanner. The correct method which avoids strain and twisting the hose, is as follows:

Unscrew the metal pipe line union nut from its connection with the hose. Hold the adjacent hexagon on the hose with a spanner while unscrewing the locknut securing the hose to the bracket. The hose can now be turned without twisting the flexible portion by using a spanner on the hexagon at the other end.

11:12 Fault diagnosis

(a) 'Spongy' brake pedal

1 Leak in hydraulic system
2 Worn master cylinder
3 Leaking wheel cylinder
4 Air in the hydraulic circuit
5 Gaps between rear brakes shoes and linings

(b) Excessive pedal movement

1 Check 1 and 4 in (a)
2 Self-adjusting mechanism not operating
3 Very low fluid level in reservoir

(c) Brakes grab or pull to one side

1 Distorted or badly worn discs or drums
2 Wet or oily friction linings
3 Disc loose on hub
4 Worn suspension or steering connections
5 Mixed linings, wrong grade, differing thicknesses
6 Unequal tyre pressures
7 Broken shoe return springs
8 Wheel cylinder not free on backplate
9 Seized piston in one brake cylinder
10 Loose caliper mountings

(d) Excessive pedal pressure required

1 Defective servo unit
2 Leak in vacuum hose
3 Servo filter blocked
4 Wet brake linings
5 Incorrect friction lining material
6 Glazed linings or excessively worn
7 Defect in one hydraulic circuit

(e) Loss of pedal pressure

1 Defective master cylinder
2 Leaking wheel cylinder or booster unit
3 Leaking brake pipes or connections
4 Empty fluid reservoir

CHAPTER 12

THE ELECTRICAL SYSTEM

12:1 Description

The electrical system is 12 volt with the negative side of the battery earthed. Current is supplied by an alternator mounted on the righthand side of the engine and driven by the fan belt from the crankshaft pulley. A separate regulator of the non-adjustable type is used.

A Bosch starter is fitted to the German and USA models and is of the pre-engaged type in which an in-built solenoid engages the drive pinion with the starter ring gear before the main starting current is applied. A Lucas inertia type is fitted to the UK models.

A four lamp headlamp system is employed on the 2000 USA models in which all four lamps are illuminated for main beam, but only the dipped filaments in the two outer units for town driving or meeting oncoming traffic. All trim pack L, XL and GT models have rectangular headlamps.

The standard instrument layout consists of a speedometer and a combined fuel and temperature gauge cluster, all fed with a steady 5 volt supply from an instrument voltage regulator. There are also four warning lights for turn indicators (green), main headlamp beam (blue), charge condition (red) and oil pressure (amber). On GT models there is also a tachometer, odometer, trip meter, oil pressure gauge, and an electric clock. A battery condition indicator gauge is also included.

The wiring for the car's electrical services is mainly carried in three harnesses. The first includes the wiring from the various instruments and switches on the panel and is connected to the engine harness and the front lamp harness by means of multiple connectors. A further loom carries the wiring associated with the fuel tank gauge and the lights at the rear of the car.

In this chapter will be found details of several of the electrical components used in the car, but it is stressed that the instruments and equipment necessary for servicing and adjusting them correctly are unlikely to be available to the private owner and it may be more satisfactory and economical in time and money, to replace defective components with new or reconditioned units.

The following precautions must be observed when working on cars fitted with an alternator.

Strict polarity must be observed at all times when making any connections in the electrical circuit.

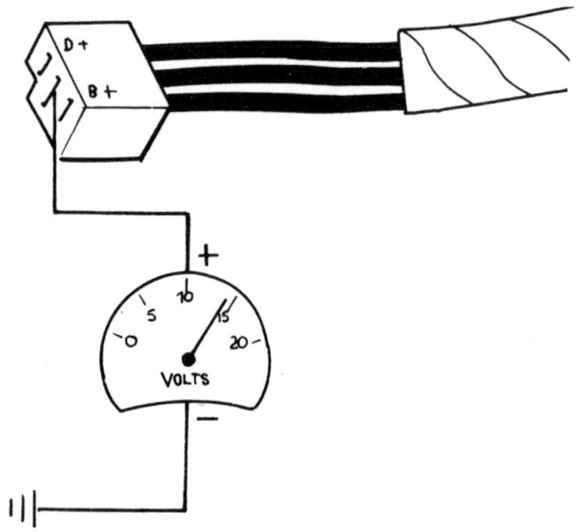

FIG 12:1 Alternator wiring continuity check

When refitting the battery, always connect the positive cable first and then the negative (ground) cable to the battery.

Never run the engine while the battery is disconnected, nor with the main alternator outout cable removed.

When arc welding on the car, always isolate the alternator by removing the moulded connectors.

12:2 The battery

In view of the importance of the battery in the operation of any automobile, its correct maintenance is of the first priority, particularly in winter when greater demands are made on the electrical system.

Maintenance:

Always keep the top of the battery clean and dry. If there are any signs of corrosion or acid split on the parts, the areas affected should be washed with a weak solution of ammonia.

A frequent cause of insufficient current to operate the starter motor is a high resistance joint on the battery terminals. These should be kept clean and smeared lightly with petroleum jelly before making the connection, which must be kept tight and also smeared over with vaseline.

At regular intervals the level of the electrolyte in the cells must be checked and if necessary topped up with distilled water to just above the tops of the plate separators.

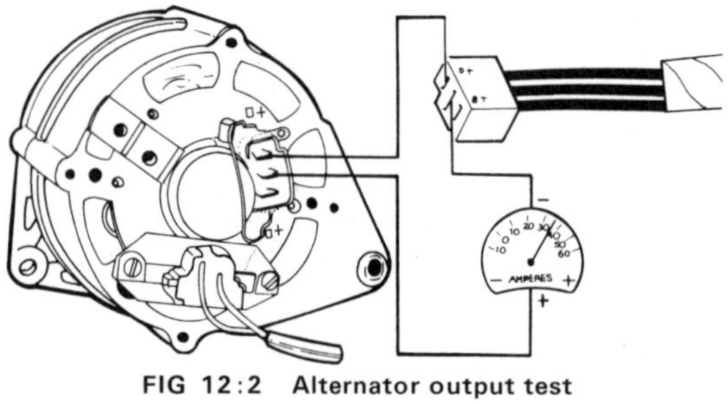

FIG 12:2 Alternator output test

Do not use neat acid to replace loss. If electrolyte is to be used for this purpose, it should be ready mixed to the correct specific gravity before use and remember: NEVER add water to acid, ALWAYS acid to water, when mixing, otherwise the resulting reaction may cause serious injury.

If the car is to stand idle for a long period or the battery removed for storage, the battery should be given a freshening change at about four weekly intervals, otherwise sulphation may occur and the battery ruined.

Testing:

Service stations have a number of instruments for battery testing, but the best method available to the owner driver is the specific gravity test made with a hydrometer.

The end of the hydrometer is inserted into each cell in turn and an adequate sample of electrolyte drawn up to enable the float to swim freely so that a reading may be taken.

Indications are as follows:

For climates below 32°C (90°F)

Cell fully charged	Specific gravity 1.270 to 1.290
Cell half charged	Specific gravity 1.190 to 1.210
Cell discharged	Specific gravity 1.110 to 1.130

Use electrolyte of 1.270 S.G. for topping up.

For climates above 32°C (90°F)

Cell fully charged	Specific gravity 1.210 to 1.230
Cell half charged	Specific gravity 1.130 to 1.150
Cell discharged	Specific gravity 1.050 to 1.070

Use electrolyte of 1.210 S.G. for topping up.

The above figures are given assuming a standard electrolyte temperature of 16°C (60°F). Convert the actual reading to standard by adding .002 for each 3°C (5°F) increase of actual electrolyte temperature above standard. Similarly, subtract .002 for each similar valve below the standard temperature.

If the readings are reasonably uniform the battery should be healthy, but if they are low, the need is shown for a bench charge or a long daylight run. If the readings are irregular with one or more cells .050 lower than the rest, the battery is no longer serviceable and should be renewed.

12:3 The alternator

The alternator is mounted low down on the righthand side of the engine and driven at 1.88 times engine speed by the fan belt. If there is any serious fault in the alternator the owner is advised to take it to the service station for repair or replacement but there are a few simple tests he may wish to make himself to locate the trouble before removing the machine from the car.

Continuity test:

Disconnect the terminal plug from the rear of the alternator and connect a voltmeter negative lead to ground.

With the ignition switched ON, connect the voltmeter positive lead to each of the connector wires in turn as shown in **FIG 12:1**.

In each case the voltmeter should show full battery voltage. If it does not do so, trace each wire to locate the fault.

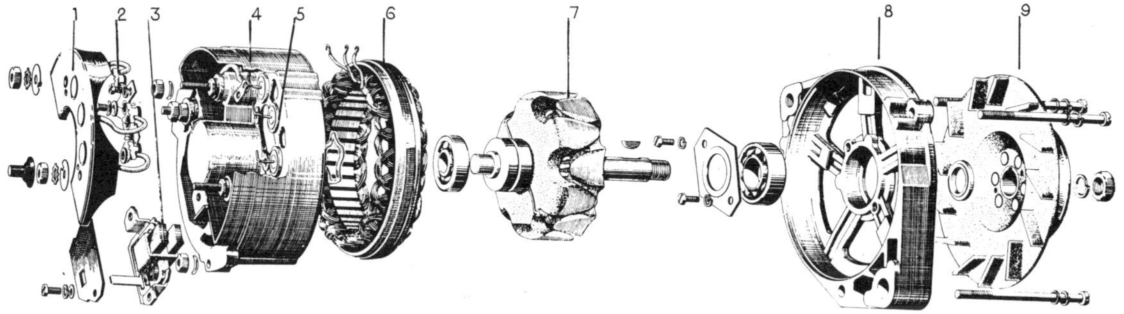

FIG 12:3 Components of a Bosch alternator

Key to Fig 12:3 1 Rectifier and diode plate 2 Magnetizing rectifier 3 Brush holder 4 Slip ring end shield 5 Rectifier 6 Stator 7 Rotor 8 Drive end shield 9 Fan and pulley

Voltage drop test:

Connect the voltmeter between the negative terminal of the battery and the alternator housing.

Start the engine and run it at about 300 rev/min. If the voltmeter reading exceeds .25 volts, a high resistance in the negative side of the charging circuit is indicated.

In this event, check for loose, dirty or corroded connections and rectify them.

Output test:

Disconnect the terminal plug from the alternator and connect an ammeter in series between the centre connector terminal on the alternator and the corresponding socket on the plug.

Connect also a wire between the alternator D+ terminal and its corresponding socket on the connector plug. See **FIG 12:2**.

Start the engine and run it at 3000 rev/min, giving an alternator speed of approximately 6000 rev/min. Switch on the headlamps and leave on for about 5 minutes.

The ammeter should give a reading of 35 amps at normal operating temperature.

Regulator control voltage check:

Connect a voltmeter across the battery terminals and an ammeter in series between the B+ terminals on the alternator and the corresponding terminal on the connector plug. Connect also a lead between the alternator D+ terminal and the corresponding terminal on the connector plug.

Run the engine at 3000 rev/min until the indicated charging rate drops below 10 amps. The voltmeter should then read between 14.1 and 14.4 volts.

If these readings cannot be obtained the regulator is faulty and must be renewed.

12:4 Removing the alternator

Disconnect the battery ground cable. Disconnect the clip securing the plug connector to the rear of the alternator and pull out the plug.

Disconnect the wiring from the regulator at the alternator.

Disconnect the heater hose bracket from the alternator.

Loosen the three mounting bolts and swing the alternator in towards the engine so that the driving belt may be removed.

Pull out the mounting bolts and lift off the alternator from the engine.

Refitting is a reversal of the above procedure, noting that the fan belt should be tensioned to give $\frac{1}{2}$ inch free movement at a point mid-way between the alternator and the fan pulley.

12:5 Dismantling the alternator

The alternator is a component for which professional attention is advised, but the following information is given for those who may feel competent to carry out the work at home. Refer to **FIG 12:3** which shows the components of a typical Bosch alternator.

1a (Bosch) Remove the brush and connector plug assembly (see **FIG 12:4**) from the rear housing and mark the front and rear housings to ensure correct alignment when assembling.

1b (Lucas) Remove two screws securing the rear plastic cover. Make a note of the connections and disconnect the leads from the regulator to the brush gear. Remove two screws and take off the regulator.

2 (Both) Undo the pulley retaining nut and remove the lockwasher, pulley and fan. Extract the key from the rotor shaft.

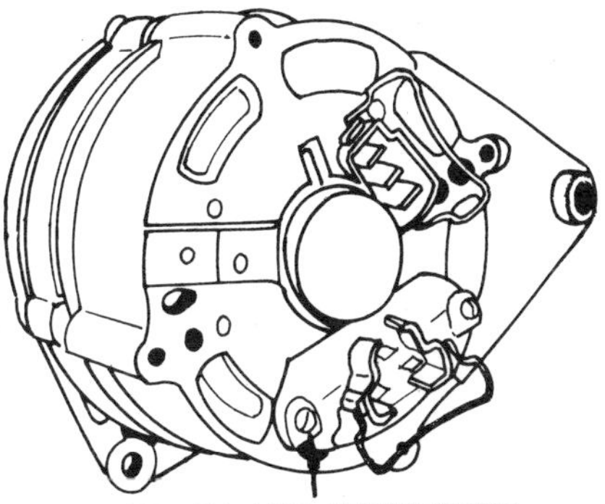

FIG 12:4 Brush and connector plug assembly

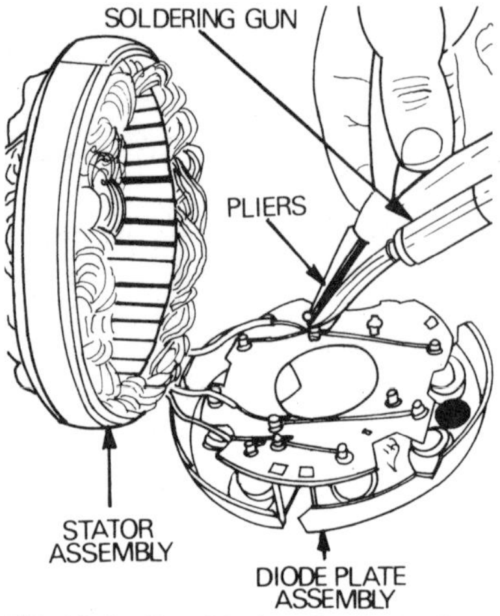

FIG 12:5 Unsoldering the diode plate

3a (Bosch) Remove four bolts holding the two housings together and pull off the front housing complete with rotor.

3b (Lucas) Remove lead connecting brush gear to rectifier pack and then the two screws securing the brushgear. Lift off the brushgear.

4a (Bosch) Press out the rotor and shaft assembly and remove the front retainer ring from the front housing and the rear spacer from the rotor shaft. The front bearing may be removed if required by taking out the securing screws and removing the bearing retainer plate. Use a puller to extract the bearing.

4b (Lucas) Unscrew and withdraw the three through bolts, press the drive end bracket off the rotor shaft and retrieve the spacer. Remove the circlip securing the bearing in the bracket and press the bearing out. Retain the grease seals.

5a (Bosch) If it is necessary to remove the diode plate, remove the four screws which will release both stator and diode plate. Retrieve the waved washer in the bore of the rear housing.

5b (Lucas) Loosen the nut securing the rectifier pack and if necessary unsolder the leads on the rectifier pack using a pair of long nosed pliers to act as a heat sink. Note the connections.

6a (Bosch) If necessary, unsolder the three wires from the diodes using a pair of long nosed pliers as described in item 5b (see also **FIG 12:5**).

6b (Lucas) To separate the slip ring end bracket from the rotor, slide a 3 inch long metal sleeve over the slip ring moulding, to engage the outer ring of the bearing and drive it out. If necessary unsolder the field winding connections from the slip ring moulding. Slide off the moulding and the bearing. Carefully prise the stator out of the end bracket.

7 (Both) Clean and inspect all components, renewing any worn or damaged bearings. The carbon brushes should be renewed if they are less than .2 inch (5 mm) in length and care taken to see that new brushes slide easily in their holders. The brush springs may be checked for tension which should be 10.6 to 14.1 oz (300 to 400 g) on the Bosch and 7 to 10 oz (198 to 283 g) on the Lucas.

Testing:

Test the rotor windings for a short circuit by connecting an ohmeter between the two slip rings. The resistance indicated should be 3.4 to 3.74 ohms.

Test the rotor insulation with a test lamp (less than 40 volts), by placing one lead on a slip ring and the other on the rotor shaft. The test lamp should not illuminate.

Test the stator windings for short circuit by connecting any two of the three stator wires in series with an ohmmeter. Repeat the test with the third wire. Resistance should be .25 to .275 ohms at 68°F.

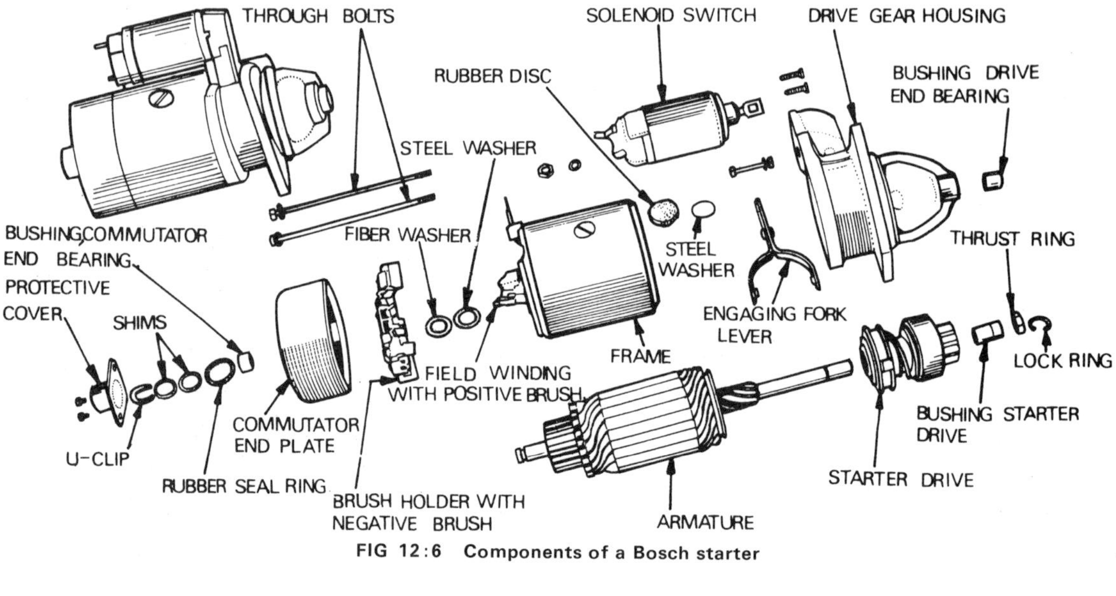

FIG 12:6 Components of a Bosch starter

Test the stator windings for earthing with the test lamp rig. Place one test lead on the housing and the other in turn with the three winding ends. The lamp should not light up.

Stator continuity is tested by placing the test lamp rig across any two of the three wiring ends and then again using the third wire in place of one of the first two tested. The lamp should light in each case.

Test the diodes with a 1.5 watt test bulb and a 12 volt supply across each diode in turn. Reverse the connections to the diode and note that the lamp should light in one direction only. If the bulb lights in both tests or not in either the diode is faulty. If any one diode is faulty the entire diode plate assembly must be renewed.

Reassembling:

1a (Bosch) Resolder the starter wires to the diodes and fit the stator/diode assembly into the rear housing and retain with the four screws.

1b (Lucas) Replace stator in slip ring end bracket ensuring that the slots in the stator line up with the bolt holes.

2 (Both) Grease the rear bearing and press it onto the rotor shaft with the shielded side of the bearing towards the slip ring.

3a (Bosch) Fit the front bearing in the front housing with its shielded side forward. Fit the retainer plate.

3b (Lucas) Re-engage the slip ring moulding with the slot in the rotor shaft. Resolder the field to the slip rings.

4a (Bosch) Place the spacer ring on the rotor shaft and fix the rotor into the front housing. Place the front bearing retainer ring on the rotor shaft and press into the front housing.

4b (Lucas) Press the bearing into the slip ring bracket and replace the inner grease seal in the drive end bracket. Grease the bearing and press it into the bracket. Refit the outer grease seal and the circlip. Press the bracket onto the rotor shaft and secure with through bolts.

5a (Bosch) Coat the bore of the rear housing with grease and fit the waved washer. Fit the front housing, with the rotor, onto the rear housing aligning the marks made earlier and install the four bolts.

5b (Lucas) Replace and solder the leads to the rectifier pack (use long nosed pliers). Tighten the nut which secures the rectifier pack to the alternator. Refit the brush gear and secure with the two screws. Reconnect the brush gear to the rectifier pack. Refit the regulator and reconnect the leads to the brush gear. Refit the plastic cover.

6 (Both) Position the key in the rotor shaft and fit the fan pulley, lockwasher and nut. Tighten to 25-29 lb ft (3 to 4 kgm).

12:6 The starter motor

Bosch:

This is a pre-engaged type in which the drive pinion is engaged with the starter ring gear before the drive shaft starts to rotate. An exploded view of the component parts is shown in **FIG 12:6** and any maintenance will be similar to that required for any other electric motor.

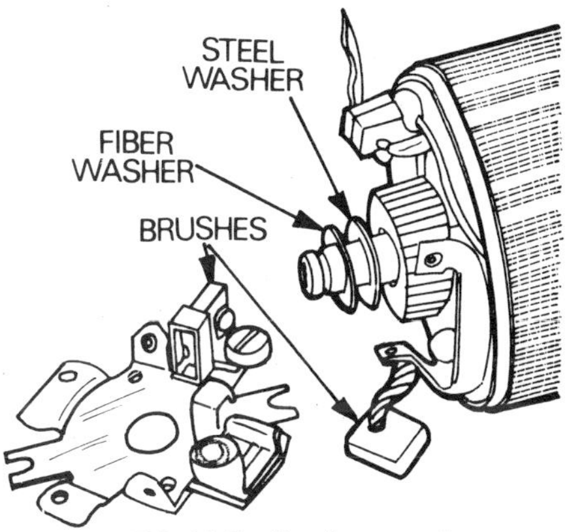

FIG 12:7 Brush removal

Removal:

Disconnect the battery ground cable and also the cables from the starter solenoid switch.

Remove the three mounting bolts and lift off the starter.

Fitting is the reverse of the above after cleaning and checking the ring gear and pinion for wear.

Dismantling:

Disconnect the field winding cable from the solenoid, unscrew the solenoid retaining screws and lift off.

Unscrew the two screws and remove the small protective cover, U clip, spacer washers and rubber gasket ring.

Remove the through bolts and the rear end plate.

Use a wire hook to pull the brushes out of their holder, then remove the brush holder, fibre and steel washers as shown in **FIG 12:7**.

Withdraw the housing from the drive end, unscrew the engaging lever guide screw, remove the rubber and steel washers from the drive end frame and then remove the armature complete with the engaging lever out of the frame.

Use a sleeve to push the thrust ring inwards towards the pinion and remove the lock ring with a pair of suitable pliers.

Check the groove in the armature shaft and remove any roughness with a very fine file. Pull off the thrust ring and pinion.

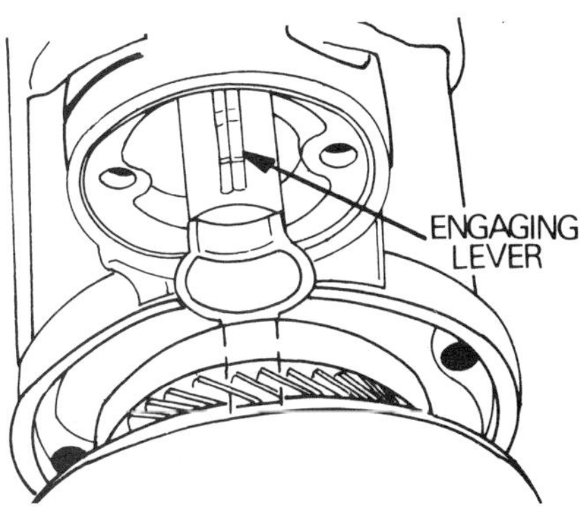

FIG 12:8 Fitting the engaging lever and armature

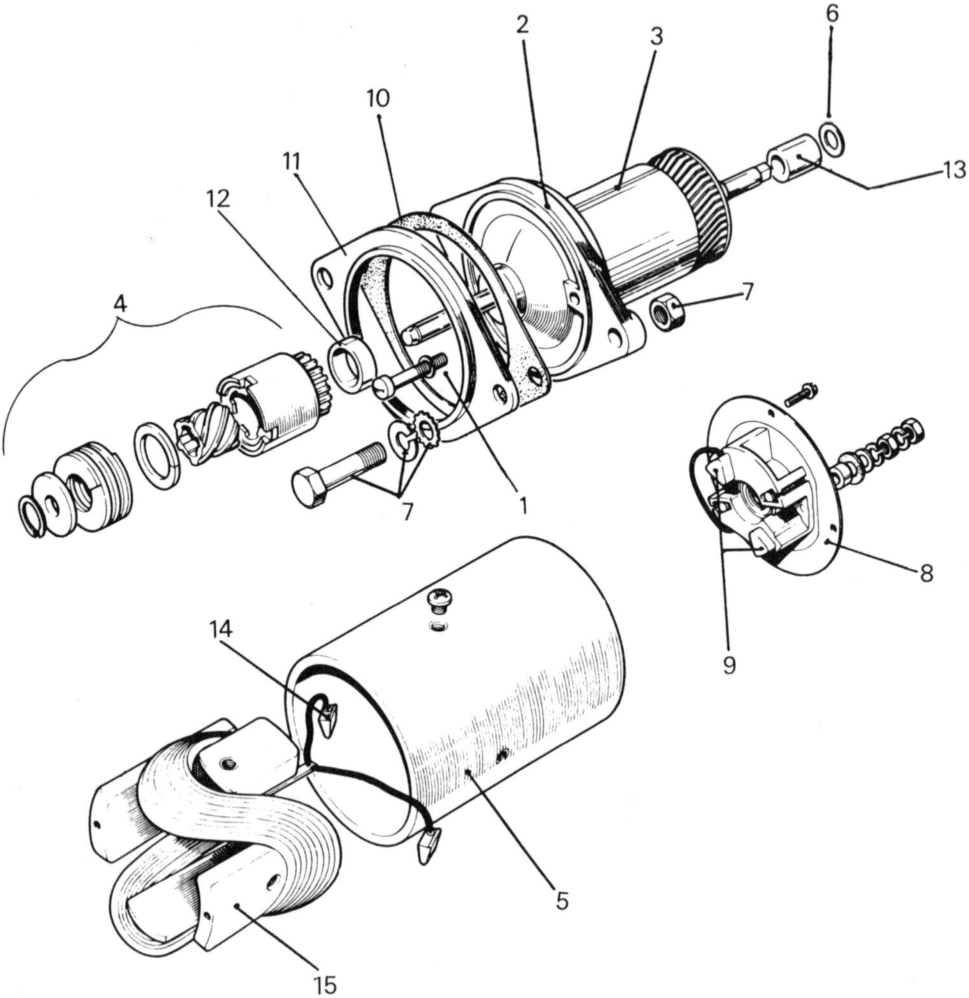

FIG 12:9 Components of starter motor

Key to Fig 12:9 1 Slot-headed bolts 2 Drive-end bracket 3 Armature 4 Inertia drive assembly 5 Yoke 6 Thrust washer 7 Mounting bolts 8 Commutator end bracket 9 Brush 10 Shim 11 Packing 12 Bush 13 Bush 14 Brush 15 Field coil

After cleaning all the parts, replace any that show excess wear or damage and allow any bushings to soak in oil until required. This will impregnate the porous metal to provide its self lubricating properties.

The four carbon brushes should be examined at this time and measured for length. The minimum dimension is .375 inch and the brushes should be renewed if any are worn down to this figure. Check also that the brush springs have a pressure of 42.3 oz, and that the brushes are able to move freely in their bores. If they are not, a fine file may be used to obtain the necessary clearance.

Reassembly:

Smear some silicon grease on the coarse thread of the armature shaft and the engaging ring of the drive gear, and then slide the drive gear, stop ring and snap ring onto the armature shaft.

Press the snap ring into the groove on the armature shaft, then press on the stop ring against the snap ring using a press or claw puller.

Position the engaging lever onto the engaging ring and insert into the drive end plate together with the armature. See **FIG 12:8**. Attach the engaging lever with the guide screw.

Fit the steel washer into the drive end plate and then the rubber washer with the tab pointing towards the armature. Install the housing and place in the rubber washer. Slide the steel and fibre washers onto the armature shaft.

Place the brush holder in position and, using a wire hook, lift up the springs and insert the carbon brushes.

Mount the rear end plate and position the insulator rubber, then fit the rubber washer, shims and U clip. Fit the protective cover and secure with its two screws.

Fit and tighten the through bolts and then check the armature shaft end play. This should be between .004 and .012 inch and may be corrected by using shims if necessary.

Couple up the solenoid to the engaging lever and secure with the two mounting screws. Connect the field winding cable.

Seal all joints and screw heads with lacquer and check the starter operation.

Lucas:

A Lucas, series wound, four brush motor with an extended shaft carrying an inertia drive, is fitted to the British OHC models. The armature shaft rotates in two porous bronze bushes, one end of the shaft is squared and protrudes from the commutator drive end to accept a spanner fitting so that it can be turned to clear any jamming. A face-type moulded commutator is a feature of this type, which means the four brushes bear on the end face of the commutator rather than the perimeter.

A plastic brushbox is riveted to the commutator end bracket which holds four wedge-shaped brushes and captive coil springs. The brushes are keyed to ensure a correct fitting.

The field winding is a continuously wound strip with no joints. One end is attached to two brush flexibles and the other end is earthed to the yoke or body.

The yoke has no inspection windows, which means the starter will have to be removed to check the brush gear. There are no through bolts, instead, the commutator end bracket is held by four screws and the drive end bracket is attached by two slot-headed bolts. The tappings for the screws and bolts are in the yoke.

Removing the starter:

1 Disconnect the battery and the single lead from the terminal post on the starter.

2 Note the position of the starter, shims if fitted and the packing in relation to the clutch housing.

3 Jack up the front of the car and support with safety stands. From above the engine remove the upper mounting bolt and nut. Working below the engine remove the lower mounting bolt and nut, support the starter and withdraw it downwards complete with packing and shims if fitted.

Dismantling, reassembling starter

1 Refer to **FIG 12:9** and remove the two slot-headed bolts 1 and spring washers. Withdraw the drive end bracket 2, armature 3 and the inertia drive assembly 4 from the yoke 5. Take off the thrust washer 6.

2 Unscrew the four 4BA bolts and lift off the commutator end bracket 8, take the two field winding brushes 9 out of their holders.

3 To separate the armature 3 from the drive end bracket 2, the inertia drive assembly 4 must first be removed.

Removing inertia drive:

4 Refer to **FIG 12:10** and using a suitable hand press, compress the spring 3 and ease the jump ring 1 off the shaft. For information, a special tool and adaptor are used to compress the spring.

5 Withdraw the components from the shaft.

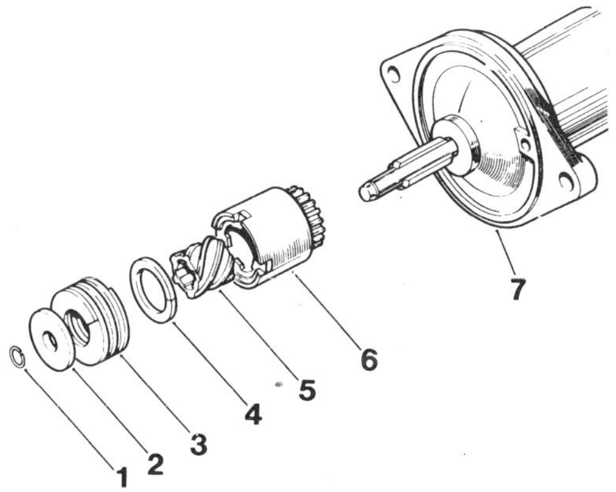

FIG 12:10 Components of inertia drive

Key to Fig 12:10 1 Jump ring 2 Collar 3 Spring 4 Washer 5 Sleeve 6 Pinion and barrel 7 Drive end bracket

Inspecting:

The brushes:

6 Renew the brushes if they are near or less than .375 inch (9.53 mm) in length.

Clean the brushes and the brush box with a petrol moistened cloth, check that the brushes move freely in the brush box by holding the flexibles and sliding the brushes backwards and forwards in their housings. If the brushes stick, polish their sides with a fine file. Examine the springs and test the spring pressure, this should be done with a new brush as follows. Position the brush so that the top protrudes .06 inch (1.5 mm) above the brush box, obtain a spring balance and push down on the brush and spring. The spring pressure should be 28 oz (800 grams). Repeat the test on the remaining three springs, if the pressure is low on any of the springs, renew the commutator end bracket. The springs are not supplied separately as a service item.

To change old brushes for new ones and dealing first with the two brushes attached to the terminal end post on the commutator bracket, brushes are supplied attached to a new terminal post. Remove the outer attachments on the terminal post, withdraw the terminal post and take off the insulation piece. When assembling the new ones, retain the longer flexible under the clip.

The field winding brushes are supplied attached to a common flexible. Severe the old flexibles .25 inch (6 mm) from the joint. Solder the new flexibles to the ends of the old flexibles. Do not try to solder direct to the field winding strip, it may be manufactured from aluminium.

The commutator and armature:

7 Inspect the armature laminations for score marks. These marks will indicate either a bent shaft, worn bearings or a loose pole shoe. If the shaft is bent (this can be checked by using a dial gauge with the armature mounted between centre stocks) renew the armature complete. Worn bearings can be renewed be referring to operation 8. Loose pole screws

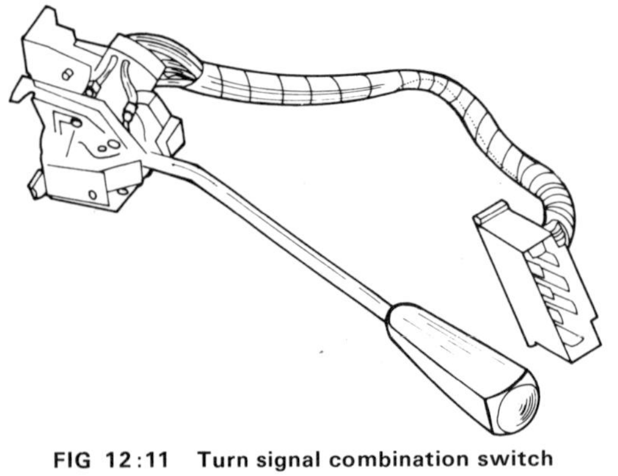

FIG 12:11 Turn signal combination switch

must be tightened with a wheel type screwdriver, if this tool is unobtainable consult your service garage.

Clean the commutator with a petrol moistened cloth, its condition should be smooth and without pits or burnt spots. If not, skim the commutator by mounting it in a lathe, use a high speed and a sharp tool. Take only a light cut each time and do not exceed a minimum commutator thickness of .080 inch (2.03 mm). Polish the skimmed surface with fine glass-paper, not emerycloth, and do not undercut the insulators between the segments. Clean with a petrol moistened cloth.

The bronze bush bearings:

8 To renew the commutator end bracket bush, drill out the two rivets which retain a plate and felt seal around the bearing orifice. Scrap the plate and seal and obtain new ones complete with rivets. Screw a $\frac{1}{2}$ inch tap into the bush to withdraw it. A new bush should be immersed in thin oil for a period of 24 hours before it is fitted. Using a highly polished shouldered mandrel with the spigot end a clearance fit in the bush, press the new bush into the end bracket. Do not ream the bush after fitting otherwise the porosity may be impaired. Fit the new felt seal and plate and secure with the rivets.

Renew the drive end bracket bush using the same method. Instead of using a tap, the bush can be pressed out of the bracket.

FIG 12:12 Fitting a headlight bulb

Field windings:

9 Checking the field windings in the yoke requires a 110-volt AC test lamp circuit. This type of test should be a job for your service garage or a Lucas agency. If there is a fault, renewing the field windings requires a special wheel-type screwdriver to loosen and tighten the securing screws.

The inertia drive:

10 Refer to **FIG 12:10** and inspect the parts for wear. Renew the sleeve 5 and pinion 6 as a pair, not individually, if either one is suspect. Before assembling, lightly lubricate the bronze bush in the drive end bracket. Assemble the parts in the order shown in the illustration. Don't use oil or grease on the splines or the components, otherwise dirt and grit will stick to the rubbing surfaces and promote rapid wear.

Reassembling:

11 Reassemble the remaining components in the reverse order of dismantling, operations 1 and 2.

12:7 The headlights

Four headlights are fitted to USA 2000 cars, using sealed beam units. On main, or high, beam all four lights are used, but on dip only the low beam filament of the outboard units is in operation.

The numeral 2 is moulded in the glass lens of the outboard units, which also have locating tabs moulded in the glass to permit their mounting in the outboard position only. The single filament (No. 1) units also have tabs moulded in the glass to allow their mounting only in the inboard support frames.

All other OHC models have two rectangular headlamps of the semi-sealed beam type.

The headlight dipper switch, which is incorporated with the turn indicator switch and horn button, is shown in **FIG 12:11** and is mounted on the steering column. The switch in the USA 2000 model is on the left of the instrument panel has three positions for OFF, headlights and parking, tail and marker lights. The European models have ON:OFF press switches to operate the head and side lights.

Removal (Circular):

Disconnect the battery ground cable.

Remove the four screws securing the headlight bezel and lift it off.

Slacken the three retaining screws turn the lamp anti-clockwise and lift out the sealed beam unit as shown in **FIG 12:12**.

Disconnect the wiring plug from the rear of the unit.

The lamp is refitted in the reverse order and the beam setting adjusted if necessary.

Rectangular:

1 Open the bonnet and disconnect the battery.
2 From above the headlamp remove the single crosshead screw from the retaining clip.
3 Depress the clip, gently pull the headlamp forward and lift out.

4 Disconnect the mult-plug at the rear of the lamp or the side light bulb. Remove the rubber grommet, disengage and remove the bulb retaining spring and lift the bulb out of the reflector.
5 Fit a new bulb and assemble in the reverse order.
6 If it is necessary, due to other faults, to separate the surround from the lamp assembly remove the four screws.

Beam setting:

This should preferably be carried out using an optical aiming instrument, but if this is not available the following procedure should give satisfactory results.

With the car at normal curb weight and the tyres correctly inflated, position it square on to a wall at a distance of 10 feet (3 m) and mark on the wall a vertical line as shown in **FIG 12:13**, corresponding to the centre line of the car and a horizontal line parallel to the ground at a height equal to the height of the headlight centres minus $\frac{1}{2}$ inch (12.7 mm).

Remove each headlight outer bezel and switch on the headlights.

By means of the horizontal and vertical adjusting screws, adjust each lamp so that the centres of brightest illumination lie on the horizontal aiming line 43.2 inch (109.7 cm) apart and equidistant from the centre line.

Switch off the lights and refit the bezels.

12:8 Service lights

Front parking and turn indicator light (USA model):

To replace a lens and/or bulb, remove the two cross headed screws and remove the glass.

To remove the lamp assembly, first remove the radiator opening panel (5 screws) and then remove the bulb socket and the two lamp body retaining nuts.

European:

To renew the turn indicator bulb refer to the USA model.

To remove the lamp assembly, unscrew and remove the two screws securing the lamp to the bumper. Disconnect the feed wire.

Rear, stop and turn indicator lights:

Access to these is from inside the luggage compartment and the units are secured by two or four retaining nuts. Pull off the rear light trim cover or shroud and pull out the spring loaded bulb holders.

Marker light—front (USA 2000):

From behind the front fender remove the two securing nuts and pull off the unit, pull back the rubber boot over the bulb holder, turn the holder a little anti-clockwise and pull out. See **FIG 12:14**.

Marker light—rear (USA 2000):

Access to this is from inside the luggage compartment.

Remove two nuts and lift off the lamp protective bracket, hold the lamp body and turn the bulb holder slightly anti-clockwise to remove. The bulb is pulled straight out of the holder.

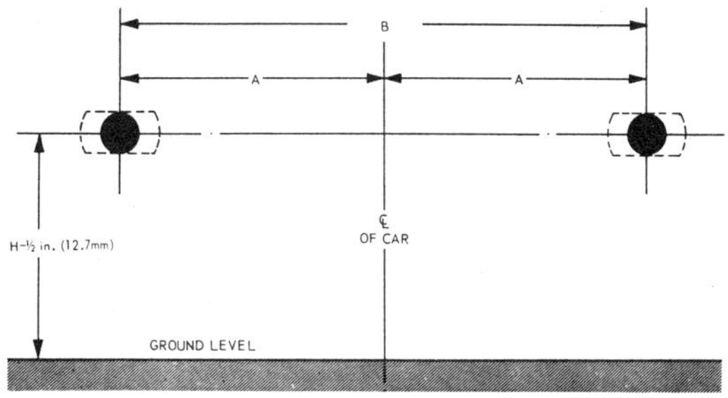

FIG 12:13 Headlight alignment diagram

Key to Fig 12:13 H=Centre of headlight height from ground B=43.2 inch (108.7 cm) A=21.6 inch (54.85 cm)

License light:

This is mounted in the rear bumper and the battery should be disconnected before removing the lamp.

Disconnect the ground and feed cables inside the luggage trunk and pull the wires through the hole in the floor.

From underneath the bumper press the two retaining levers inwards (see **FIG 12:15**) and pull out the lamp body. Remove the bulb from the assembly.

Replacement is carried out in the reverse order, but do not forget the sealing grommet when passing the wires through the trunk floor.

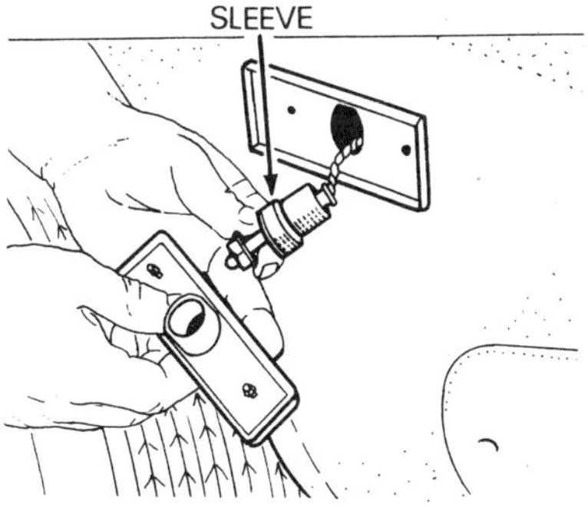

FIG 12:14 Side marker light—front

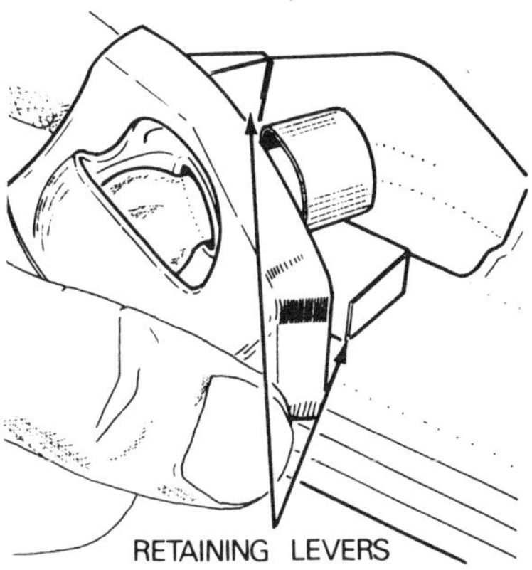

FIG 12:15 Licence plate light

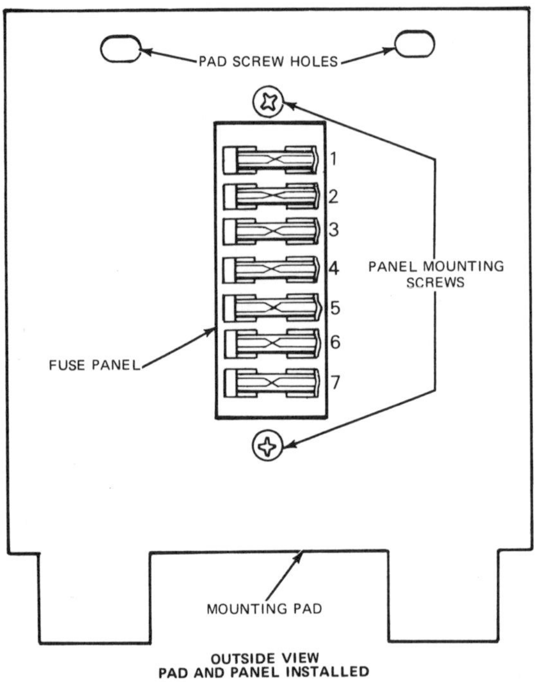

FIG 12:16 The fuse panel

Key to Fig 12:16 1 (8 amp) Interior lights, cigar lighter, hazard flasher 2 (8 amp) Left side marker lights, left tail light, instrument panel illumination bulbs 3 (8 amp) Right side marker lights, right tail light, licence plate light 4 (8 amp) Headlights—high beam 5 (8 amp) Headlights—low beam 6 (8 amp) Stop lights, heater, turn signal, gauges and back up lights 7 (8 amp) Windshield wiper

Back-up light (USA 2000):

To replace the bulb, simply undo the lens retaining screws and lift off.

The angular bracket for the back-up light switch is mounted on the gearshift housing and is adjusted as follows:

Loosen the mounting screw and move the gearshift lever into reverse, then move the switch towards the lever until the back-up lights illuminate and then tighten the screw.

12:9 Fuses

The fuse panel may be mounted either on top of the side panel in the engine compartment or to the lower righthand edge of the instrument panel. On early cars the fuse panel contained six fuses of 8 amps, later cars have 7 fuses. A typical installation is shown in **FIG 12:16**.

To obtain access to the fuses it is only necessary to snap off the transparent cover.

12:10 Windshield wipers

The two-speed wiper system is shown in **FIG 12:17**. This is supplemented by a washer system, that is either electrically operated or the footpump which is located on the floor adjacent to the left side trim panel. Exerting a steady pressure on the pump will cause both washer and wiper to operate together. A light pressure on the pump operates just the wipers, while just tapping the pump lightly moves the wipers through one cycle.

Removing the motor:

Disconnect the battery. Remove the two wiper arms and the nuts securing the wiper pivots to the body.

Remove the front parcel tray and the hose from the heater to the windshield defroster vent.

Disconnect the two control cables from the heater and the wiper wires, noting their positions carefully.

Remove the screws securing the motor to its mounting bracket and lift off the motor assembly.

Refitting:

Hold the motor in position behind the instrument panel and secure it to the body with the two wiper pivot nuts.

Reconnect the motor wiring, position the motor and fit the mounting screws.

Reconnect the two heater control cables and complete the operation by reversing the removal procedure.

The linkage:

Carefully prise the short wiper link off the motor output arm and remove the plastic pivot bush.

Separate the motor from the linkage by removing the three securing screws.

Carefully prise the long wiper link from the two plastic pivot bushings which hold the link to the pivots and remove the long link and the bushings.

Prise the short wiper link from the plastic bushing at the lefthand wiper pivot and remove the bushing and spring washer.

Remove two snap rings securing the pivots to the main link frame and remove both pivots.

When reassembling, position both wiper pivots in the main frame and secure with a snap ring.

Fit the spring washer and plastic bush to the lefthand pivot and then fit the short link.

Fit the long link plastic bushes to the pivots and fit the long link. Attach the motor to the linkage.

12:11 Turn signals and hazard flasher

The turn signal switch is incorporated with the headlight dipper switch and is shown in **FIG 12:11**. The turn signals operate only when the ignition is switched on.

The hazard flasher switch in the 2000 USA model is mounted on the right of the instrument panel and when switched on causes all four of the turn signals to operate simultaneously as a warning to other traffic. The indicator light is to the right of the standard instrument cluster or next to the headlight switch on GT models.

Removing the turn signal switch:

Disconnect the battery.

Disconnect the bolts securing the steering column to the underside of the instrument panel and lower the column.

Remove the steering column shrouds by taking out the two retaining screws. Remove the two screws securing the switch to the column. Disconnect the multi-pin plug and remove the switch.

Refit the switch in the reverse order.

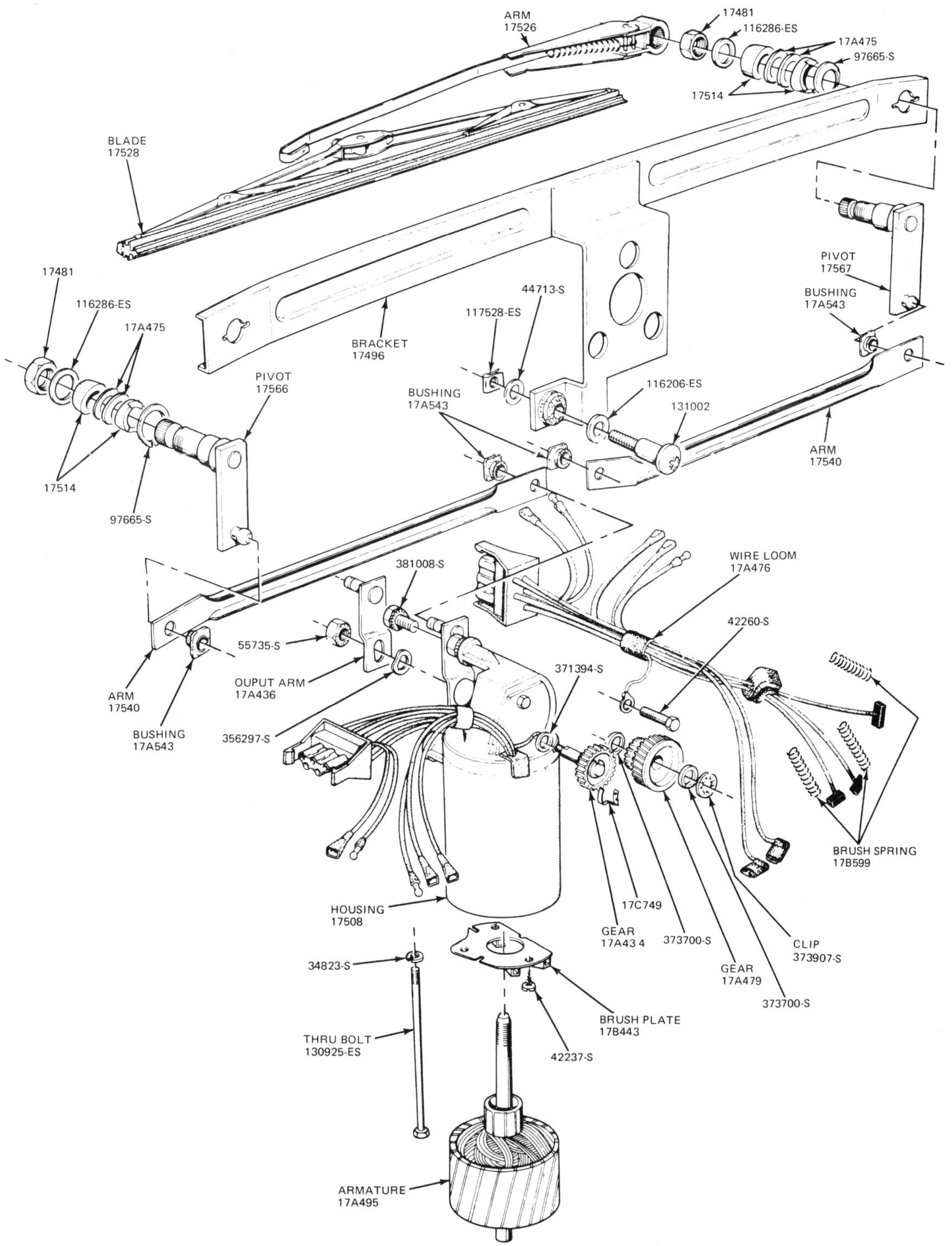

FIG 12:17 Components of the windshield wiper system

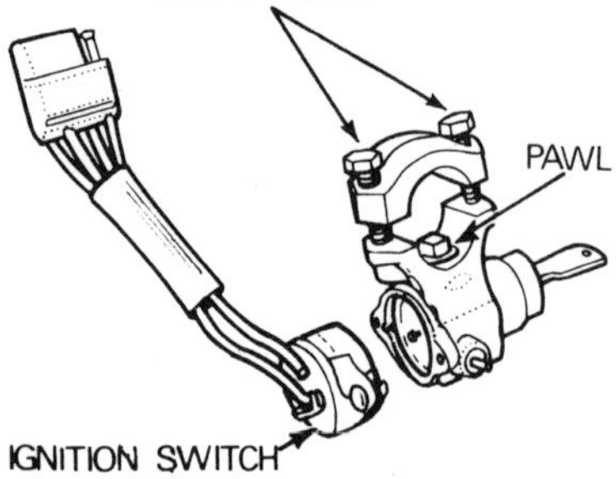

FIG 12:18 Ignition and steering lock

12:12 Ignition switch and steering lock (2000 USA model):

This anti-theft device has four positions: Lock (0), Accessories (I), Ignition (II) and Start (III). The steering is locked by removing the key at the lock position when a pawl is released and, with a slight rotation of the steering wheel, enters a recess in the steering shaft to prevent any further movement. To unlock the shaft, push the key in and turn to the accessories position.

At (II) the ignition is switched on and the starter operates when the key is moved to (III). If the engine does not start the key must be returned to the off or accessory position before the starter can be operated again. This prevents operation of the starter while the engine is running.

A buzzer mounted on the steering column bracket will sound if the drivers door is opened while the key is in any position in the lock.

Removal. Ignition switch:

Disconnect the battery and remove the steering column shroud.

Turn the ignition key to the 0 position. Mark the leads to the switch and disconnect them.

Remove the two securing screws and withdraw the switch from the lock.

Fitting is the reverse of the above, but make sure that the key remains in the 0 position and is the right way up.

Steering lock:

After removing the steering column shroud, remove the upper screws retaining the steering column and turn the column to gain access to the headless bolts.

Disconnect the leads from the ignition switch and lock body, being careful to note their respective positions.

Drill out or use an extractor to remove the headless bolts and lift away the lock assembly.

To refit, position the new lock assembly, with the key in the lock, to the steering column and withdraw the lock to allow the pawl to enter the steering shaft. See **FIG 12:18**.

Place the half clamp in position and tighten the shear bolts evenly until the heads shear off. Check for free operation of the pawl while tightening the bolts.

Reconnect all the leads to their respective terminals then turn the steering column back to its correct position and replace the screws securing the column and the shroud. Reconnect the battery cable.

12:13 The instrument clusters

Standard LH Steer:

The components of the standard instrument panel cluster, LH steer, are shown in **FIG 12:19** and the procedure for its removal are as follows:

Disconnect the battery. Remove the two bolts securing the steering column to the underside of the dashboard and lower the column.

Remove the five crossheaded screws securing the cluster and pad assembly to the instrument panel, then pull the cluster carefully back sufficiently to gain access to the connections at the rear of the panel. Disconnect the cable connections at the rear of the gauges and switches and also the speedometer drive cable.

The cluster and pad assembly may now be removed from the car and separated by taking out the four cluster-to-pad attaching screws.

G.T. models LH steer. (See FIG 12:20):

The procedure here is similar to that for standard LH steer models, but the two heater control knobs must be removed and also the access cover at the righthand side of the instrument panel by taking out four screws.

Remove three screws and loosen only one nut retaining the cluster and pad assembly to the instrument panel. Release the fuse panel (two screws) and then pull the assembly forward to disconnect all the connections at the rear, being careful not be bend the tube to the oil pressure gauge.

Refitting the instrument cluster is a reversal of the removal procedure.

Reference to the two exploded illustrations should facilitate any further dismantling which may be required.

Control panel RH steer:

The control panel and instrument cluster illustrations of the LH steer are instrumentally identical except that they are positioned the other way round. Removal is very similar in both cases.

1. Open the bonnet and disconnect the battery.
2. Remove two screws and remove the lower half of the steering column shroud. The upper shroud is secured by a pin moulded into the assembly. Push the shroud upwards to remove it.
3. Remove eight screws from the underside panel and after easing over the ignition switch, allow it to hang down.
4. If a radio is fitted pull off the two control knobs.
5. Remove three screws, disconnect the switch multplug(s) and detach the facia frame. Remove four screws and ease the cluster forward from its location.
6. Disconnect the speedometer cable, loom, multiplug and oil pressure gauge feed pipe to detach the cluster assembly.

12:14 The heating system

The components of the heating and ventilation system are shown in **FIG 12:21**. Fresh air is drawn in the way of a grille in front of the windshield and, by suitably positioning the two control levers, can be directed in varying ratios to the windshield or the car interior and can either be heated or allowed to pass directly into the interior.

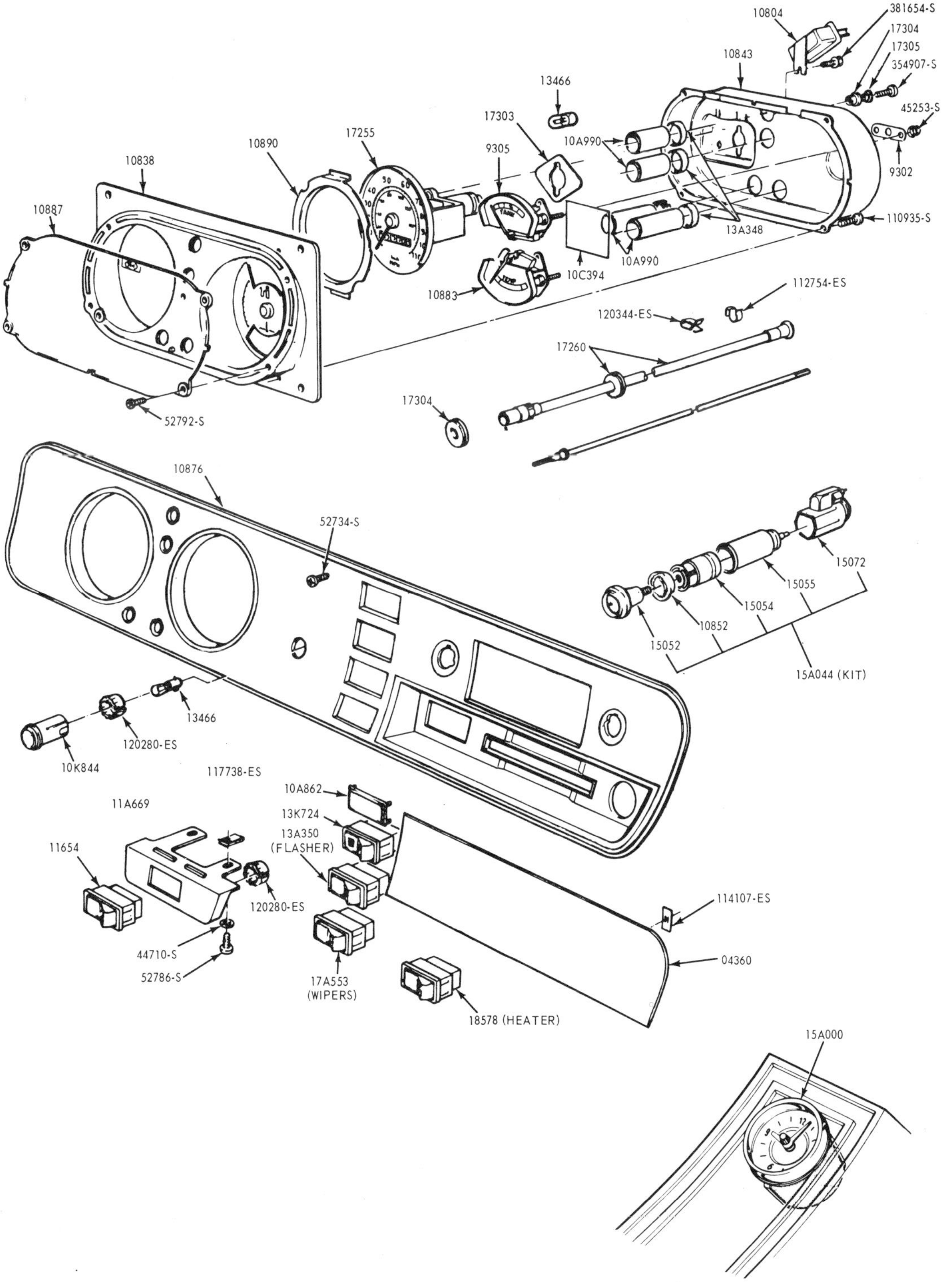

FIG 12:19 Components of a standard instrument cluster assembly

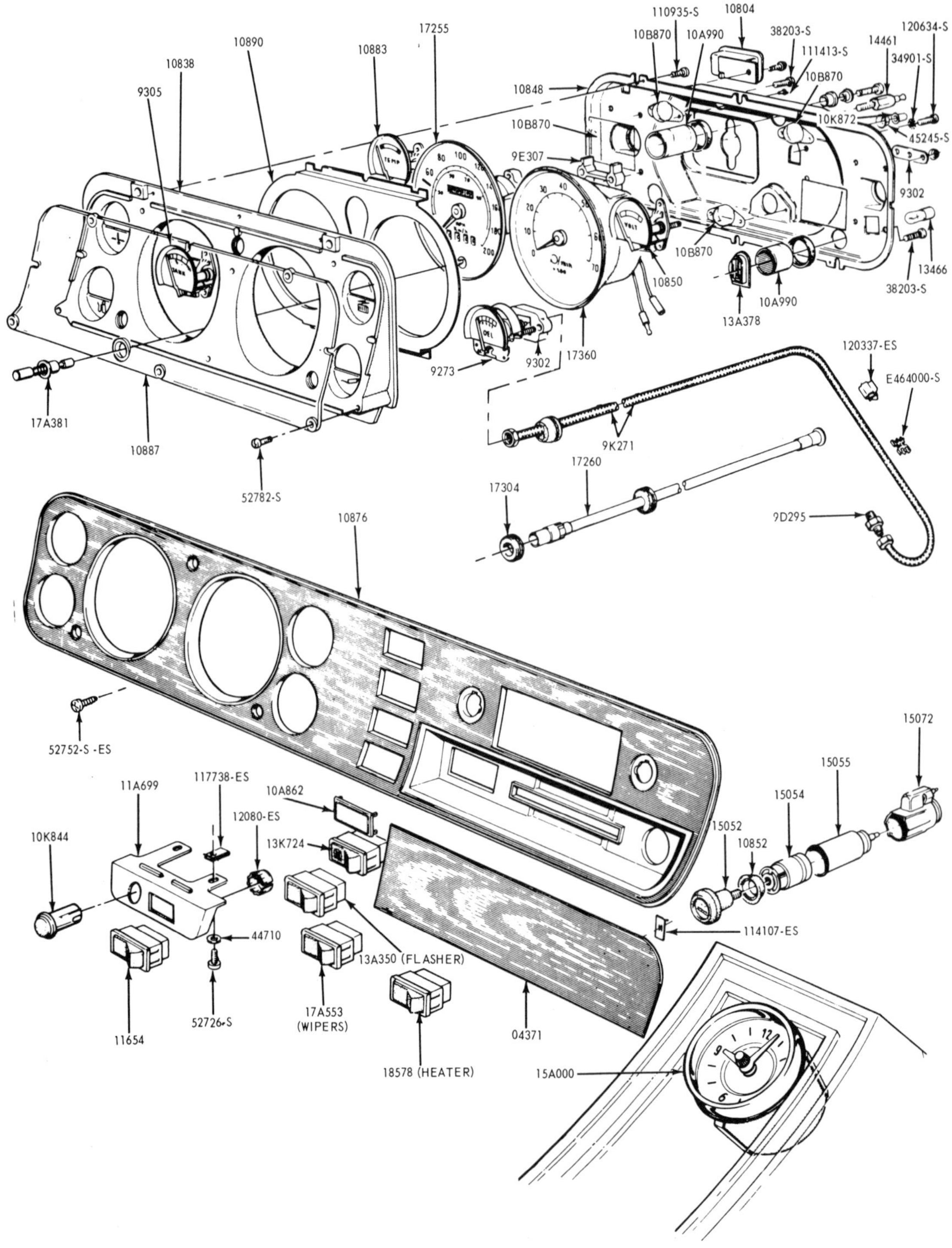

FIG 12:20 Components of a G.T. instrument cluster assembly

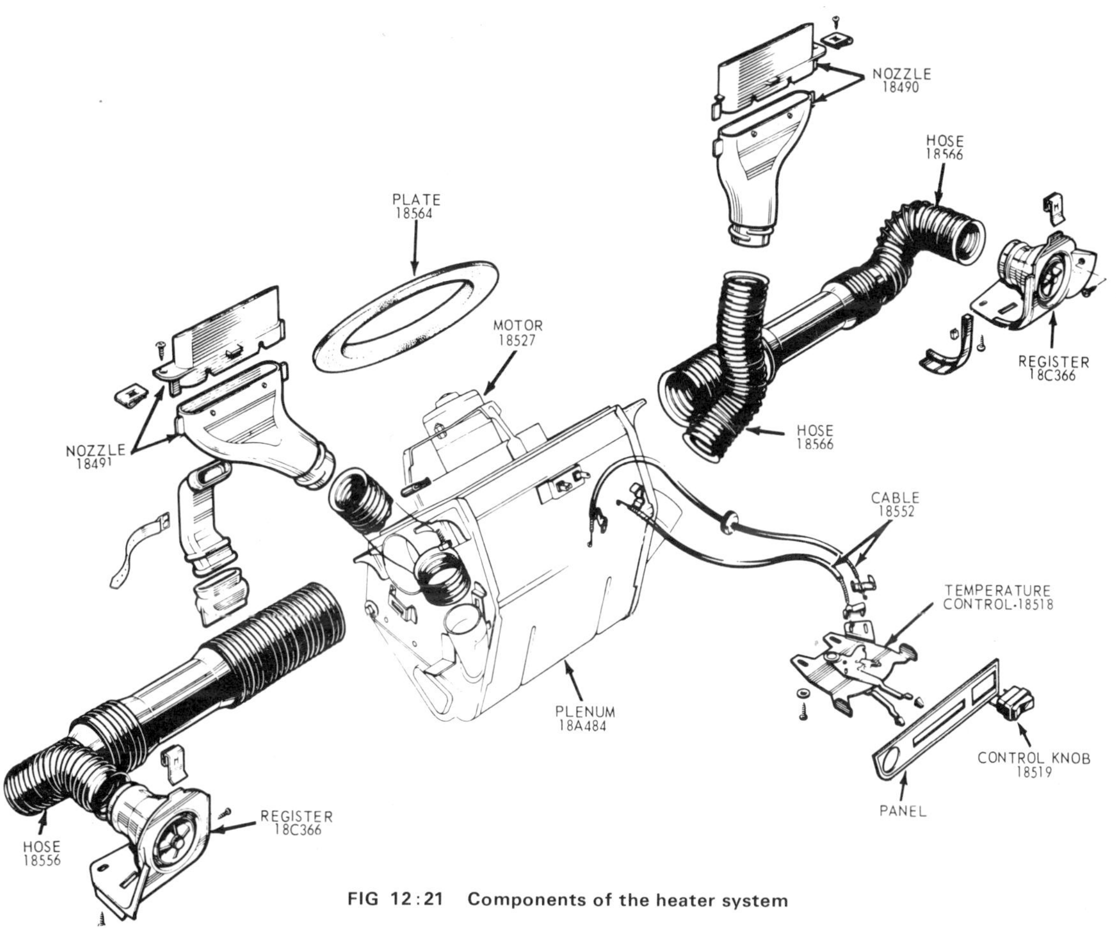

FIG 12:21 Components of the heater system

Adjustable vents at either end of the instrument panel allow the amount and direction of face level air to be closely controlled. Stale air is exhausted through a grille below the rear window and ensures a constant flow of fresh or heated air through the car.

Adjusting controls. (See FIG 12:22):

These operations should be required only if the cables have been disconnected for any reason.

Directional control:

This is the lower lever and should first be pushed fully to the left or OFF position and then the spring clip securing the cable to the heater removed.

Move the floor/defrost door to the full OFF position by turning its operating lever fully upwards as shown by the arrow.

Slide the end of the cable housing to the lever and secure it with the spring clip.

Temperature control:

Move the upper lever to the extreme left or maximum heat position and then remove its securing spring clip from the heater.

Move the temperature blend door to its max. heat position by turning its operating lever fully anti-clockwise as shown.

Hold it in this position while sliding the cable housing to the lever and secure the cable housing with its clip on the heater.

Removing the controls:

Disconnect the battery, remove the ashtray and pull off the two control lever knobs.

Remove the two screws securing the control quadrant to the panel and pull out the controls from below the panel.

Remove the two cable clips from the quadrant plate and remove the cables from their levers.

The controls are re-installed by reversing the above procedure.

Removing the heater assembly:

Disconnect the battery and drain the cooling system. Disconnect the two heater hoses from the heater core tubes and remove the coverplate and gasket from around the core tubes at the dash panel by taking out two screws.

Inside the car, remove the parcel tray and if a console is fitted it must be removed as follows:

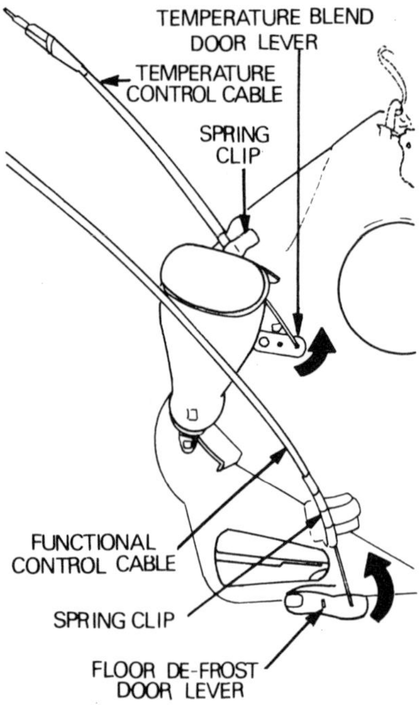

FIG 12:22 Heater cable adjustments

Take out the two screws securing the front end of the console to the floor and also two screws from underneath the rubber boot on the gearshift lever. Remove two screws under the rear panel.

Carefully lift the clock panel and disconnect two electrical connectors and an illumination bulb, then remove the main screw at the back of the area under the clock panel.

Remove the plastic brace under the handbrake lever by sliding it forward then lift the console out of the car.

Disconnect the cables from the control levers, three wire connectors from the terminals on the heater and the bullet connector on the other wire.

Disconnect the two panel vent ducts and the two windshield ducts from the heater.

Remove the four securing screws from the heater and lift it off. It may be necessary to remove the windshield wiper motor to gain access to one of the lefthand mounting screws.

Refitting is a reversal of the removal procedure after which the cooling system must be refilled and bled of any air. Run the engine for a few minutes with the radiator cap removed, check for leaks and top up as necessary. Replace the filler cap and if any air remains in the system it will be necessary to loosen a heater hose at the core until water flows out when the clip may be re-tightened.

12:15 Fault diagnosis

(a) Battery discharged

1 Terminal connections loose or dirty
2 Short circuits in lighting circuits
3 Alternator not charging
4 Regulator faulty
5 Battery internally defective

(b) Insufficient charging current

1 Check 1 and 4 in (a)
2 Drive belt slipping
3 Defective rectifier

(c) Battery will not hold charge

1 Electrolyte level too low
2 Battery plates sulphated
3 Case leaking
4 Plate separators defective

(d) Battery overcharged

1 Defective regulator

(e) Alternator output low or nil

1 Belt broken or slipping
2 Defective regulator
3 Worn bearings
4 Slip rings dirty or worn
5 Armature worn or bent
6 Brushes sticking, springs weak or broken
7 Rotor or stator coils broken, shorted or earthed
8 Rectifier defective

(f) Starter motor lacks power or will not operate

1 Battery discharged, terminals loose or corroded
2 Starter pinion jammed
3 Starter switch or solenoid faulty
4 Brushes worn or sticking
5 Commutator worn or dirty
6 Armature shaft bent

(g) Starter runs but does not turn engine

1 Pinion not engaging
2 Broken teeth on pinion or flywheel gears

(h) Starter inoperative

1 Check 1, 3 and 4 in (f)
2 Broken rotor or stator windings
3 Defective solenoid

(j) Starter motor rough or noisy

1 Worn bearings
2 Mounting bolts loose
3 Damaged teeth on pinion or flywheel

(k) Lamps inoperative or erratic

1 Bulb broken
2 Battery low
3 Faulty earth connection to lamp or battery
4 Faulty switch or bad connections
5 Fuse blown

(l) Wiper motor sluggish

1 Faulty armature
2 Defective brushes, commutator dirty
3 Linkage or spindles binding (lubrication or damage)

CHAPTER 13

THE BODYWORK

13:1 Bodywork finish

The high gloss exterior paintwork of the Capri is produced by an Acrylic resin-based enamel which is stoved on. It is specially formulated so that scratches which do not penetrate to the primer can be removed by rubbing down with a fine cutting compound followed by a polish to restore the original finish.

The finish is a stable one which can be repaired using conventional materials such as cellulose lacquers or air-drying acrylic lacquers which are now readily obtainable in all current standard colours.

Any stopping or priming which may be used to fill minor blemishes should be carefully rubbed down until the surface is smooth and flush with the surrounding area. When spraying keep the central area wet and the outer edges light and dry. Leave to dry for a few hours and then use a fine cutting compound to remove the dry spray. Finish off with polish.

Always remove any traces of wax polish before attempting to apply any paint. Usually a white spirit will be satisfactory, but silicone polishes are best removed with a very fine abrasive.

To maintain the high finish the paintwork should be washed frequently with plenty of water. Never wipe the surface with a dry cloth, this will rub the dust into the surface and have a sandpaper effect on the paint.

To remove stains from the vinyl roof, apply a cleaner to the affected area covering an area of not more than a radius of 12 inches at a time. Brush in circles with a medium hard brush and allow the cleaner to evaporate. If necessary, repeat the procedure and when the stains have been removed, wash the car and wipe the roof with a damp sponge. Always remove immediately any cleaner which may splash on the paintwork.

13:2 Removing door trim panels

Unscrew the knob on the door interior lock and carefully lever out the black plastic handle trim from the chrome escutcheon.

Remove the screw securing the door opening handle escutcheon and lift it off.

Remove the window regulator handle, lever out the plastic cover and undo the retaining screw. Remove two screws and lift off the armrest.

Carefully prise the trim panel away from the door panel to release the spring clips. Remove the panel and the waterproof sheet.

To refit the panel, first apply a coat of adhesive to the inner door panel for a minimum width of 1 inch and stick the waterproof sheet in place, making sure that the edges are sealed all round. Refit all the other pieces in the reverse order of dismantling.

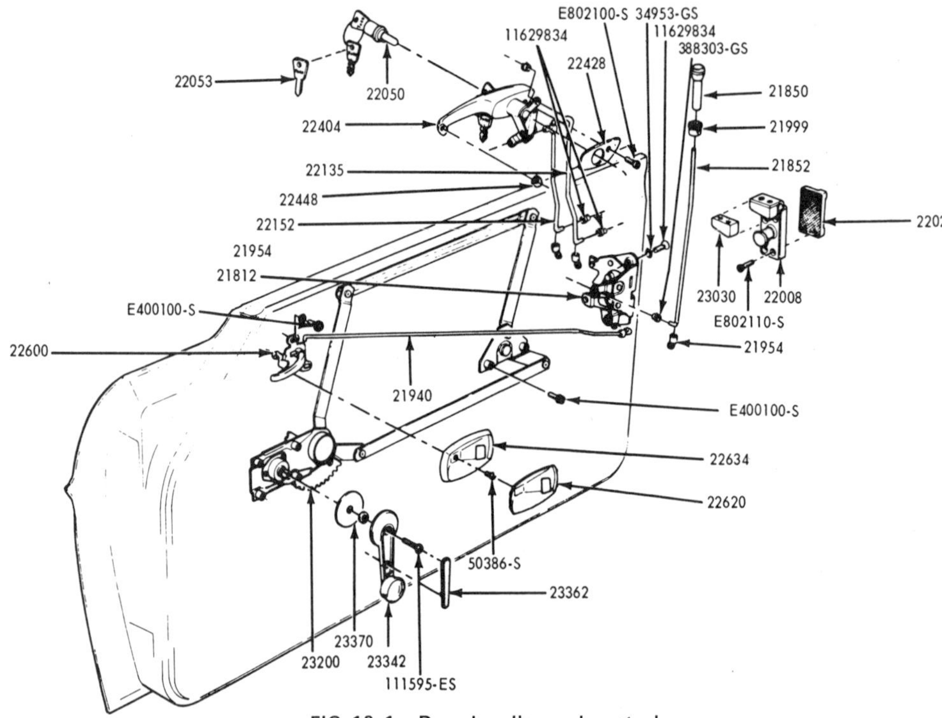

FIG 13:1 Door handles and controls

13:3 Door locks and handles

Exterior handle:

Remove the door trim panel as described in **Section 13:2** and then wind the window up. Pull down the waterproof sheet and disconnect the spring clip securing the operating rod to the handle and remove the rod. See **FIG 13:1**.

Disconnect the spring clip and remove the locking rod from the handle.

Through the door access hole remove the front screw securing the exterior handle and slacken the rear screw. Pull the handle forwards to release the rear end and lift it away with the sealing gaskets. See **FIG 13:2**.

Remove the rear screw, gaskets and remote rod clip. Tap out the pivot pin and remove the crankarm and return spring.

Remove the circlip from the end of the barrel to release the locking plate return spring and lock barrel. Pull off the spacer washer and remove the return spring from the end of the cylinder.

Remove the rubber ring from its groove in the handle push button, tap out the pin and remove the lock cylinder from the push button.

The handle is reassembled and refitted in the reverse order to the above.

Door lock assembly:

With the trim panel removed, wind the window up, disconnect the remote control rod from the operating arm on the interior handle as shown in **FIG 13:3**.

Disconnect the push button rod, the exterior operating rod and the locking rod from the lock. Release the window channel by removing two screws.

Remove the three retaining screws and remove the lock assembly.

To refit the lock, first replace the four rod connecting clips on the lock, place the lock in position on the door and secure it with the three screws. Secure the window channel.

Reconnect the four control rods and check the operation of the lock.

Remote control assembly:

Remove the spring clip securing the operating rod to the lock mechanism and disconnect the rod.

Prise out the nylon guide from the door inner panel. Remove the three securing screws securing the remote control to the inner door panel and lift away through the access hole.

Refit in the reverse order.

Door striker plate:

A cranked service tool is used to release the three screws securing the striker plate in position and it may be adjusted as follows:

With the securing screws loosened, press the door outside push button and slowly close the door to the full catch position. Move the door in or out until it is flush with the body panels.

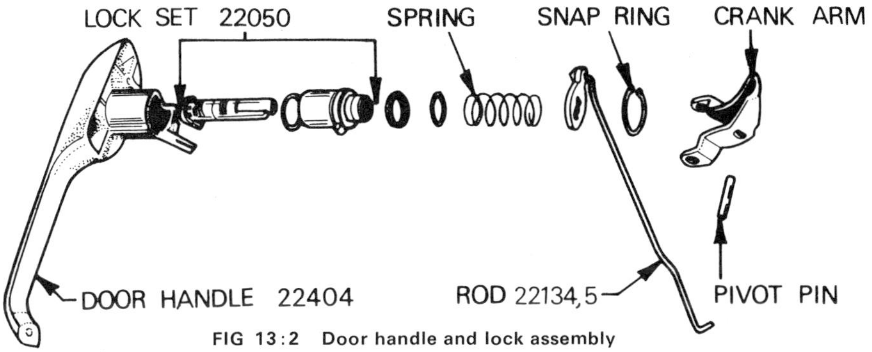

FIG 13:2 Door handle and lock assembly

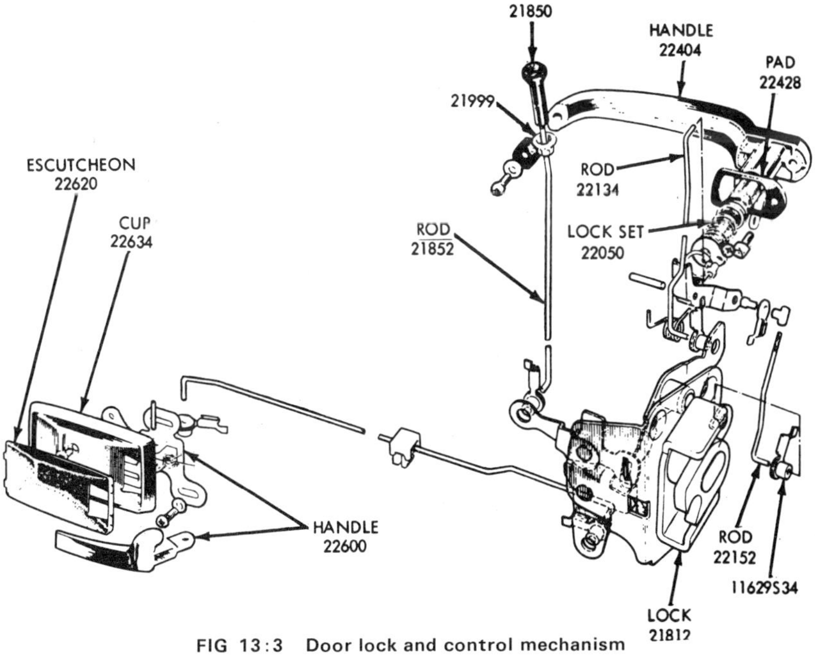

FIG 13:3 Door lock and control mechanism

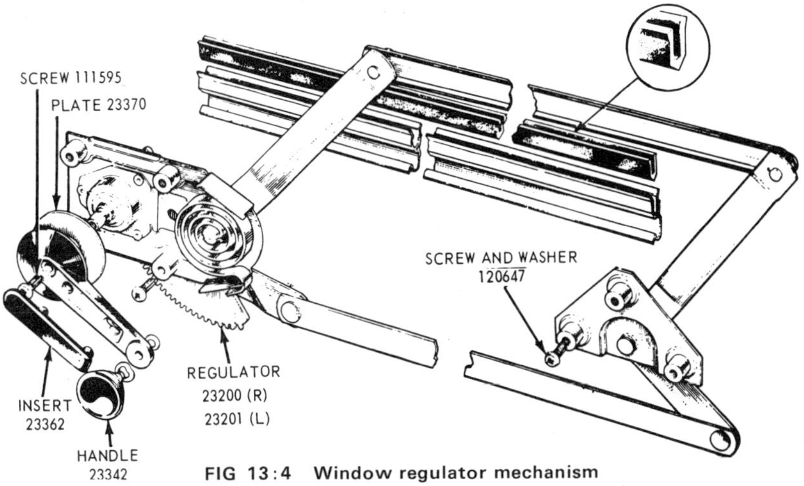

FIG 13:4 Window regulator mechanism

FIG 13:5 Removing a door glass

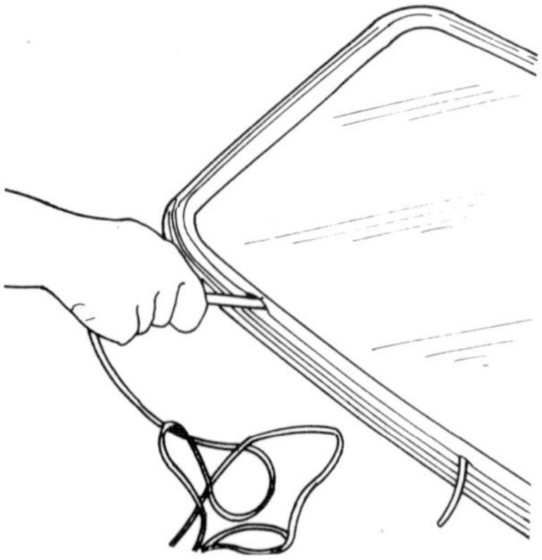

FIG 13:6 Showing the use of a drawcord when fitting windshield

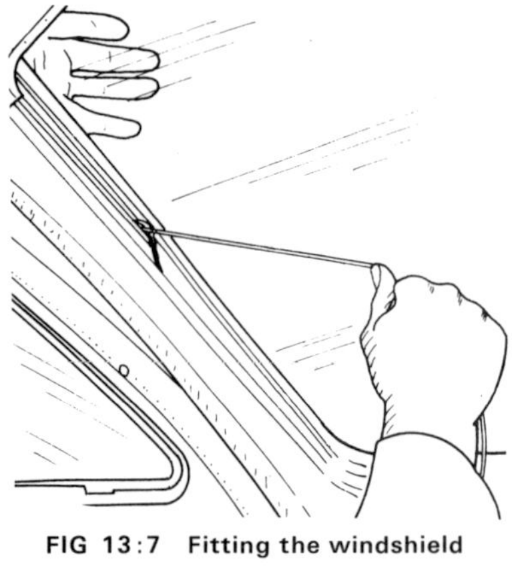

FIG 13:7 Fitting the windshield

Press in the button and carefully open the door and check that the striker plate is vertical. Tighten the securing screws and check that the door closes correctly and does not rattle, making a further slight adjustment if necessary.

13:4 Window regulators

The window regulating mechanism is shown in **FIG 13:4** and access is gained by removing the interior door trim as described earlier.

Wind down the window and remove the seven screws and washers securing the mechanism to the door.

Carefully pull the assembly towards the rear of the door to release the operating arm from the window glass.

Push the window up and either secure it or take it out of its recess by rotating it through 90 deg. and lifting out, see **FIG 13:5**.

Remove the regulator through the door acess aperture.

Window frame:

Remove the chrome door moulding and weatherstrip.

Remove the two bolts securing the front of the frame and one bolt and two screws securing the rear. Lift out the frame and channel assembly from the door and prise out the silent channel strip.

Refit by reversing the above order.

13:5 Replacing a windshield

Cover the adjacent body panels with a sheet to prevent scratching. Remove the wiper arms and blades.

Using a suitable tool push the lip of the rubber weatherstrip under the top and sides of the windshield aperture flange. The glass can now be pushed out from the inside of the car complete with the weatherstrip.

Prise out the joint cover clip and pull the finisher strip away from the weatherstrip.

If a glass is being fitted on account of breakage, take great care to see that all traces of broken glass and sealer are removed from the body flanges and the de-mister vents, from which the fragments may be blown when the car heater is switched on.

Fit the weatherstrip around the new glass and with a pressure gun apply a suitable sealing compound (C5AZ-19554-A) in the weatherstrip groove which fits the body flange.

Fit a drawcord in the rubber to body groove as shown in **FIG 13:6** allowing a crossover of about 6 inches at the bottom.

Place the glass in the body aperture with the cord ends inside the car, and while hand pressure is applied to the outside of the glass, lift the rubber lip over the body flange by pulling on the cord as shown in **FIG 13:7**.

Again using the gun, apply sealer to the rubber to glass groove.

Fit the finisher strip in its groove using a lipping tool if necessary and replace the joint cover clip.

Clean off any surplus sealer and refit the wiper arms and blades.

Back window:

A similar procedure is used for removing and replacing a back window.

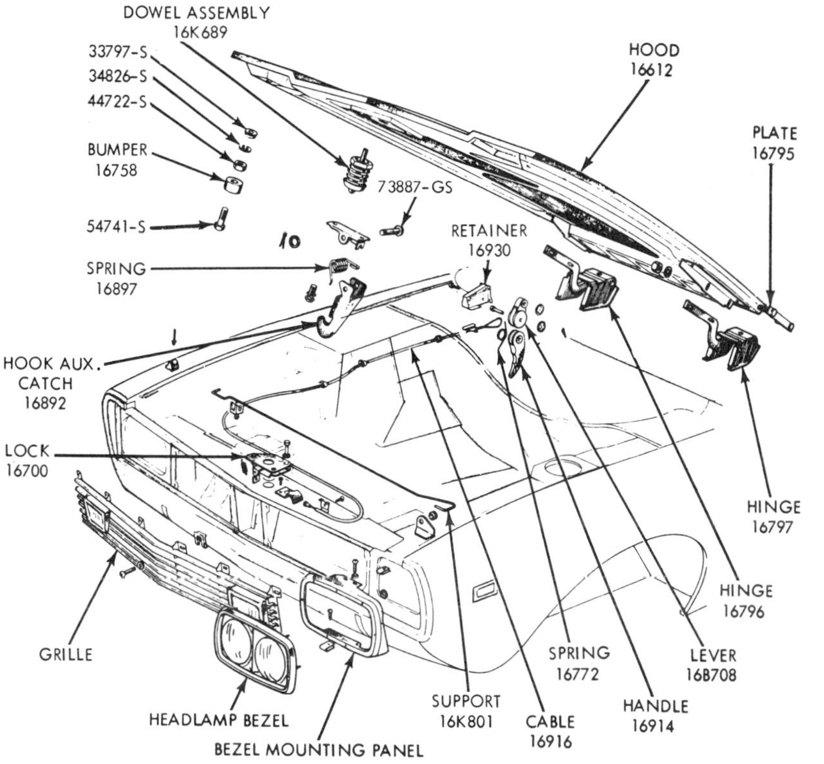

FIG 13:8 Hood and front end assembly

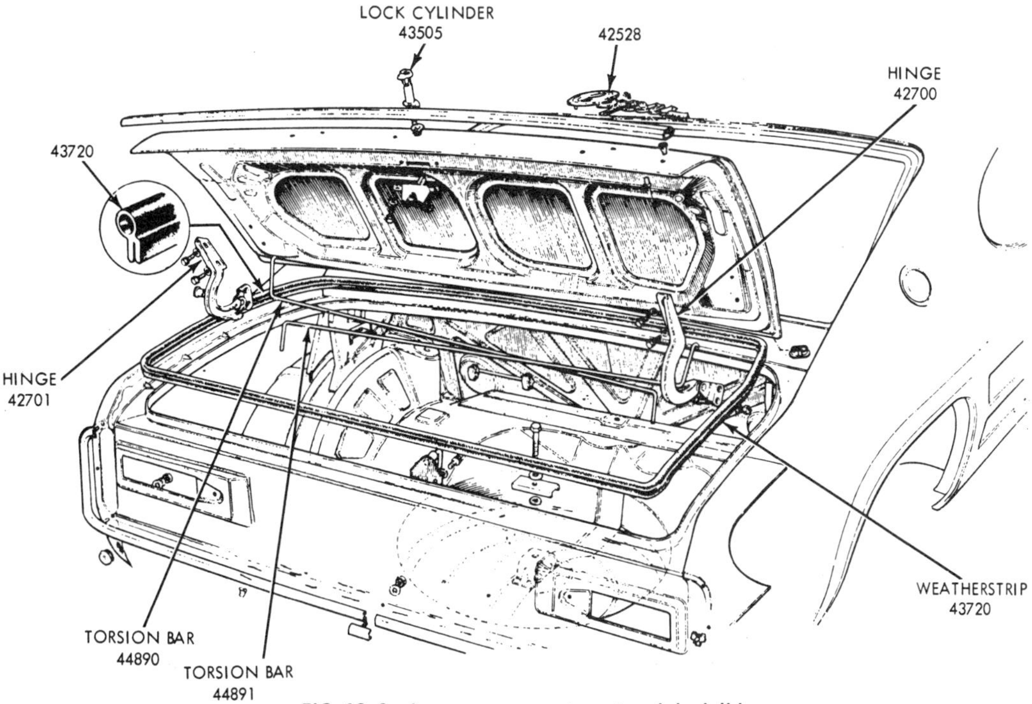

FIG 13:9 Luggage compartment and deck lid

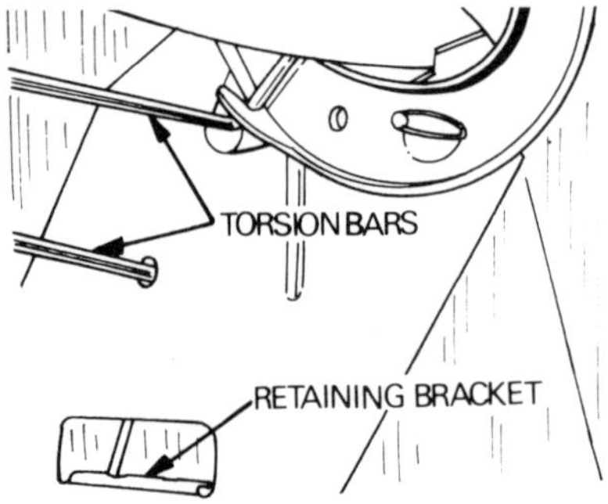

FIG 13:10 Torsion bar mountings

13:6 The hood

Before starting to remove the hood from the engine compartment it will be advisable to scribe a line around the hinges to ensure their correct location when re-fitting.

Remove the two retaining nuts and washers on each side, remove the two bolt plates and lift off the hood. See **FIG 13:8**.

When refitting, first position the hood on the hinges and replace the two bolt plates and nuts, but do not tighten fully until the hinges have been aligned to the scribed markings made earlier.

Striker:

This is adjustable in order to ensure correct fitting of the hood to the surrounding body panels. Release the locknut and screw the striker in or out as required, then tighten the locknut.

Release cable:

Prise out the clips and remove the radiator trim panel. From inside the car remove both clevis pins and spring and disconnect the cable from the control lever.

Slacken the cable adjuster and release the cable from the hood lock. Remove the body clips and pull the cable through the bulk head.

The hood lock is secured in position by three bolts and is easily removed.

After refitting, adjust the release cable before replacing the radiator cowl panel.

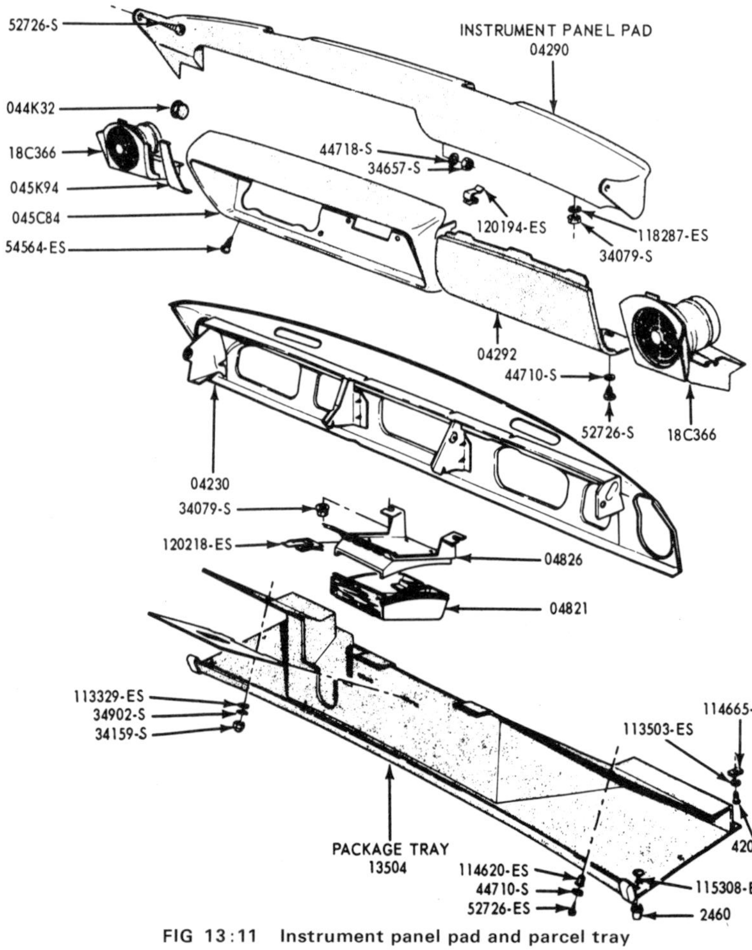

FIG 13:11 Instrument panel pad and parcel tray

13:7 Luggage compartment deck lid

As with the hood, always mark the position of the hinges before removing the securing screws to ensure correct fitting on re-installation.

The weatherstrip is retained by an internal toothed channel and is removed by carefully prising it off the aperture flanges. See **FIG 13:9**. It is refitted by tapping into place with a rubber mallet and the joint in the weather strip should be sealed with a length of one inch wide body tape.

Torsion bars:

The mounting for the torsion bars which control the opening of the deck lid is shown in **FIG 13:10**.

To remove them it is necessary to use a pair of adjustable spanners and release the cranked end from its retaining bracket on the body.

Disconnect the double cranked end from the hinge and remove the torsion bar. Repeat for the other torsion bar.

To refit: Engage the double cranked end in the hinge and use a pair of adjustable spanners to locate the other end of the bar in its retaining bracket.

Lock:

With the lid open remove the spring clip from the end of the lock spindle, remove three screws and washers and remove the lock.

Use a pair of long nosed pliers through the hole in the lid to compress the legs of the spring clip retaining the lock cylinder and pull it out.

A new cylinder is simply pressed in until the spring clip engages.

13:8 Instrument panel pad

This is shown in **FIG 13:11** together with the parcel tray and removal is effected as follows:

Take out two screws one each side and remove the left and right A post garnish mouldings, then remove each corner screw which is now uncovered.

Remove the instrument cluster panel pad assembly as described in **Chapter 12**.

Remove the two nuts and washers which will be found directly above the opening for the instrument cluster and also the remaining nut on the righthand side of the panel pad.

Lift the panel pad away from the instrument panel.

To refit, first position the pad and retaining clips on the instrument panel assembly—then fit the three retaining nuts and washers.

Fit the left and righthand corner screws and garnish moulding. Refit the instrument panel pad as described earlier.

NOTES

APPENDIX

NOTES

TECHNICAL DATA

Unless otherwise stated dimensions are in inches (millimeters in brackets)

Engine:

Type	4-in-line OHC
Bore, 2.0 litre	3.575 (90.80)
1.6 litre	3.453 (87.65)
1.3 litre	3.113 (79.00)
Stroke, 2.0 litre	3.029 (76.93)
1.6 and 1.3 litre	2.600 (66.00)
Capacity, 2.0 litre	1999 cc
1.6 litre	1593 cc
1.3 litre	1294 cc
Compression ratio	9.2:1 (HC) or 8.2:1 (LC)
Firing order	1-3-4-2 (No. 1 in front)

Crankshaft:

Journal diameter, standard, red	2.2441 to 2.2437 (57.00 to 56.99)
blue	2.2437 to 2.2433 (56.99 to 56.98)
Undersizes, red or blue	—.010 (—.25)
Following first regrind, common undersides of	2.2244 to 2.2240 (56.50 to 56.49) 2.2146 to 2.2142 (56.25 to 56.24) 2.2047 to 2.2043 (56.00 to 55.99)
Crankpin diameter, standard, red	2.0472 to 2.0468 (52.00 to 51.99)
blue	2.0468 to 2.0465 (51.99 to 51.98)
Undersizes, red or blue	—.010 (—.25)
Following first regrind, common undersizes of	2.0276 to 2.0272 (51.50 to 51.49) 2.0177 to 2.0173 (51.25 to 51.24) 2.0079 to 2.0075 (51.00 to 50.99)
End thrust	.003 to .001 (.08 to .28)
Thrust washer thickness, standard	.091 to .092 (2.30 to 2.35)
oversize	.099 to .100 (2.50 to 2.55)
Main bearing shell to crankshaft clearance, aluminium type	.0006 to .0019 (.014 to .048)
compound type	.0004 to .0019 (.010 to .048)
Big-end shell to crankshaft clearance, aluminium type	As main bearing
compound type	As main bearing

Connecting rod and piston pin:

Small-end bore diameter	.9435 to .9439 (23.964 to 23.976)
Piston pin diameter, red	.9446 to .9448 (23.994 to 23.997)
blue	.9448 to .9449 (23.997 to 24.000)
yellow	.9449 to .9450 (24.000 to 24.003)

Interference fit to connecting rod	.0007 to .0015 (.018 to .039)
Clearance fit in piston	.0002 to .0004 (.005 to .011)

Camshaft:

Bearings	Three
Journal diameter 1	1.6539 to 1.6531 (42.01 to 41.99)
2	1.7606 to 1.7528 (44.72 to 44.52)
3	1.7720 to 1.7713 (45.01 to 44.99)
Bearing bore 1	1.656 to 1.655 (42.055 to 42.035)
2	1.760 to 1.759 (44.675 to 44.655)
Retaining plate thickness, type 1	.158 (4.01)
type 2	.157 (3.98)
3	1.775 to 1.774 (45.055 to 45.035)
Location. Front edge of bearing towards the rear from front face of block or pedestal	.059
End play	.0012 to .0047
Bearing clearance	.0010 to .0025
Colour code, where applicable	1300:White, 1600:Yellow

Cylinder block:

Bore diameter, standard, 2000	3.5748 to 3.5763 (90.799 to 90.838)	
Oversizes, 2000	+.020 (+.5), +.040 (+1.00)	
Bore diameter	*1300*	*1600*
Standard, grade 1	3.1126 to 3.1130 (79.000 to 79.010)	3.4534 to 3.4538 (87.650 to 87.660)
grade 2	+.0004 (+.010)	above grade 1
grade 3	+.0008 (+.020)	above grade 1
grade 4	+.0012 (+.030)	above grade 1
Overside, grade A	3.1327 to 3.1331 (79.510 to 79.520)	3.4735 to 3.4739 (88.160 to 88.170)
grade B	+.0004 (+.010)	above grade A
grade C	+.0008 (+.020)	above grade A
Standard service supply	3.1138 to 3.1142 (79.030 to 79.040)	3.4546 to 3.4550 (87.680 to 87.690)
Oversize service	+.020 +.040	(+.50) (+1.00)
Gasket surface flatness	.003 in 6	(.076 in 152)

Pistons:

Standard diameter, 2000	3.5749 to 3.5740 (90.80 to 90.78)	
Oversizes, 2000	+.020 (+.50), +.040 (+1.00)	
Standard diameter	*1300*	*1600*
Grade 1	3.1108 to 3.1112 (78.955 to 78.965)	3.4516 to 3.4520 (87.605 to 87.615)
2	+.0004 (+.010)	above grade 1
3	+.0008 (+.020)	above grade 1
4	+.0012 (+.030)	above grade 1
Standard service supply	3.1118 to 3.1128 (78.980 to 79.005)	3.4526 to 3.4536 (87.630 to 87.655)
Oversize service	+.020 +.040	(+.50) (+1.00)
Piston clearance, fitted	.001 to .002	(.025 to .060)

Piston rings:

Gap, fitted, compression, 2000	.002 to .003 (.05 to .07)
1600	.015 to .023 (.38 to .58)
1300	.015 to .023 (.38 to .58)
Oil control, all	.016 to .056 (.40 to 1.4)

Valves:

Head diameter, inlet, 2000	1.65 ± .008 (42 ± .2)		
1600	1.654 ± .008 (42 ± .2)		
1300	1.516 ± .008 (38.5 ± .2)		
Head diameter, exhaust, 2000	1.417 ± .008 (36 ± .2)		
1600	1.340 ± .008 (34 ± .2)		
1300	1.180 ± .008 (30 ± .2)		
Face angle	45°		
Stem diameter, inlet, standard	.3169 to .3162 (8.043 to 8.025)		
Stem diameter, exhaust, standard	.3159 to .3152 (8.017 to 7.000)		
Oversizes	+.008 (+.20), +.016 (+.40)		
Stem clearance in guide, inlet	.0008 to .0025 (.020 to .063)		
Stem clearance in guide, exhaust	.0018 to .0035 (.046 to .089)		
Valve timing	*1300*	*1600*	*2000*
Inlet opens, BTDC	22°	24°	18°
Inlet closes, ABDC	54°	64°	70°
Exhaust opens, BBDC	64°	70°	64°
Exhaust closes, ATDC	12°	18°	24°
Valve clearances (Cold)			
Inlet	.008 (.20)		
Exhaust	.010 (.25)		

Valve springs:

Free length	1.77 approx.
Assembled height	1.417
Length at pressure	1.417 at 60.64 lbs

Oil pump:

Relief valve spring	1.39 at 13.6 to 14.7 lbs
Clearance, shaft to housing	.001 to .002
Relief valve clearance	.001 to .002
Rotor end play	.001 to .004

FUEL SYSTEM

Carburetter:

Type, 2000	Motorcraft 5200 or Weber 32/36 DFAV	
	Primary	*Secondary*
Bore	1.260	1.417
Venturi	1.024	1.063
Main jet (stamped)	137	145
Idle jet (stamped) Manual	55	50
Automatic	50	50
Main air bleed (stamped)	71	67
Float setting dry	.45	
Float drop	1.9	
Vacuum pulldown clearance	.26	
Dechoke clearance	.295 to .335	
Idle speed. Manual	730 to 780 rev/min	
Automatic (D)	630 to 680 rev/min	
Fast idle	1800 rev/min	
1300 LC, emission controlled	Ford 71-HW-9510-AA	
HC, emission controlled	Ford 71-HW-9510-BA	

1600	Ford 71-HW-9510-AJA used with automatic transmission, or Ford 71-HW-9510-AGA used with manual transmission
1600 emission controlled	Ford 71-HW-9510-YA used with manual transmission, or Ford 71-HW-9510-AHA used with automatic transmission
1600 GT	Weber 71-HF-9510-BA used with manual transmission, or Weber 71-HF-9510-CA used with automatic transmission

71-HW-9510-AA and BA:

Venturi diameter	1.02 (26.0)
Main jet	130
Float level	1.08 (27.43)
travel	.26 (6.60)
Choke plate pull down	.10 (2.54)
Piston link hole	Outer
Spring slot	Centre
Idling speed	750 rev/min
Fast idle	1700 to 1900 rev/min

71-HW-9510-AJA and AHA:

Venturi diameter	1.10 (28.0)
Main jet	137
Float level	1.10 (27.93)
travel	.26 (6.60)
Choke plate pull down	.15
Piston link hole	Outer
Spring slot	Centre
Idling speed, AJA	730 rev/min
AHA	770 rev/min
Fast idle, AJA	2000 rev/min
AHA	2200 rev/min

71-HW-9510-AGA and YA:

Venturi diameter	1.10 (28.0)
Main jet	137
Float level	1.10 (27.93)
Float travel	.26 (6.57)
Choke plate pull down	.15 (3.81)
Piston link hole	Outer
Spring slot	Centre
Idling speed, AGA	730 rev/min
YA	770 rev/min
Fast idle, AGA	1650 rev/min
YA	1850 rev/min

71-HF-9510-BA and CA:

Venturi diameter, primary	1.02 (26.0)
secondary	1.06 (27.0)
Main jet, primary	140
secondary	135
Air correction jet, primary	170
secondary	140
Emulsion tube, primary	F50
secondary	F6

Idling jet, primary	55
secondary	45
Idling speed, BA	800 rev/min
CA	700 rev/min
Fast idle, on high cam, BA	3200 rev/min
CA	3000 rev/min
Fuel pump:	
Type	Mechanical from camshaft
Pressure	3.8 to 5.0 lb/sq in
Flow minimum	1 pint in 43 sec at 500 rev/min

IGNITION SYSTEM

Distributor:	
Type, 2000	Bosch dual diaphragm
others	Bosch or Autolite single diaphragm
Contact breaker gap	.025 (.64 mm)
Rotor rotation	Clockwise
Timing	6° BTDC
Vehicles in the state of California, automatic transmission	10° BTDC
Engine applicability:	
1600 GT, (colour red)	Autolite 71-BB-12100-UB
or (colour blue)	Bosch 71-HM-12100-DA
1600 (colour black)	Bosch 71-HM-12100-SA or Autolite
1300 HC (colour white)	Bosch 71-HM-12100-AA
1300 LC (colour yellow)	Bosch 71-HM-12100-BA
Spark plugs:	
Type	Autolite BRF32
Gap	.025

COOLING SYSTEM

Type:	Pressurized, pump assisted
Radiator cap release pressure	13 lb/sq in
Thermostat:	
Starts to open	178° to 199°F
Fully open	203° to 223°F

CLUTCH

Type	Single dry plate, diaphragm spring. Cable operated
Diameter, 2000, 1600 GT	$8\frac{1}{2}$
1600, 1300	$7\frac{1}{2}$
Lining wear limit	.039 (1.0)
No. of torsion springs, 2000 and 1600, GT	6
1300, 1600	4
Cable free play at abutment bracket	.118 to .138 (3.0 to 3.5)

MANUAL TRANSMISSION

Type	Four forward, one reverse
Synchromesh	All forward ratios
Vehicle applicability:	
1600 LC or HC	Type 'C' transmission
1300 HC	Type 'H' transmission
1600 GT	Type C or H transmission
2000	Type H transmission

Ratio:	Type C	Type H
1st	2.97:1	3.65:1
2nd	2.01:1	1.97:1
3rd	1.40:1	1.37:1
4th	1.00:1	1.00:1
Reverse	3.32:1	3.66:1

AUTOMATIC TRANSMISSION

Type:	Borg Warner 35
Ratios:	
1st	2.393:1
2nd	1.450:1
3rd	1.000:1
Reverse	2.094:1
Fluid:	ESW-M2C33-F (Type F)

REAR AXLE

Type	Hypoid bevel
Ratios, 1.3 litre	4.125:1
1.6 litre	3.777:1
1.6 GT	3.75:1
2.0 litre	3.44:1

FRONT SUSPENSION

Type	Independent McPherson strut. Track control arms, stabilizer bar, coil springs and telescopic hydraulic dampers
Springs, 1300 and 1600	Standard or heavy duty
Identification colour	Green:orange or Brown:green
Suspension units 1300 and 1600	
Identification colour, RH	Green
LH	Red
Damper fluid type	M-100502-E
capacity	326 cc

REAR SUSPENSION

Type:	Semi-elliptic leaf springs, twin radius arms. Rigid axle
Control:	Telescopic, hydraulic shock absorbers
Length between eye centres	47
Length from front to axle	19.15
Width of spring leaves	2.0

STEERING

Type:	Rack and pinion
Steering wheel turns (lock to lock):	$3\frac{1}{2}$
Ratio:	17.7:1
Geometry:	
Castor	$-\frac{1}{2}$ to $+1\frac{1}{2}°$
Camber	$-\frac{1}{4}°$ to $-\frac{3}{4}°$
King pin inclination	7° 30′ to 8° 30′
Toe-in	0 to $\frac{1}{4}$
Lock setting	20° and 18° 15′ to 19° 45′
Turning circle	31.5 feet

BRAKES

Type:	Disc front, drum rear, twin circuit
Operation:	Hydraulic with vacuum booster. Mechanical handbrake
Discs:	
Diameter, 2000 and 1600	9.625 (24.45 cm), 1300 to 9.59 (24.13 cm)
Thickness, 2000 and 1600	.50 (12.6) 1300 to .376 (9.5)
Run-out	.0035
Pad coding	Blue-white-white-white-blue or DON 223, but all fitted must be of same type
Drums:	
Diameter, 2000 and 1600	9.0 (22.9 cm), 1300 to 8.0 (20.3 cm)
Width, 2000 and 1600	1.75 (44.5), 1300 to 1.50 (38.1)
Lining thickness	.188
Lining thickness minimum	.03

ELECTRICAL EQUIPMENT

System type:	12 volt, negative ground
Battery:	
Type	Lead acid
Capacity (Manual) 2000	55 amp hours, standard-38 amp hrs
(Automatic) 2000	66 amp hours or optional
Specific Gravity (Charged)	1.275 to 1.290
(Low limit)	1.105
Alternator:	
Type	Bosch K-1 or Lucas 17 ACR
Drive ratio	1.88:1
Output max	35 amps 36 amps
Brush min length	.2
Spring tension	10.6 to 14.1 oz 7 to 10 oz
Belt tension	½ inch free movement
Regulator setting	10 amps max at 5000 rev/min
voltage	14.1 to 14.4 volts
Starter:	
Type, 2000, 1600 GT	Bosch GF 1.0 pre-engaged type
1300, 1600 HC	Bosch EFO.7 PE type
1600 LC	Lucas M35J inertia type
No. of brushes	4, copper based
Minimum length	.40 (10 mm)
Spring pressure, Bosch	2.7 lbs (1.2 kg)
Lucas	3.8 lbs (1.76 kg)
Teeth on pinion	10
ring gear	135
Light bulbs:	
Headlight outer, 2000	40 to 50 watts
inner, 2000	37.5 watts
rectangular	40 to 45 watts
Turn indicator, front, 2000	32 to 4 CP, others 21 watt
rear, 2000	32 CP, others 21 watt
Tail and stop, 2000	32 to 4 CP, others 21 to 5 watt
Licence plate, 2000	5 CP, others 4 CP
Back up light	21 CP
Cluster illumination	2.2 watt

CAPACITIES

Full tank	12.7 US gals (10$\frac{1}{2}$ imp) 48 litres
Engine oil pan (with filter)	5 US qts (6.6 pts imp) 3.75 litres
Manual transmission, 'H' type	2.8 US pts (2.55 imp) 1.45 litres
'C' type	(1.76 imp) 1.00 litre
Automatic transmission	6$\frac{3}{4}$ US qts (11.26 imp pts) 6.4 litres
Rear axle, German	2.3 US pts (1.10 imp) 1.94 litres
British	(1.14 imp) 2.05 litres
Steering gear	.3 US pts (.25 imp) .14 litres
Cooling system	8 US qts (6$\frac{1}{2}$ imp) 3.7 litres

TORQUE WRENCH SETTINGS

Values are in lb ft unless otherwise stated

Engine:	
Camshaft gear bolt	32 to 36
Camshaft thrust plate	5 to 8
Carburetter to manifold	12 to 15
Connecting rod nuts	29 to 34
Crankshaft pulley	39 to 43
Cylinder head	See text
Decel valve nut	27 to 30
Exhaust manifold	12 to 15
Flywheel	47 to 51
Fuel pump	12 to 15
Inlet manifold	12 to 15
Main bearing cap	65 to 75
Oil pump to block	12 to 15
Oil pan	See text
Oil filter to block	10 to 15
Rocker arm ball stud	32 to 36
Rocker arm cover	See text
Rocker oil pipe	4 to 6
Waterpump to block (M8)	12 to 15
(M10)	26 to 31
Clutch and gearbox:	
Pressure plate	11 to 14
Housing to transmission	40 to 47
Drain and filler plug	25 to 30
Top cover	5 to 8
Housing to engine	22 to 27
Extension housing	30 to 35
Automatic transmission:	
Centre support	10 to 18
Extension housing	30 to 33
Drive plate to converter	40 to 45
Inhibitor switch	4 to 6
Oil pan	8 to 13
Suspension:	
Unit upper mounting	15 to 18
Lower control arm ball nut	30 to 35
Stabilizer bar to control arm	15 to 45
Attachment clamps	15 to 18
Crossmember to side member	25 to 30
Radius arm	25 to 30
Shock absorber to body	15 to 20
to axle	40 to 45

U bolts	18 to 26
Spring axle shackle	8 to 10
Front hanger	27 to 32
Steering:	
Coupling to pinion	12 to 15
Gear to crossmember	15 to 18
Steering wheel nut	20 to 25
Track rod and ball joint	10 to 20
Track control arm ball joint	30 to 60
Brakes:	
Caliper to suspension unit	45 to 50
Backplate to axle	15 to 18
Disc to hub	30 to 34
Hydraulic union	5 to 7
Wheel nuts	50 to 55

SPECIAL TOOLS

	UK	*USA*	*Germany*
Engine:			
Engine lifting tackle	P6171	T53L300A	GS6000
Cylinder head bolt wrench	21002	T71P6065A	21002
Camshaft bearing remover		T71P6250A	
Valve stem seal replacer	21006	VSIT-1	21006
Crankshaft front seal remover	21008	T71P6150A	21008
Crankshaft front seal replacer	21009	T71P6150B	21009
Auxiliary shaft bearing remover		T58L101A	
Auxiliary shaft bearing replacer		T57T7003AF	
Piston pin remover		T72C6135	
Piston pin replacer	21014	T72C6135	21014
Main bearing shell remover, replacer		6331	
Crankshaft rear seal remover	21010		21010
replacer	21011	T71P6701A	21011
Clutch disc locator (mandrel)	P7137	T71P7137A	
Pilot bearing remover	P7600A-7	T58L101A	P7600A-7
replacer	P7137	T71P7137C-H	P7137
Gearbox:			
Dummy countershaft	P7113	T71P7111B	G27020
Input shaft bearing remover	P4090-10	T69P4621A	G37025
replacer	P4000-39		G24621B
Dummy bearing tool (ext. housing)	P7154	T70P7154	
Input shaft seal replacer	P7136	T71P7050B	
Extension housing bush remover	P7149	T71P7697A	G37041A
replacer	P7150	T71P7095B	G47041B
Extension housing seal remover	P7657-4	T71P7657A	GE7657B1
replacer	P7095	T71P7095B	G27657B
Rear axle:			
Axle shaft remover	P3072	T6614234A	
Bearing remover	P4090-2 & 6	T69P4621A	
Sliding hammer	P3072A	T50T100A	
Pinion bearing remover	P4000-28	T69P4621A	
Pinion bearing race remover	P4015		
installer	P4013-3	T70P4127	
Dummy pinion	P4075-4	T70P4133	
Master spacer pinion shaft		T70P4137	
Pinion flange holding tool	P4097	T70P4067A	G24851B
Pinion seal installer		T70P4129	
Spring shackle bush remover	P5029	T70P-5029	

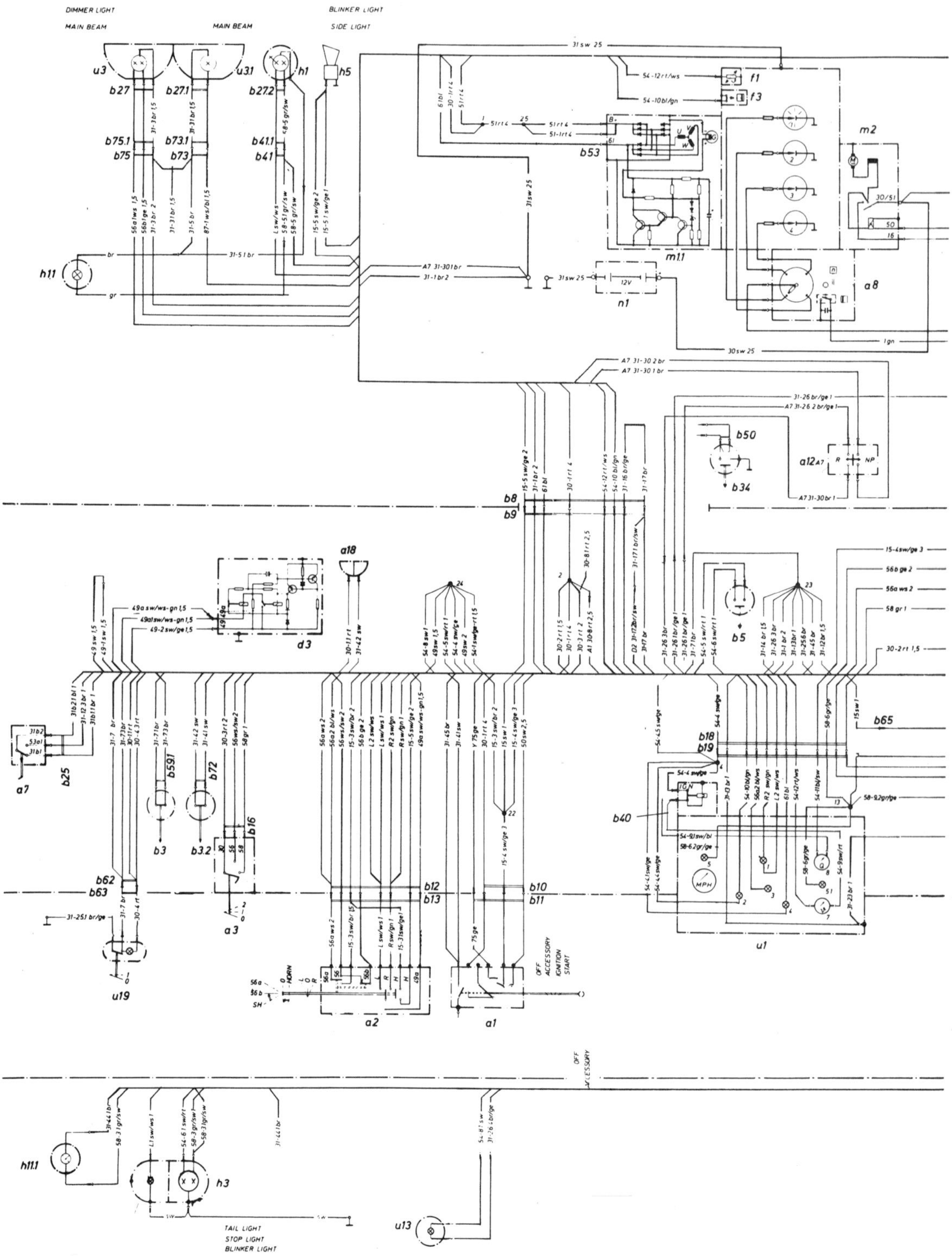

FIG 14:1 Wiring diagram for Capri 2000

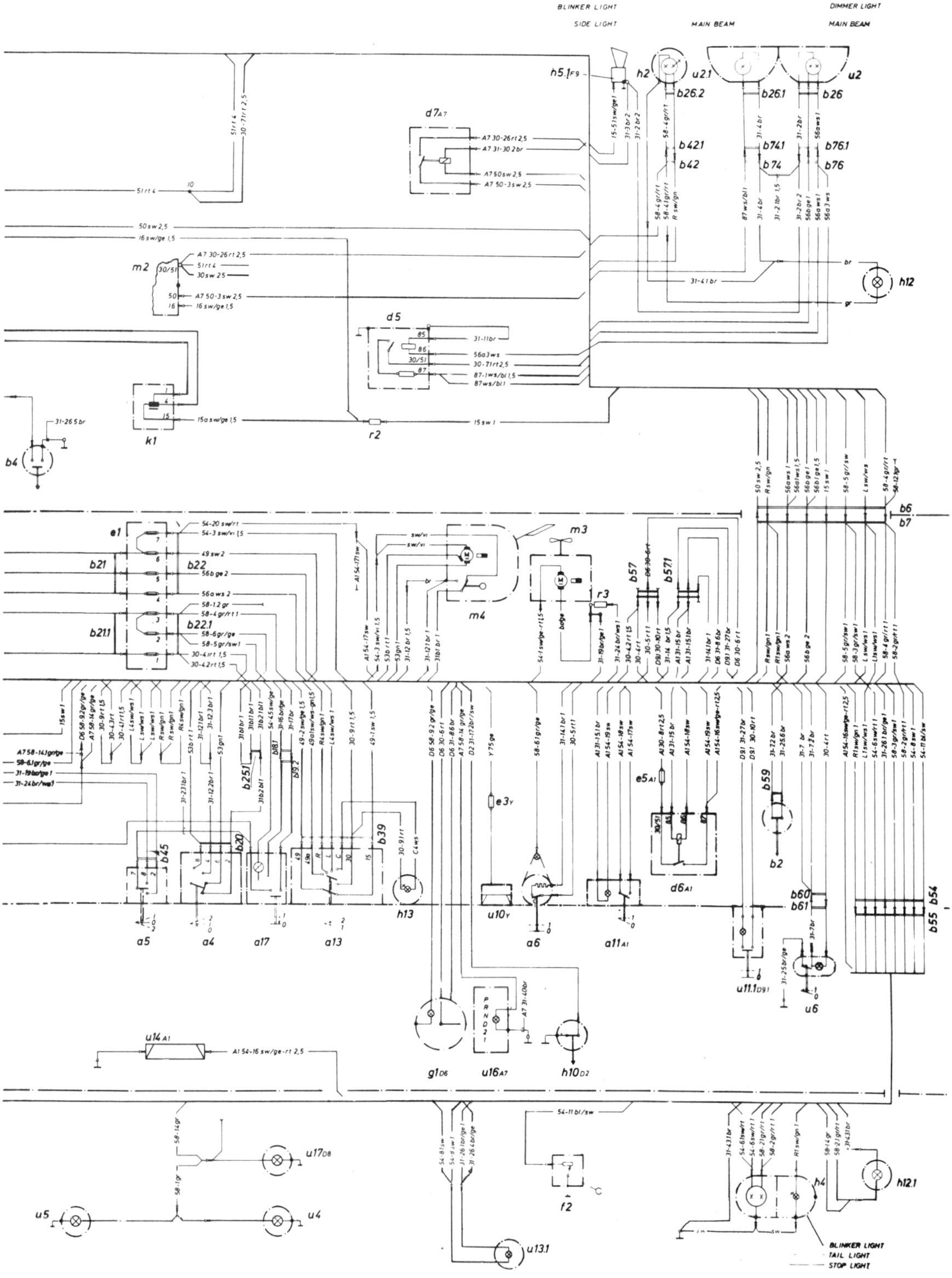
BLINKER LIGHT
SIDE LIGHT
MAIN BEAM
DIMMER LIGHT
MAIN BEAM
h5.1
h2
u2.1
u2
b26.2
b26.1
b26
b42.1
b42
b74.1
b74
b76.1
b76
d7
m2
h12
d5
k1
r2
b4
e1
b21
b22
b21.1
b22.1
m4
m3
r3
b57
b57.1
b6
b7
b25.1
b20
b45
b18.1
b19.2
b39
e3
e5
b59
b2
d6
h13
a5
a4
a17
a13
u10
a6
a11
b60
b61
b54
b55
u11.1
u6
u14
g1
u16
h10
u17
u5
u4
u13.1
f2
h4
h12.1
BLINKER LIGHT
TAIL LIGHT
STOP LIGHT

FIG 1 Schematic code and equipment titles

Key to Fig 14:1

a1 Steering/ignition lock
a2 Blinker switch
a3 Light switch
a4 Windshield wiper motor switch—two stage
a5 Heating blower switch—two stage
a6 Cigar lighter
a7 Foot operated switch windshield wiper motor
a8 Ignition distributor
a13 Blinker switch warning system
a17 Switch-control-light—two circuit brake system
a18 Buzzer
b2 Door contact interruptor RH interior light
b3 Door contact interruptor LH interior light
b3.2 Door contact interruptor buzzer
b4 Back-up light switch
b5 Stop light switch
b6 Multiple connector—Dash board, R
b7 Multiple connector—Dash board, R
b8 Multiple connector—dash board, L
b9 Multiple connector—Dash board, L
b10 Multiple connector—steering/ignition lock
b11 Multiple connector—Steering/ignition lock
b12 Multiple connector—blinker switch
b13 Multiple connector—blinker switch
b16 Multiple connector—light switch
b18 Multiple connector—instrument cluster
b18.1 Multiple connector—switch control light—two circuit brake system
b19 Multiple connector—instrument cluster
b19.2 Multiple connector—switch-control light—two circuit brake system
b20 Multiple connector—Windshield wiper motor switch
b21 Multiple connector—fuse box
b21.1 Multiple connector—fuse box
b22 Multiple connector—fuse box
b22.1 Multiple connector—Fuse box
b25 Multiple connector foot operated switch windshield wiper motor
b25.1 Multiple connector wiper wash system
b26 Multiple connector main beam headlight, R
b26.1 Multiple connector remote headlight, R
b26.2 Multiple connector blinker—side light, R
b27 Multiple connector main beam headlight, L
b27.1 Multiple connector remote headlight, L
b41.1 Multiple connector blinker—side light, L
b42 Multiple connector blinker—side light, R
b42.1 Multiple connector blinker—side light, R
b45 Multiple connector heating blower switch
b50 Multiple connector warning light switch—two circuit brake system
b53 Multiple connector alternator
b54 Multiple connector—instrument panel, R
b55 Multiple connector—instrument panel, R
b57 Multiple connector
b57.1 Multiple connector
b59 Door contact switch, R
b59.1 Door contact switch, L
b60 Multiple connector—interior light, R
b61 Multiple connector—interior light, R
b62 Multiple connector—interior light, L
b63 Multiple connector—interior light, L
b65 Connector wire 15
b72 Multiple connector buzzer switch
b73 Multiple connector remote headlight, L
b73.1 Multiple connector remote headlight, L
b74 Multiple connector remote headlight, R
b74.1 Multiple connector remote headlight, R
b75 Multiple connector main beam headlight, L
b75.1 Multiple connector main beam headlight, L
b76 Multiple connector main beam headlight, R
b76.1 Multiple connector main beam headlight, R
d3 Blinker unit
d5 Relay remote headlights
e1 Fuse box
f1 Transmitter water temperature gauge
f2 Transmitter fuel gauge
f3 Oil pressure control switch
h1 Blinker—side light, L
h2 Blinker—side light, R
h3 Combined tail light, L
h4 Combined tail light, R
h5 Horn, L
h11 Side marker front, L
h11.1 Side marker back, L
h12 Side marker front, R
h12.1 Side marker back, R
h13 Warning indicator—control light
k1 Ignition coil
m1.1 Alternator
m2 Starter
m3 Heating blower motor
m4 Windshield wiper motor
n1 Battery

Wire codes

54-16 sw/ge-rt 2-5

- 2-5: Wire cross section in mm^2
  Unmarked wires have 0,56 mm^2 cross-section
- rt: Wire colour code – secondary colours
- sw/ge: Wire colour code – main colour
- 54-16: Wire number

Colour codes – Key

sw = black	rs = pink	ge = yellow	gr = grey
ws = white	gn = green	bl = blue	br = brown
rt = red			vi = violet

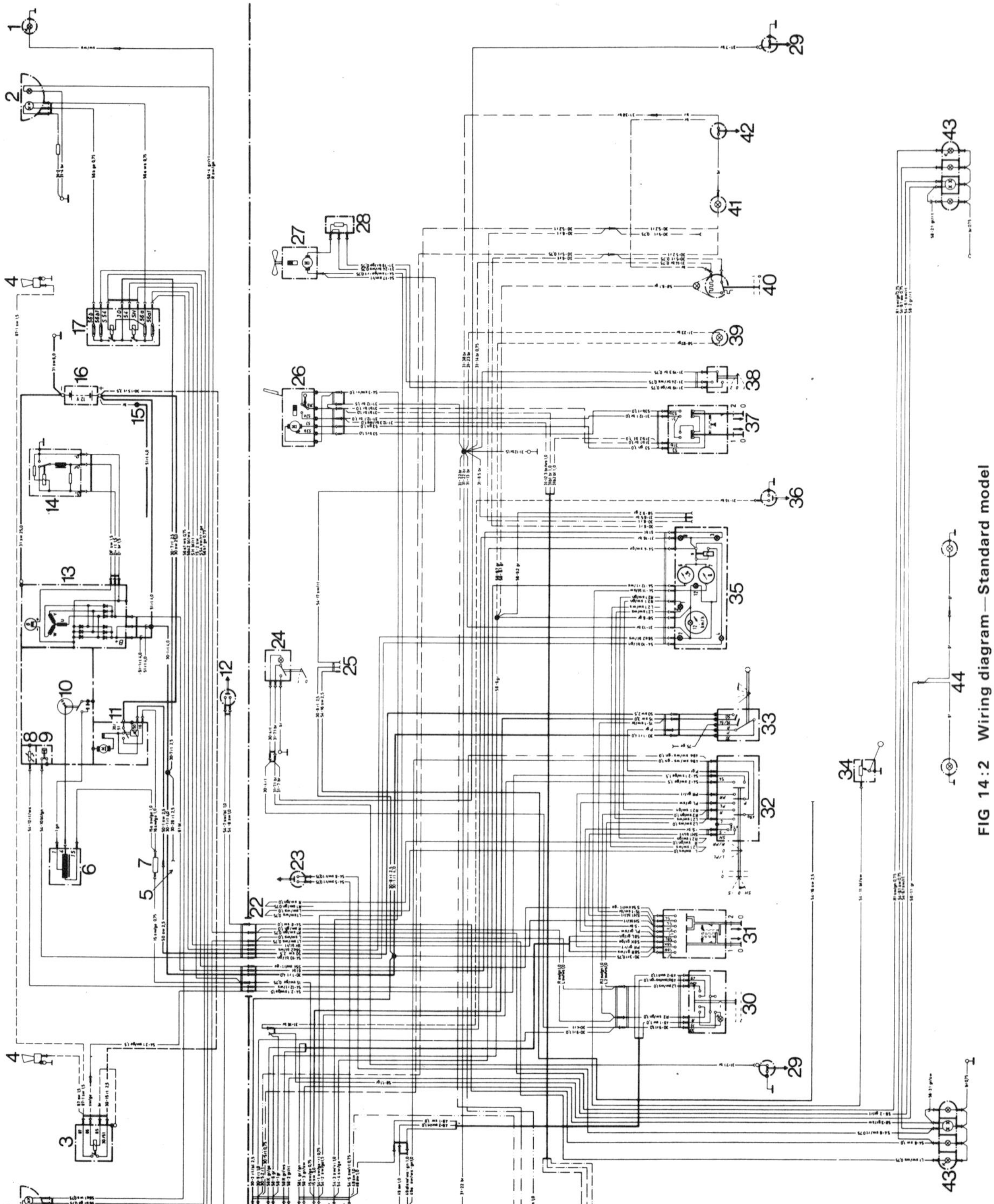

FIG 14:2 Wiring diagram—Standard model

Key to Fig 14:2 1 Front indicator 2 Headlamp 3 Relay horn 4 Horn 5 Relay—auto trans. 6 Ignition coil 7 Series resistance—ignition coil 8 Temperature gauge sender unit 9 Oil pressure switch 10 Distributor 11 Starter motor 12 Back-up lamp switch 13 Alternator 14 Regulator 15 Fuse wire—alternator (FORD U.K.) 16 Battery 17 Headlamp relay 18 Fuse block 19 Flasher unit 20 Flasher unit (FORD U.K.) 21 Wiper motor—foot switch 22 Vehicles without hazard flasher system 23 Stop light switch 24 Interior light 25 Heated rear window 26 Wiper motor 27 Heater motor 28 Series resistance, heater motor 29 Courtesy light switch 30 Hazard flasher switch 31 Light switch 32 Indicator switch 33 Steering lock ignition switch 34 Fuel gauge sender unit 35 Instrument cluster: 1 Flasher warning light (red), 2 Main beam warning light (blue), 3 Ignition warning light (green), 4 Oil pressure warning light (red), 6 Temperature gauge, 7 Fuel gauge, 8 Handbrake warning light, 9 Voltage regulator, 12 Instrument lighting 36 Handbrake warning light switch 37 Wiper motor switch 38 Heater blower switch 39 Lighting, heater blower switch 40 Cigarette lighter 41 Glove box lamp 42 Glove box lamp switch 43 Rear lamp assembly 44 Number plate lamps

Wiring Loom on Standard instrument panel has no connections for any auxiliary instrumentation

Fuses (fuse block): 1 Interior lights, hazard flasher system, cigarette lighter, electric clock, glove box lamp 2 Instrument lighting, number plate lamps 3 Side light RH, rear lamp RH 4 Side light LH, rear lamp LH 5 Heater blower motor, horn, heated rear window 6 Wiper motor, back-up lamps, instrument cluster 7 Indicator lamp, brake light

Unmarked fuses are 8 amps

———————— Standard-, L and XL
—··—··—··—··— Standard only
— — — — — — — XL
—·—·—·—·—·— L and XL

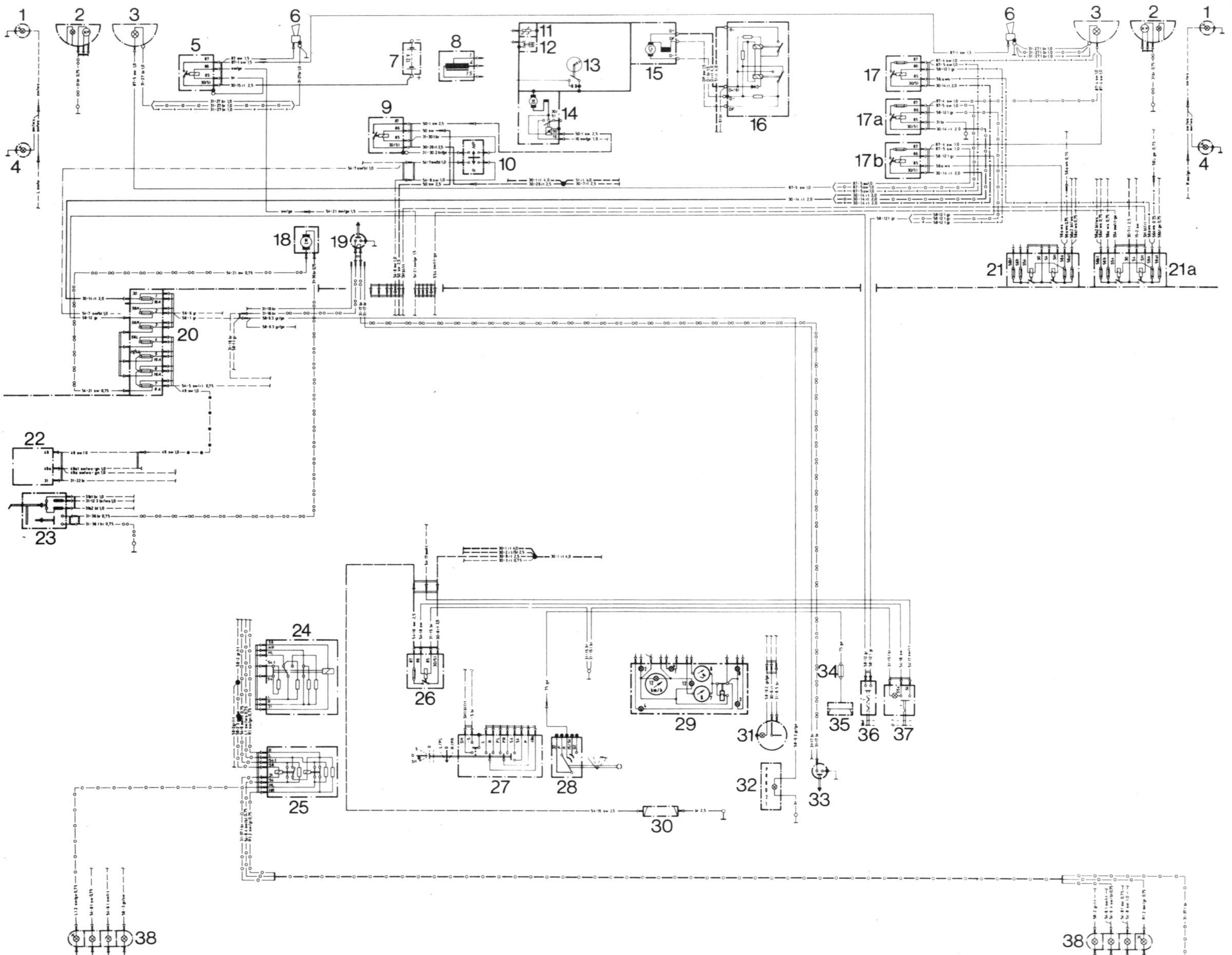

FIG 14:3 Supplementary wiring diagram—standard model

Key to Fig 14:3 1 Front indicator 2 Headlamp 3 Fog lamp 4 Front side repeater lamp 5 Horn relay 6 Horn 7 Battery 8 Ignition coil 9 Relay—auto trans. 10 Inhibitor switch—auto trans. 11 Temperature gauge sender unit 12 Oil pressure sender unit 13 Distributor 14 Starter motor 15 Alternator 16 Regulator 17 Relay—fog lamp (France) 17a Relay—fog lamp (FORD U.K.) 17b Relay—fog lamp (special equipment) 18 Washer motor 19 Dual braking system warning light switch 20 Fuse block 21 Headlamp relay 21a Headlamp relay (Italy and France) 22 Flasher unit 23 Wiper foot switch 24 and 25 Operational relays for double lighting intensity (FORD U.K.) 26 Heater rear window relay 27 Indicator switch 28 Steering lock/ignition switch 29 Instrument cluster 30 Heater rear window 31 Clock 32 Quadrant lamp 33 Handbrake warning light switch 34 Fuse—radio (medium delay action) 35 Radio 36 Fog lamp switch 37 Heater rear window switch 38 Rear lamp assembly switch

Fuses (Fuse block): 1 Interior lights, hazard flasher system, cigarette lighter, clock, glove box lamp 2 Instrument lighting, number plate lamps, quadrant lamp 3 Side light—RH, rear lamp—RH 4 Side light—LH, rear lamp—LH 5 Heater blower motor, horn, heated rear window 6 Wiper motor, back-up lamps, instrument cluster 7 Indicator lamp, brake light

All unmarked fuses are 8 amps

————————	Wire for special equipment
— — — — — — — — — — — —	Standard wire (as shown in wiring diagram for standard model)
—o—o—o—o—o—o—o—	Ford U.K.
—.—.—.—.—.—.—.—	Italy, Portugal and France
—..—..—..—..—..—..—	Italy
—oo—oo—oo—oo—oo—oo—oo	Sweden
—+—+—+—+—+—+—+—+—	France

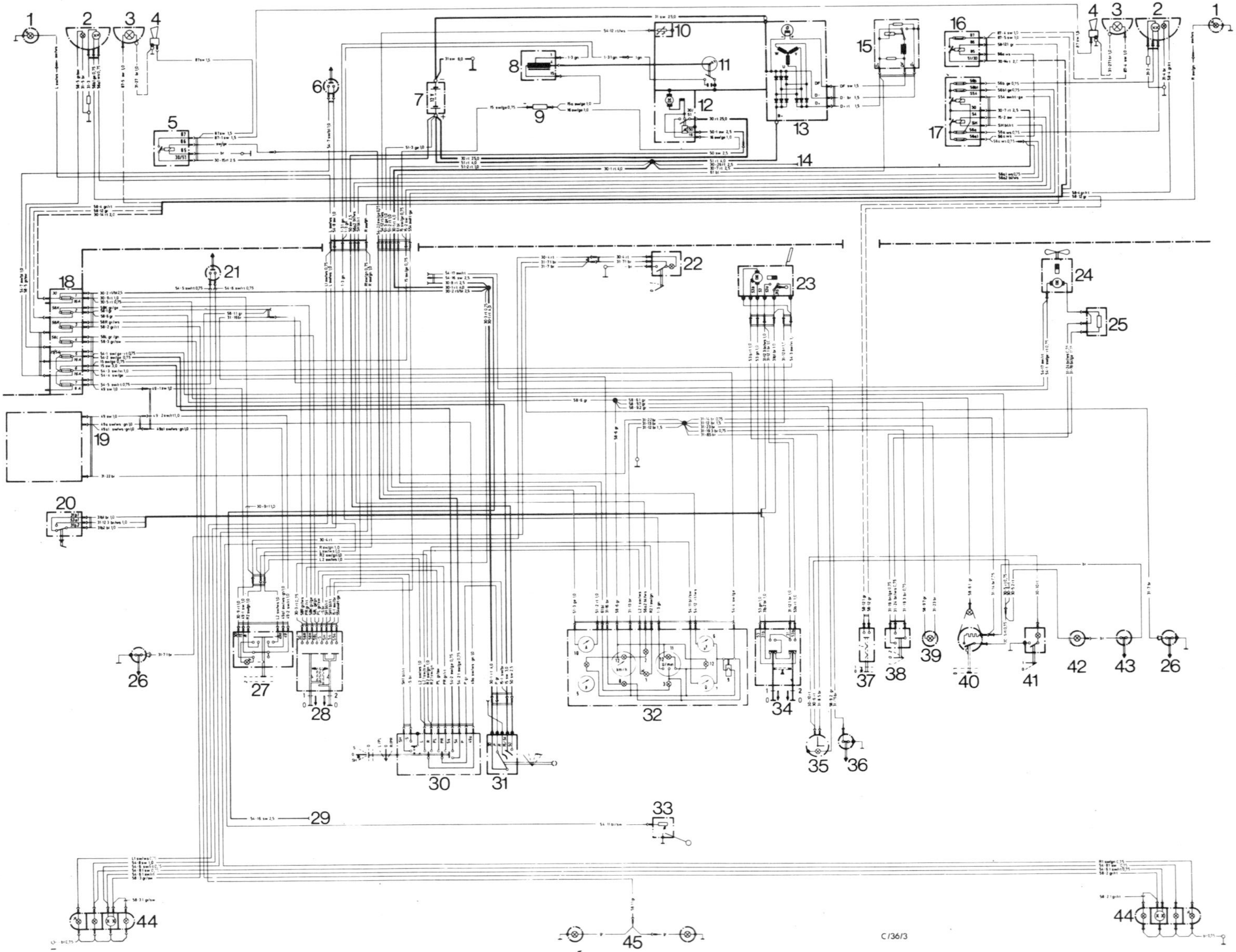

FIG 14 : 4 Wiring diagram—model GT (1600)

Key to Fig 14:4 1 Front indicator 2 Headlamp 3 Fog lamp 4 Horn 5 Two-tone horn relay 6 Dual braking system warning light switch 7 Battery 8 Ignition coil 9 Series resistance--ignition coil 10 Temperature gauge sender unit 11 Distributor 12 Starter motor 13 Alternator 14 Relay auto trans. 15 Regulator 16 Relay fog lamp 17 Headlamp relay 18 Fuse block 19 Flasher unit 20 Wiper foot switch 21 Brake light switch 22 Interior light 23 Wiper motor 24 Heater blower motor 25 Series resistance, heater blower motor 26 Courtesy light switch 27 Hazard light switch 28 Light switch 29 Heated rear window 30 Direction indicator lamp switch 31 Steering lock ignition switch 32 Instrument cluster: 1 Indicator warning light (red), 2 Main beam warning light (blue), 3 Ignition warning light (green), 5 Oil pressure gauge, 6 Temperature gauge, 7 Fuel gauge, 8 Brake warning light (red), 9 Voltage regulator, 10 Ammeter, 11 Tachometer, 12 Instrument lights 33 Fuel gauge sender unit 34 Wiper motor switch 35 Clock 36 Handbrake warning light switch 37 Fog lamp switch 38 Heater motor switch 39 Lighting, heater motor switch 40 Cigarette lighter 41 Map reading light 42 Glove compartment lamp 43 Glove compartment lamp switch 44 Rear lamp assembly 45 Number plate lamps

Fuses (Fuse block): 1 Interior lights, hazard flasher system, cigarette lighter, clock, glove box lamp 2 Instrument lighting, number plate lamps 3 Side light—RH, rear lamp—RH 4 Side light—LH, rear lamp—LH 5 Heater blower motor, horn, heated rear window 6 Wiper motor, back-up lamps, instrument cluster 7 Indicator lamp, brake light

All unmarked fuses are 8 amps

———— Model GT and GTR

– – – – GTR only

FIG 4 Schematic code and equipment titles

r2	Series resistance wire ignition
r3	Series resistor heating blower
u1	Instrument cluster
u2	Main beam headlight, R
u2.1	Remote headlight, R
u3	Main beam headlight, L
u3.1	Remote headlight, L
u4	License plate light, R
u5	License plate light, L
u6	Interior light, R
u13	Back-up light, L
u13.1	Back-up light, R
u19	Interior light, L
a11	Heating plate switch
d6	Working current relay heating plate
e5	Fuse heating plate
u14	Heating plate
a12	Blocking—switch automatic transmission
u16	Transmission control selector dial
d7	Working current relay automatic transmission
h10	Handbrake warning switch
g1	Clock
u17	Luggage compartment light
u11.1	Reading light
h5.1	Horn, R
e3	Fuse radio
u10	Radio
b27.2	Multiple connector blinker—side light, L
b34	Warning light switch two circuit brake system
b39	Multiple connector blinker switch warning system
b40	Voltage divider
b41	Multiple connector blinker—side light, L
30	Interior lights Reading lights Four way hazard flasher Clock Buzzer Cigar lighter
58	Tail light, L Side light front and back, L Illumination—instrument cluster Illumination—Cigar lighter Illumination—transmission control selector dial Illumination—clock Tail light, R Side light front and back, R Luggage compartment lights License plate lights
56a	Main beam Relay remote headlights
56b	Low beam
15	Back-up lights Heating blower motor Blinker system Stop light Voltage divider Control light—two circuit brake system Control light charging current Control light oil pressure
15	Windshield wiper motor Current circuit heating plate
	Interior wiring diagram and symbol according to DIN. A. IEC.
A1	In combination with heating plate
A7	In combination with automatic gear
D2	In combination with two circuit brake system
D6	In combination with clock
D8	In combination with luggage compartment light
D9	In combination with interior light, L
D9.1	In combination with reading light
F9	In combination with horn, R
Y	In combination with radio

Colour code **Bl** Blue **Br** Brown **Bk** Black **G** Green **LG** Light Green **O** Orange **P** Purple **Pk** Pink **R** Red **W** White **Y** Yellow

Inches	Decimals	Millimetres	Inches to Millimetres		Millimetres to Inches	
			Inches	mm	mm	Inches
1/64	.015625	.3969	.001	.0254	.01	.00039
1/32	.03125	.7937	.002	.0508	.02	.00079
3/64	.046875	1.1906	.003	.0762	.03	.00118
1/16	.0625	1.5875	.004	.1016	.04	.00157
5/64	.078125	1.9844	.005	.1270	.05	.00197
3/32	.09375	2.3812	.006	.1524	.06	.00236
7/64	.109375	2.7781	.007	.1778	.07	.00276
1/8	.125	3.1750	.008	.2032	.08	.00315
9/64	.140625	3.5719	.009	.2286	.09	.00354
5/32	.15625	3.9687	.01	.254	.1	.00394
11/64	.171875	4.3656	.02	.508	.2	.00787
3/16	.1875	4.7625	.03	.762	.3	.01181
13/64	.203125	5·1594	.04	1.016	.4	.01575
7/32	.21875	5.5562	.05	1.270	.5	.01969
15/64	.234375	5.9531	.06	1.524	.6	.02362
1/4	.25	6.3500	.07	1.778	.7	.02756
17/64	.265625	6.7469	.08	2.032	.8	.03150
9/32	.28125	7.1437	.09	2.286	.9	.03543
19/64	.296875	7.5406	.1	2.54	1	.03937
5/16	.3125	7.9375	.2	5.08	2	.07874
21/64	.328125	8.3344	.3	7.62	3	.11811
11/32	.34375	8.7312	.4	10.16	4	.15748
23/64	.359375	9.1281	.5	12.70	5	.19685
3/8	.375	9.5250	.6	15.24	6	.23622
25/64	.390625	9.9219	.7	17.78	7	.27559
13/32	.40625	10.3187	.8	20.32	8	.31496
27/64	.421875	10.7156	.9	22.86	9	.35433
7/16	.4375	11.1125	1	25.4	10	.39370
29/64	.453125	11.5094	2	50.8	11	.43307
15/32	.46875	11.9062	3	76.2	12	.47244
31/64	.484375	12.3031	4	101.6	13	.51181
1/2	.5	12.7000	5	127.0	14	.55118
33/64	.515625	13.0969	6	152.4	15	.59055
17/32	.53125	13.4937	7	177.8	16	.62992
35/64	.546875	13.8906	8	203.2	17	.66929
9/16	.5625	14.2875	9	228.6	18	.70866
37/64	.578125	14.6844	10	254.0	19	.74803
19/32	.59375	15.0812	11	279.4	20	.78740
39/64	.609375	15.4781	12	304.8	21	.82677
5/8	.625	15.8750	13	330.2	22	.86614
41/64	.640625	16.2719	14	355.6	23	.90551
21/32	.65625	16.6687	15	381.0	24	.94488
43/64	.671875	17.0656	16	406.4	25	.98425
11/16	.6875	17.4625	17	431.8	26	1.02362
45/64	.703125	17.8594	18	457.2	27	1.06299
23/32	.71875	18.2562	19	482.6	28	1.10236
47/64	.734375	18.6531	20	508.0	29	1.14173
3/4	.75	19.0500	21	533.4	30	1.18110
49/64	.765625	19.4469	22	558.8	31	1.22047
25/32	.78125	19.8437	23	584.2	32	1.25984
51/64	.796875	20.2406	24	609.6	33	1.29921
13/16	.8125	20.6375	25	635.0	34	1.33858
53/64	.828125	21.0344	26	660.4	35	1.37795
27/32	.84375	21.4312	27	685.8	36	1.41732
55/64	.859375	21.8281	28	711.2	37	1.4567
7/8	.875	22.2250	29	736.6	38	1.4961
57/64	.890625	22.6219	30	762.0	39	1.5354
29/32	.90625	23.0187	31	787.4	40	1.5748
59/64	.921875	23.4156	32	812.8	41	1.6142
15/16	.9375	23.8125	33	838.2	42	1.6535
61/64	.953125	24.2094	34	863.6	43	1.6929
31/32	.96875	24.6062	35	889.0	44	1.7323
63/64	.984375	25.0031	36	914.4	45	1.7717

UNITS	Pints to Litres	Gallons to Litres	Litres to Pints	Litres to Gallons	Miles to Kilometres	Kilometres to Miles	Lbs. per sq. In. to Kg. per sq. Cm.	Kg. per sq. Cm. to Lbs. per sq. In.
1	.57	4.55	1.76	.22	1.61	.62	.07	14.22
2	1.14	9.09	3.52	.44	3.22	1.24	.14	28.50
3	1.70	13.64	5.28	.66	4.83	1.86	.21	42.67
4	2.27	18.18	7.04	.88	6.44	2.49	.28	56.89
5	2.84	22.73	8.80	1.10	8.05	3.11	.35	71.12
6	3.41	27.28	10.56	1.32	9.66	3.73	.42	85.34
7	3.98	31.82	12.32	1.54	11.27	4.35	.49	99.56
8	4.55	36.37	14.08	1.76	12.88	4.97	.56	113.79
9		40.91	15.84	1.98	14.48	5.59	.63	128.00
10		45.46	17.60	2.20	16.09	6.21	.70	142.23
20				4.40	32.19	12.43	1.41	284.47
30				6.60	48.28	18.64	2.11	426.70
40				8.80	64.37	24.85		
50					80.47	31.07		
60					96.56	37.28		
70					112.65	43.50		
80					128.75	49.71		
90					144.84	55.92		
100					160.93	62.14		

UNITS	Lb ft to kgm	Kgm to lb ft	UNITS	Lb ft to kgm	Kgm to lb ft
1	.138	7.233	7	.967	50.631
2	.276	14.466	8	1.106	57.864
3	.414	21.699	9	1.244	65.097
4	.553	28.932	10	1.382	72.330
5	.691	36.165	20	2.765	144.660
6	.829	43.398	30	4.147	216.990

HINTS ON MAINTENANCE AND OVERHAUL

There are few things more rewarding than the restoration of a vehicle's original peak of efficiency and smooth performance.

The following notes are intended to help the owner to reach that state of perfection. Providing that he possesses the basic manual skills he should have no difficulty in performing most of the operations detailed in this manual. It must be stressed, however, that where recommended in the manual, highly-skilled operations ought to be entrusted to experts, who have the necessary equipment, to carry out the work satisfactorily.

Quality of workmanship:

The hazardous driving conditions on the roads to-day demand that vehicles should be as nearly perfect, mechanically, as possible. It is therefore most important that amateur work be carried out with care, bearing in mind the often inadequate working conditions, and also the inferior tools which may have to be used. It is easy to counsel perfection in all things, and we recognize that it may be setting an impossibly high standard. We do, however, suggest that every care should be taken to ensure that a vehicle is as safe to take on the road as it is humanly possible to make it.

Safe working conditions:

Even though a vehicle may be stationary, it is still potentially dangerous if certain sensible precautions are not taken when working on it while it is supported on jacks or blocks. It is indeed preferable not to use jacks alone, but to supplement them with carefully placed blocks, so that there will be plenty of support if the car rolls off the jacks during a strenuous manoeuvre. Axle stands are an excellent way of providing a rigid base which is not readily disturbed. Piles of bricks are a dangerous substitute. Be careful not to get under heavy loads on lifting tackle, the load could fall. It is preferable not to work alone when lifting an engine, or when working underneath a vehicle which is supported well off the ground. To be trapped, particularly under the vehicle, may have unpleasant results if help is not quickly forthcoming. Make some provision, however humble, to deal with fires. Always disconnect a battery if there is a likelihood of electrical shorts. These may start a fire if there is leaking fuel about. This applies particularly to leads which can carry a heavy current, like those in the starter circuit. While on the subject of electricity, we must also stress the danger of using equipment which is run off the mains and which has no earth or has faulty wiring or connections. So many workshops have damp floors, and electrical shocks are of such a nature that it is sometimes impossible to let go of a live lead or piece of equipment due to the muscular spasms which take place.

Work demanding special care:

This involves the servicing of braking, steering and suspension systems. On the road, failure of the braking system may be disastrous. Make quite sure that there can be no possibility of failure through the bursting of rusty brake pipes or rotten hoses, nor to a sudden loss of pressure due to defective seals or valves.

Problems:

The chief problems which may face an operator are:

1 External dirt.
2 Difficulty in undoing tight fixings
3 Dismantling unfamiliar mechanisms.
4 Deciding in what respect parts are defective.
5 Confusion about the correct order for reassembly.
6 Adjusting running clearances.
7 Road testing.
8 Final tuning.

Practical suggestion to solve the problems:

1 Preliminary cleaning of large parts—engines, transmissions, steering, suspensions, etc.,—should be carried out before removal from the car. Where road dirt and mud alone are present, wash clean with a high-pressure water jet, brushing to remove stubborn adhesions, and allow to drain and dry. Where oil or grease is also present, wash down with a proprietary compound (Gunk, Teepol etc.,) applying with a stiff brush—an old paint brush is suitable—into all crevices. Cover the distributor and ignition coils with a polythene bag and then apply a strong water jet to clear the loosened deposits. Allow to drain and dry. The assemblies will then be sufficiently clean to remove and transfer to the bench for the next stage.

On the bench, further cleaning can be carried out, first wiping the parts as free as possible from grease with old newspaper. Avoid using rag or cotton waste which can leave clogging fibres behind. Any remaining grease can be removed with a brush dipped in paraffin. If necessary, traces of paraffin can be removed by carbon tetrachloride. Avoid using paraffin or petrol in large quantities for cleaning in enclosed areas, such as garages, on account of the high fire risk.

When all exteriors have been cleaned, and not before, dismantling can be commenced. This ensures that dirt will not enter into interiors and orifices revealed by dismantling. In the next phases, where components have to be cleaned, use carbon tetrachloride in preference to petrol and keep the containers covered except when in use. After the components have been cleaned, plug small holes with tapered hard wood plugs cut to size and blank off larger orifices with grease-proof paper and masking tape. Do not use soft wood plugs or matchsticks as they may break.

2 It is not advisable to hammer on the end of a screw thread, but if it must be done, first screw on a nut to protect the thread, and use a lead hammer. This applies particularly to the removal of tapered cotters. Nuts and bolts seem to 'grow' together, especially in exhaust systems. If penetrating oil does not work, try the judicious application of heat, but be careful of starting a fire. Asbestos sheet or cloth is useful to isolate heat.

Tight bushes or pieces of tail-pipe rusted into a silencer can be removed by splitting them with an open-ended hacksaw. Tight screws can sometimes be started by a tap from a hammer on the end of a suitable screwdriver. Many tight fittings will yield to the judicious use of a hammer, but it must be a soft-faced hammer if damage is to be avoided, use a heavy block on the opposite side to absorb shock. Any parts of the steering system which have been damaged should be renewed, as attempts to repair them may lead to cracking and subsequent failure, and steering ball joints should be disconnected using a recommended tool to prevent damage.

3 If often happens that an owner is baffled when trying to dismantle an unfamiliar piece of equipment. So many modern devices are pressed together or assembled by spinning-over flanges, that they must be sawn apart. The intention is that the whole assembly must be renewed. However, parts which appear to be in one piece to the naked eye, may reveal close-fitting joint lines when inspected with a magnifying glass, and, this may provide the necessary clue to dismantling. Left-handed screw threads are used where rotational forces would tend to unscrew a right-handed screw thread.

Be very careful when dismantling mechanisms which may come apart suddenly. Work in an enclosed space where the parts will be contained, and drape a piece of cloth over the device if springs are likely to fly in all directions. Mark everything which might be reassembled in the wrong position, scratched symbols may be used on unstressed parts, or a sequence of tiny dots from a centre punch can be useful. Stressed parts should never be scratched or centre-popped as this may lead to cracking under working conditions. Store parts which look alike in the correct order for reassembly. Never rely upon memory to assist in the assembly of complicated mechanisms, especially when they will be dismantled for a long time, but make notes, and drawings to supplement the diagrams in the manual, and put labels on detached wires. Rust stains may indicate unlubricated wear. This can sometimes be seen round the outside edge of a bearing cup in a universal joint. Look for bright rubbing marks on parts which normally should not make heavy contact. These might prove that something is bent or running out of truth. For example, there might be bright marks on one side of a piston, at the top near the ring grooves, and others at the bottom of the skirt on the other side. This could well be the clue to a bent connecting rod. Suspected cracks can be proved by heating the component in a light oil to approximately 100°C, removing, drying off, and dusting with french chalk, if a crack is present the oil retained in the crack will stain the french chalk.

4 In determining wear, and the degree, against the permissible limits set in the manual, accurate measurement can only be achieved by the use of a micrometer. In many cases, the wear is given to the fourth place of decimals; that is in ten-thousandths of an inch. This can be read by the vernier scale on the barrel of a good micrometer. Bore diameters are more difficult to determine. If, however, the matching shaft is accurately measured, the degree of play in the bore can be felt as a guide to its suitability. In other cases, the shank of a twist drill of known diameter is a handy check.

Many methods have been devised for determining the clearance between bearing surfaces. To-day the best and simplest is by the use of Plastigage, obtainable from most garages. A thin plastic thread is laid between the two surfaces and the bearing is tightened, flattening the thread. On removal, the width of the thread is compared with a scale supplied with the thread and the clearance is read off directly. Sometimes joint faces leak persistently, even after gasket renewal. The fault will then be traceable to distortion, dirt or burrs. Studs which are screwed into soft metal frequently raise burrs at the point of entry. A quick cure for this is to chamfer the edge of the hole in the part which fits over the stud.

5 **Always check a replacement part with the original one before it is fitted.**

If parts are not marked, and the order for reassembly is not known, a little detective work will help. Look for marks which are due to wear to see if they can be mated. Joint faces may not be identical due to manufacturing errors, and parts which overlap may be stained, giving a clue to the correct position. Most fixings leave identifying marks especially if they were painted over on assembly. It is then easier to decide whether a nut, for instance, has a plain, a spring, or a shakeproof washer under it. All running surfaces become 'bedded' together after long spells of work and tiny imperfections on one part will be found to have left corresponding marks on the other. This is particularly true of shafts and bearings and even a score on a cylinder wall will show on the piston.

6 Checking end float or rocker clearances by feeler gauge may not always give accurate results because of wear. For instance, the rocker tip which bears on a valve stem may be deeply pitted, in which case the feeler will simply be bridging a depression. Thrust washers may also wear depressions in opposing faces to make accurate measurement difficult. End float is then easier to check by using a dial gauge. It is common practice to adjust end play in bearing assemblies, like front hubs with taper rollers, by doing up the axle nut until the hub becomes stiff to turn and then backing it off a little. Do not use this method with ballbearing hubs as the assembly is often preloaded by tightening the axle nut to its fullest extent. If the splitpin hole will not line up, file the base of the nut a little.

Steering assemblies often wear in the straight-ahead position. If any part is adjusted, make sure that it remains free when moved from lock to lock. Do not be surprised if an assembly like a steering gearbox, which is known to be carefully adjusted outside the car, becomes stiff when it is bolted in place. This will be due to distortion of the case by the pull of the mounting bolts, particularly if the mounting points are not all touching together. This problem may be met in other equipment and is cured by careful attention to the alignment of mounting points.

When a spanner is stamped with a size and A/F it means that the dimension is the width between the jaws and has no connection with ANF, which is the designation for the American National Fine thread. Coarse threads like Whitworth are rarely used on cars to-day except for studs which screw into soft aluminium or cast iron. For this reason it might be found that the top end of a cylinder head stud has a fine thread and the lower end a coarse thread to screw into the cylinder block. If the car has mainly UNF threads then it is likely that any coarse threads will be UNC, which are not the same as Whitworth. Small sizes have the same number of threads in Whitworth and UNC, but in the $\frac{1}{2}$ inch size for example, there are twelve threads to the inch in the former and thirteen in the latter.

7 After a major overhaul, particularly if a great deal of work has been done on the braking, steering and suspension systems, it is advisable to approach the problem of testing with care. If the braking system has been overhauled, apply heavy pressure to the brake pedal and get a second operator to check every possible source of leakage. The brakes may work extremely well, but a leak could cause complete failure after a few miles.

Do not fit the hub caps until every wheel nut has been checked for tightness, and make sure the tyre pressures are correct. Check the levels of coolant, lubricants and hydraulic fluids. Being satisfied that all is well, take the car on the road and test the brakes at once. Check the steering and the action of the handbrake. Do all this at moderate speeds on quiet roads, and make sure there is no other vehicle behind you when you try a rapid stop.

Finally, remember that many parts settle down after a time, so check for tightness of all fixings after the car has been on the road for a hundred miles or so.

8 It is useless to tune an engine which has not reached its normal running temperature. In the same way, the tune of an engine which is stiff after a rebore will be different when the engine is again running free. Remember too, that rocker clearances on pushrod operated valve gear will change when the cylinder head nuts are tightened after an initial period of running with a new head gasket.

Trouble may not always be due to what seems the obvious cause. Ignition, carburation and mechanical condition are interdependent and spitting back through the carburetter, which might be attributed to a weak mixture, can be caused by a sticking inlet valve.

For one final hint on tuning, never adjust more than one thing at a time or it will be impossible to tell which adjustment produced the desired result.

NOTES

GLOSSARY OF TERMS

Allen key Cranked wrench of hexagonal section for use with socket head screws.

Alternator Electrical generator producing alternating current. Rectified to direct current for battery charging.

Ambient temperature Surrounding atmospheric temperature.

Annulus Used in engineering to indicate the outer ring gear of an epicyclic gear train.

Armature The shaft carrying the windings, which rotates in the magnetic field of a generator or starter motor. That part of a solenoid or relay which is activated by the magnetic field.

Axial In line with, or pertaining to, an axis.

Backlash Play in meshing gears.

Balance lever A bar where force applied at the centre is equally divided between connections at the ends.

Banjo axle Axle casing with large diameter housing for the crownwheel and differential.

Bendix pinion A self-engaging and self-disengaging drive on a starter motor shaft.

Bevel pinion A conical shaped gearwheel, designed to mesh with a similar gear with an axis usually at 90 deg. to its own.

bhp Brake horse power, measured on a dynamometer.

bmep Brake mean effective pressure. Average pressure on a piston during the working stroke.

Brake cylinder Cylinder with hydraulically operated piston(s) acting on brake shoes or pad(s).

Brake regulator Control valve fitted in hydraulic braking system which limits brake pressure to rear brakes during heavy braking to prevent rear wheel locking.

Camber Angle at which a wheel is tilted from the vertical.

Capacitor Modern term for an electrical condenser. Part of distributor assembly, connected across contact breaker points, acts as an interference suppressor.

Castellated Top face of a nut, slotted across the flats, to take a locking splitpin.

Castor Angle at which the kingpin or swivel pin is tilted when viewed from the side.

cc Cubic centimetres. Engine capacity is arrived at by multiplying the area of the bore in sq cm by the stroke in cm by the number of cylinders.

Clevis U-shaped forked connector used with a clevis pin, usually at handbrake connections.

Collet A type of collar, usually split and located in a groove in a shaft, and held in place by a retainer. The arrangement used to retain the spring(s) on a valve stem in most cases.

Commutator Rotating segmented current distributor between armature windings and brushes in generator or motor.

Compression The ratio, or quantitative relation, of the total volume (piston at bottom of stroke) to the unswept volume (piston at top of stroke) in an engine cylinder.

Condenser See capacitor.

Core plug Plug for blanking off a manufacturing hole in a casting.

Crownwheel Large bevel gear in rear axle, driven by a bevel pinion attached to the propeller shaft. Sometimes called a 'ring gear'.

'C'-spanner Like a 'C' with a handle. For use on screwed collars without flats, but with slots or holes.

Damper Modern term for shock-absorber, used in vehicle suspension systems to damp out spring oscillations.

Depression The lowering of atmospheric pressure as in the inlet manifold and carburetter.

Dowel Close tolerance pin, peg, tube, or bolt, which accurately locates mating parts.

Drag link Rod connecting steering box drop arm (pitman arm) to nearest front wheel steering arm in certain types of steering systems.

Dry liner Thinwall tube pressed into cylinder bore

Dry sump Lubrication system where all oil is scavenged from the sump, and returned to a separate tank.

Dynamo See Generator.

Electrode Terminal, part of an electrical component, such as the points or 'Electrodes' of a sparking plug.

Electrolyte In lead-acid car batteries a solution of sulphuric acid and distilled water.

End float The axial movement between associated parts, end play.

EP Extreme pressure. In lubricants, special grades for heavily loaded bearing surfaces, such as gear teeth in a gearbox, or crownwheel and pinion in a rear axle.

Fade	Of brakes. Reduced efficiency due to overheating.
Field coils	Windings on the polepieces of motors and generators.
Fillets	Narrow finishing strips usually applied to interior bodywork.
First motion shaft	Input shaft from clutch to gearbox.
Fullflow filter	Filters in which all the oil is pumped to the engine. If the element becomes clogged, a bypass valve operates to pass unfiltered oil to the engine.
FWD	Front wheel drive.
Gear pump	Two meshing gears in a close fitting casing. Oil is carried from the inlet round the outside of both gears in the spaces between the gear teeth and casing to the outlet, the meshing gear teeth prevent oil passing back to the inlet, and the oil is forced through the outlet port.
Generator	Modern term for 'Dynamo'. When rotated produces electrical current.
Grommet	A ring of protective or sealing material. Can be used to protect pipes or leads passing through bulkheads.
Grubscrew	Fully threaded headless screw with screwdriver slot. Used for locking, or alignment purposes.
Gudgeon pin	Shaft which connects a piston to its connecting rod. Sometimes called 'wrist pin', or 'piston pin'.
Halfshaft	One of a pair transmitting drive from the differential.
Helical	In spiral form. The teeth of helical gears are cut at a spiral angle to the side faces of the gearwheel.
Hot spot	Hot area that assists vapourisation of fuel on its way to cylinders. Often provided by close contact between inlet and exhaust manifolds.
HT	High Tension. Applied to electrical current produced by the ignition coil for the sparking plugs.
Hydrometer	A device for checking specific gravity of liquids. Used to check specific gravity of electrolyte.
Hypoid bevel gears	A form of bevel gear used in the rear axle drive gears. The bevel pinion meshes below the centre line of the crownwheel, giving a lower propeller shaft line.
Idler	A device for passing on movement. A free running gear between driving and driven gears. A lever transmitting track rod movement to a side rod in steering gear.
Impeller	A centrifugal pumping element. Used in water pumps to stimulate flow.
Journals	Those parts of a shaft that are in contact with the bearings.
Kingpin	The main vertical pin which carries the front wheel spindle, and permits steering movement. May be called 'steering pin' or 'swivel pin'.
Layshaft	The shaft which carries the laygear in the gearbox. The laygear is driven by the first motion shaft and drives the third motion shaft according to the gear selected. Sometimes called the 'countershaft' or 'second motion shaft.'
lb ft	A measure of twist or torque. A pull of 10 lb at a radius of 1 ft is a torque of 10 lb ft.
lb/sq in	Pounds per square inch.
Little-end	The small, or piston end of a connecting rod. Sometimes called the 'small-end'.
LT	Low Tension. The current output from the battery.
Mandrel	Accurately manufactured bar or rod used for test or centring purposes.
Manifold	A pipe, duct, or chamber, with several branches.
Needle rollers	Bearing rollers with a length many times their diameter.
Oil bath	Reservoir which lubricates parts by immersion. In air filters, a separate oil supply for wetting a wire mesh element to hold the dust.
Oil wetted	In air filters, a wire mesh element lightly oiled to trap and hold airborne dust.
Overlap	Period during which inlet and exhaust valves are open together.
Panhard rod	Bar connected between fixed point on chassis and another on axle to control sideways movement.
Pawl	Pivoted catch which engages in the teeth of a ratchet to permit movement in one direction only.
Peg spanner	Tool with pegs, or pins, to engage in holes or slots in the part to be turned.
Pendant pedals	Pedals with levers that are pivoted at the top end.
Phillips screwdriver	A cross-point screwdriver for use with the cross-slotted heads of Phillips screws.
Pinion	A small gear, usually in relation to another gear.
Piston-type damper	Shock absorber in which damping is controlled by a piston working in a closed oil-filled cylinder.
Preloading	Preset static pressure on ball or roller bearings not due to working loads.
Radial	Radiating from a centre, like the spokes of a wheel.

Radius rod	Pivoted arm confining movement of a part to an arc of fixed radius.
Ratchet	Toothed wheel or rack which can move in one direction only, movement in the other being prevented by a pawl.
Ring gear	A gear tooth ring attached to outer periphery of flywheel. Starter pinion engages with it during starting.
Runout	Amount by which rotating part is out of true.
Semi-floating axle	Outer end of rear axle halfshaft is carried on bearing inside axle casing. Wheel hub is secured to end of shaft.
Servo	A hydraulic or pneumatic system for assisting, or, augmenting a physical effort. See 'Vacuum Servo'.
Setscrew	One which is threaded for the full length of the shank.
Shackle	A coupling link, used in the form of two parallel pins connected by side plates to secure the end of the master suspension spring and absorb the effects of deflection.
Shell bearing	Thinwalled steel shell lined with antifriction metal. Usually semi-circular and used in pairs for main and big-end bearings.
Shock absorber	See 'Damper'.
Silentbloc	Rubber bush bonded to inner and outer metal sleeves.
Socket-head screw	Screw with hexagonal socket for an Allen key.
Solenoid	A coil of wire creating a magnetic field when electric current passes through it. Used with a soft iron core to operate contacts or a mechanical device.
Spur gear	A gear with teeth cut axially across the periphery.
Stub axle	Short axle fixed at one end only.
Tachometer	An instrument for accurate measurement of rotating speed. Usually indicates in revolutions per minute.
TDC	Top Dead Centre. The highest point reached by a piston in a cylinder, with the crank and connecting rod in line.
Thermostat	Automatic device for regulating temperature. Used in vehicle coolant systems to open a valve which restricts circulation at low temperature.
Third motion shaft	Output shaft of gearbox.
Threequarter floating axle	Outer end of rear axle halfshaft flanged and bolted to wheel hub, which runs on bearing mounted on outside of axle casing. Vehicle weight is not carried by the axle shaft.
Thrust bearing or washer	Used to reduce friction in rotating parts subject to axial loads.
Torque	Turning or twisting effort. See 'lb ft'.
Track rod	The bar(s) across the vehicle which connect the steering arms and maintain the front wheels in their correct alignment.
UJ	Universal joint. A coupling between shafts which permits angular movement.
UNF	Unified National Fine screw thread.
Vacuum servo	Device used in brake system, using difference between atmospheric pressure and inlet manifold depression to operate a piston which acts to augment brake pressure as required. See 'Servo'.
Venturi	A restriction or 'choke' in a tube, as in a carburetter, used to increase velocity to obtain a reduction in pressure.
Vernier	A sliding scale for obtaining fractional readings of the graduations of an adjacent scale.
Welch plug	A domed thin metal disc which is partially flattened to lock in a recess. Used to plug core holes in castings.
Wet liner	Removable cylinder barrel, sealed against coolant leakage, where the coolant is in direct contact with the outer surface.
Wet sump	A reservoir attached to the crankcase to hold the lubricating oil.

NOTES

INDEX

THE AUTOBOOK SERIES OF WORKSHOP MANUALS

Alfa Romeo Giulia 1600, 1750 1962 on
Aston Martin 1921-58
Auto Union Audi 70, 80, Super 90, 1966 on
Audi 100 1969 on
(Austin, Morris etc.) 1100 Mk. 1 1962-67
(Austin, Morris etc.) 1100 Mk. 2, 3, 1300 Mk. 1, 2, 3 America 1968 on
Austin A30, A35, A40 Farina
Austin A55 Mk. 2, A60 1958-69
Austin A99, A110 1959-68
Austin J4 1960 on
Austin Maxi 1969 on
Austin, Morris 1800 1964 on
Austin, Morris 2200 1972 on
Austin, Morris 1300, 1500 Nomad 1969 on

BMC 3 (Austin A50, A55 Mk. 1, Morris Oxford 2, 3 1954-59)
Austin Healey 100/6, 3000 1956-68
(Austin Healey, MG) Sprite, Midget 1958 on
Bedford Beagle HA Vans 1964 on
BMW 1600 1966 on
BMW 1800 1964 on
BMW 2000, 2002 1966 on
Chevrolet Corvair 1960-69
Chevrolet Corvette V8 1957-65
Chevrolet Corvette V8 1965 on
Chevrolette Vega 2300 1970 on
Chrysler Valiant V8 1965 on
Chrysler Valiant Straight Six 1966-70
Citroen DS 19, ID 19 1955-66
Citroen ID 19, DS 19, 20, 21 1966 on
Daf 31, 32, 33, 44, 55 1961 on
Datsun 1200 1970 on
Datsun 1300, 1400, 1600 1968 on
Datsun 240C 1971 on
Datsun 240Z Sport 1970 on
De Dion Bouton 1899-1907
Fiat 124 1966 on
Fiat 124 Sport 1966 on
Fiat 125 1967 on
Fiat 128 1969 on
Fiat 500 1957 on
Fiat 600, 600D 1955-69
Fiat 850 1964 on
Fiat 1100 1957-69
Fiat 1300, 1500 1961-67

Ford Anglia Prefect 100E 1953-62
Ford Anglia 105E, Prefect 107E 1959-67
Ford Capri 1300, 1600 OHV 1968 on
Ford Capri 1300, 1600, 2000 OHC 1972 on
Ford Capri 2000, 3000 1969 on
Ford Classic, Capri 1961-64
Ford Consul, Zephyr, Zodiac, 1, 2 1950-62
Ford Corsair Straight Four 1963-65
Ford Corsair V4 1965-68
Ford Corsair V4 2000 1969-70
Ford Cortina 1962-66
Ford Cortina 1967-68
Ford Cortina 1969-70
Ford Cortina Mk. 3 1970 on
Ford Escort 1967 on
Ford Falcon 6 1964-70
Ford Falcon XK, XL 1960-63
Ford Falcon 6 XR/XA 1966 on
Ford Falcon V8 (U.S.A.) 1965-71
Ford Falcon V8 (Aust.) 1966 on
Ford Pinto 1970 on
Ford Maverick 1969 on
Ford Mustang V8 1965-71
Ford Thames 10, 12, 15 cwt 1957-65
Ford Transit 1965 on
Ford Zephyr Zodiac Mk. 3 1962-66
Ford Zephyr Zodiac V4, V6, Mk. 4 1966-72
Ford Consul, Granada 1972
Hillman Avenger 1970 on
Hillman Hunter 1966 on
Hillman Imp 1963-68
Hillman Imp 1969 on
Hillman Minx 1 to 5 1956-65
Hillman Minx 1965-67
Hillman Minx 1966-70
Hillman Super Minx 1961-65
Holden V8 1968 on
Holden Straight Six 1948-66
Holden Straight Six 1966 on
Holden Torana 4 Series HB 1967-69
Jaguar XK120, 140, 150, Mk. 7, 8, 9 1948-61
Jaguar 2.4, 3.4, 3.8 Mk. 1, 2 1955-69
Jaguar 'E' Type 1961 on
Jaguar 'S' Type 420 1963-68

Jaguar XJ6 1968 on
Jowett Javelin Jupiter 1947-53
Landrover 1, 2 1948-61
Landrover 2, 2a, 3 1959 on
Mazda 616 1970 on
Mazda 1200, 1300 1969 on
Mazda 1500, 1800 1967 on
Mercedes-Benz 190b, 190c, 200 1959-68
Mercedes-Benz 220 1959-65
Mercedes-Benz 220/8 1968 on
Mercedes-Benz 230 1963-68
Mercedes-Benz 250 1965-67
Mercedes-Benz 250 1968 on
Mercedes-Benz 280 1968 on
MG TA to TF 1936-55
MGA MGB 1955-68
MGB 1969 on
Mini 1959 on
Mini Cooper 1961 on
Morgan 1936-69
Morris Marina 1971 on
Morris (Aust) Marina 1972 on
Morris Minor 2, 1000 1952-71
Morris Oxford 5, 6 1959-71
NSU 1000 1963 on
NSU Prinz 1 to 4 1957 on
Opel Ascona, Manta 1970 on
Opel GT 1900 1968 on
Opel Kadett, Olympia 993cc 1078cc 1962 on
Opel Kadett, Olympia 1492, 1698, 1897cc 1967 on
Opel Rekord C 1966 on
Peugeot 204 1965 on
Peugeot 304 1970 on
Peugeot 404 1960 on
Peugeot 504 1968-70
Porsche 356A, B, C 1957-65
Porsche 911 1964-69
Porsche 912 1965-69
Porsche 914S 1969 on
Reliant Regal 1952 on
Renault R4, R4L, 4 1961 on
Renault 6 1968 on
Renault 8, 10, 1100 1962 on
Renault 12, 1969 on
Renault R16 1965 on
Renault Dauphine Floride 1957-67
Renault Caravelle 1962-68
Rover 60 to 110 1953-64
Rover 2000 1963 on
Rover 3 Litre 1958-67
Rover 3500, 3500S 1968 on
Saab 95, 96, Sport 1960-68
Saab 99 1969 on
Saab V4 1966 on

Simca 1000 1961 on
Simca 1100 1967 on
Simca 1300, 1301, 1500, 1501 1963 on
Skoda One (440, 445, 450) 1955-70
Sunbeam Rapier Alpine 1955-65
Toyota Corolla 1100 1967 on
Toyota Corona 1500 Mk. 1 1965-70
Toyota Corona 1900 Mk. 2 1969 on
Triumph TR2, TR3, TR3A 1952-62
Triumph TR4, TR4A 1961-67
Triumph TR5, TR250, TR6 1967 on
Triumph 1300, 1500 1965 on
Triumph 2000 Mk. 1, 2.5 PI Mk. 1 1963-69
Triumph 2000 Mk. 2, 2.5 PI Mk. 2 1969 on
Triumph Dolomite 1972 on
Triumph Herald 1959-68
Triumph Herald 1969-71
Triumph Spitfire, Vitesse 1962-68
Triumph Spitfire Mk. 3, 4 1969 on
Triumph GT6, Vitesse 2 Litre 1969 on
Triumph Toledo 1970 on
Vauxhall Velox, Cresta 1957-72
Vauxhall Victor 1, 2, FB 1957-64
Vauxhall Victor 101 1964-67
Vauxhall Victor FD 1600, 2000 1967 on
Vauxhall Victor 3300, Ventora 1968 on
Vauxhall Victor FE Ventora 1972 on
Vauxhall Viva HA 1963-66
Vauxhall Viva HB 1966-70
Vauxhall Viva, HC Firenza 1971 on
Volkswagen Beetle 1954-67
Volkswagen Beetle 1968 on
Volkswagen 1500 1961-66
Volkswagen 1600 Fastback 1965 on
Volkswagen Transporter 1954-67
Volkswagen Transporter 1968 on
Volkswagen 411 1968 on
Volvo 120 1961-70
Volvo 140 1966 on
Volvo 160 series 1968 on
Volvo 1800 1960 on

NOTES